American Reform Judaism

American Reform Judaism

An Introduction

DANA EVAN KAPLAN

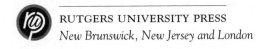

RUTGERS UNIVERSITY PRESS
New Brunswick, New Jersey and London

Library of Congress Cataloging-in-Publication Data

Kaplan, Dana Evan.
American Reform Judaism: an introduction / Dana Evan Kaplan.
p. cm.
Includes bibliographical references and index.
ISBN 0-8135-3218-3 (cloth) — ISBN 0-8135-3219-1 (pbk.)
1. Reform Judaism—United States—History—20th century. 2. Judaism—20th
century. 3. Jews—United States—Identity. 4. Jews–United States—Social
life and customs. I. Title.
BM197 .K37 2003
269.8 '341'0973—dc21
        2002012498
British Cataloging-in-Publication information is available from the British
Library.

Manufactured in the United States of America

Contents

Foreword

Let me confess at the very outset of this foreword to Dana Evan Kaplan's excellent book that I resisted writing this essay. I was eventually persuaded that I should by my respect for the author's clearheaded understanding of the contemporary situation of Reform Judaism. He knows all the nuances of the problems that liberal Jewish religion must face and he understands the positions of all the major participants in the various debates. Dana Evan Kaplan, the scholar, has done an admirable and even exemplary job of leading the reader through this piece of uncharted territory of contemporary religious history of American Jews.

Thus I had no problem with Kaplan's description of the contemporary religious situation among Reform Jews. My problem began with the question of how the contemporary crisis is to be addressed. Dana Kaplan, the rabbi, is clearly an optimist. It is evident that he is comfortable and even takes pride in the openness and experimentation within the ranks of the Reformed. The good that this affords in freedom of behavior far outweighs, so Kaplan believes, the threats of doubt and evaporation that are unchecked by any religious authority. I am on the other side of this debate. I know that the bulk of American Jews are not waiting for rabbinic permission to do whatever they want, but this contemporary situation saddens me. It is the task and responsibility of rabbis to defend and to fight for restrictions on our individual conduct. I remember having this argument for the first time more than a half century ago when I was a teenager teaching a little Talmud in a summer class under the auspices of the Baltimore Hebrew College. Its redoubtable president then, in the 1930s, Dr. Louis Kaplan, paid an unannounced visit to my class. At the end he called me aside to say that the future of American Jewish observance would be found in cherishing the positive commandments like the Passover seder or the rituals that surround Hanukkah. American Jews would not retain much attachment to the "Do nots," such as thou shall not eat shrimp. I could not shut myself up before I said to the much older man, whom I loved and admired for his personal qualities, that I did not agree with him at all: Religion, like marriage or patriotism, is best defined by the actions it forbids. Dr. Kaplan shook his head at me and said that "forbid" was not likely to be at the center of the future lexicon of American Judaism.

Dana Kaplan knows that the one element without which Reform Judaism cannot have a firm future is a unifying religious vision, but he seems to admit that this is unlikely. The most that can be hoped for is that some Reform Jews will continue to add to the number of those who are seriously involved in a Jewish piety. They will include both more ritual observance and a deepened sense of the history to which Jews belong. Put simply and fundamentally, Kaplan knows that no religious movement can exist and continue unless it is led by religious personalities. Jews cannot survive as Jews by merely enlisting in the wars of Jews against their enemies.

Some works of scholarship are instantly important because they are the preamble to a call to repent. Other books are of profound significance because they tell us the truth and force the reader to confront it. Kaplan has performed a major service by producing this honest and nuanced account of American Reform Judaism at the turn of the century. Let the reader study this book—and let each of us ponder what we see in the mirror that Kaplan has held up.

Arthur Hertzberg
Professor of Jewish Studies, New York University

Preface

I write this book as a scholar working out of a university, but it would be disingenuous to claim that I come to it from a detached, neutral perspective. I grew up in the Reform movement and feel a strong sense of attachment to it. I studied at the Hebrew Union College–Jewish Institute of Religion (HUC-JIR) in Jerusalem and have served as a Reform rabbi in Georgia, Missouri, Wisconsin, and Michigan in the United States as well as in South Africa, Australia, and Israel.

Even before I was born, my family was connected to the Reform movement. Rabbi Edward Klein at the Stephen Wise Free Synagogue in New York married my parents in 1958. After we moved farther uptown, we joined Congregation Rodeph Sholom on West Eighty-third Street. At the same time, there were substantial traditionalist influences on me as well. My mother's parents were traditional eastern European Jews, although by the time I got to know them toward the end of their lives, they had become less observant. My parents sent me to Ramaz School, an Orthodox Zionist day school on the Upper East Side. Even as a young child, there were aspects of Reform Judaism that I was very attracted to and others that I found less appealing. The astute reader may see some of these prejudices in the manuscript. I can only say that I have tried to be objective. I believe that the manuscript highlights not only the difficulties but also the rewards of trying to pioneer a Jewish liberal religious movement within contemporary American society in a global age.

I thank the Jacob Rader Marcus Center of the American Jewish Archives and its director, Gary Zola, for awarding me an Ethel Marcus Memorial Fellowship, which enabled me to spend a month doing research not only in the extensive archives, but also in the Klau Library. I thank the University of Missouri–Kansas City for awarding me a Meriweather Lewis Fellowship, which facilitated the research and the writing in its final stages. Temple B'nai Israel of Albany, Georgia, provided a warm congregational setting to participate in as well as observe Reform Judaism at its finest. Congregational leaders Robert Kraselsky and Peggy Posnick and many, many others in the Peach State were always encouraging and supportive. David Myers, my editor at Rutgers University Press, was able and willing to provide consistently helpful feedback. David's insight and vision has molded this manuscript and helped me become a better writer. Marlie Wasserman, Bobbe Needham, Nicole Manganaro, Adi Hovav, Kristi Long, and the entire staff at Rutgers University Press were all invaluable. Professor Jonathan D. Sarna of Brandeis University has always been ready to answer my every question, from my first inquiry writing from a student pulpit at Temple Shalom in Brisbane, Queensland, Australia. Professor Yaakov Ariel of the University of North Carolina at Chapel Hill and Rabbi Uri Regev of the World Union for Progressive Judaism helped me learn about the Reform movement during my years of study at HUC-JIR in Jerusalem. Professors Milton Shain of the Kaplan Centre for Jewish Studies and Research at the University of Cape Town and Yair Mazor of the Center for Jewish Studies at the University of Wisconsin–Milwaukee encouraged me during my research work at those institutions. Professor Lloyd Gartner of Tel Aviv University supervised my Ph.D. dissertation at Tel Aviv University and initiated me into the profession, along with Professors Ron Zweig and Robert Rockaway. I thank Professor Haim Shaked of the Miller Center for Contemporary Jewish Studies and Professor Jaime Suchlicki at the Institute for Cuban and Cuban-American Studies for their recent assistance. I thank Professor Arthur Hertzberg for writing the foreword to this book. I have been inspired for many years by not only his published work but also his communal activism. Rabbi Hertzberg has combined scholarship with rabbinic leadership and provided me with a model for my own life path. Rabbi Eric H. Yoffie has honored me by writing the afterword, and I likewise thank him.

I thank the many friends and colleagues who gave me advice or feedback on this manuscript in the various stages of its development:

Professors Isa Aron, Murray Baumgarten, S. Daniel Breslauer, Fred Greenspahn, Michael A. Meyer, Jacob Neusner, Marc Lee Raphael, Michael Satlow, Chaim Waxman, Zion Zohar; Rabbis Melanie Aron, Gary Bretton-Granatoor, Jacques Cukierkorn, Geoff Dennis, Denise Eger, Fred Gottschalk, Jan Katzew, Joel Levine, Paul Menitoff, Evan Moffic, Leon Morris, the late, lamented Alexander Schindler, Lance Sussman; Dru Greenwood, Sybil Kahn, and Catherine Kahn; Ron Owens; Joe Weintraub; Cantor David Bentley. Julie Angulo, Jose Boveda, Bethany Brill, Amanda Chau, Huong Dang, Lindsey Eisenbarger, Sheri Hopkins, Beth Huliska, Brad Phillips, Sophie Sherman, Neeta Soorya, and Stephanie Zwiener helped with the manuscript. Carolyn Washburne has been a friend and adviser since the conception of this project and has been invaluable in many ways. I also thank the anonymous readers who encouraged Rutgers University Press to take on this project and made a great number of valuable suggestions.

I have been fortunate in having been able to try out many of my ideas in academic journals as well as popular magazines and thank these publications and their editors for these opportunities. I have published on the Reform platforms, which are discussed in chapters 3 and 11, in "A Statement of Principles for Reform Judaism: The American Reform Movement's Most Recent Debate" (*Australian Journal of Jewish Studies* 14 [2000]: 31–53); "Reform Jewish Theology and the Sociology of Liberal Religion in America: The Platforms as Response to the Perception of Socio-Religious Crisis" (*Modern Judaism*, February 2000, 60–77); "The 1999 Pittsburgh Platform and Its Impact on American Reform Judaism" (*Scottish Journal of Religious Studies* 20, 2 [December 1999]: 135–157); "The New American Reform Pittsburgh Platform of 1999" (*Jewish Spectator*, winter 2000, 24–26); "Politics and Piety in the Religious Marketplace" (*Congress Monthly*, July/August 1999, 11–14).

On Reform Jewish education, which is discussed in chapter 7, I have published "The Educational Crisis in American Reform Judaism" (*Journal of Beliefs and Values*, 22, 2 [2001]: 183–196). On outreach, intermarriage, and conversion to Judaism, which is discussed in chapter 8, my publications include: "Opening the Gates of the Jewish Community" (*Conservative Judaism*, summer 2000, 32–46); "Conversion to Judaism: A Historical Perspective" (*Judaism*, summer 1999, 259–274, 285–289), with responses from Harold Schulweis, Ephraim Buchwald, and Steven Lerner; and "Millions of Converts?" (*Manna—Journal of the Sternberg Centre for Judaism at the Manor House*, winter 2000, 2–3).

Some of my ideas on Reform Judaism generally were first published in "Reform Judaism" in *The Companion to Judaism*, edited by Jacob Neusner (Blackwell, 2000, 291–310). Perhaps most importantly, many of my ideas on Reform Judaism developed in the process of editing two collections on the movement, *Contemporary Debates in American Reform Judaism: Conflicting Visions* (Routledge, 2001); and *Platforms and Prayer Books: Theological and Liturgical Perspectives on Reform Judaism* (Rowman and Littlefield, 2002).

I originally discussed many of the topics covered in this volume with my late aunt Ruth Moskowitz during my high school years in Waterbury, Connecticut. We spent hours talking of the future of the American Jewish community, and I owe her a great deal for stimulating this interest. My uncle Herman Moskowitz has been a source of strength for me over the past few decades. He celebrated his ninety-third birthday recently, and I hope that this volume appears in time for his ninety-fourth. My father, Dr. Norman Kaplan, has recently begun reading Judaica at a furious clip and will certainly be one of the first to read this work. I was particularly pleased that he was able to hear me speak recently at Temple Emanu-El on Fifth Avenue.

I hope this work can make a modest contribution to fair and dispassionate discourse on modern Judaism. May we all try to live up to the words of Micah 6:8: "He has told you, O man, what is good, and what the Lord requires of you: only to do justice, to love goodness, and to walk modestly with your God."

American Reform Judaism

Introduction

THIS BOOK is designed to accomplish three goals. First, I hope to provide a general introduction to the American Reform movement for readers coming from different backgrounds. Many non-Jews as well as Jews who have seen passing references to Reform Judaism may have been unable to put these stray facts into context. This volume is intended to provide that context. I have tried both to give enough background to familiarize the reader with historical events and to keep the focus primarily on contemporary developments.

A second goal is to describe the social and religious dynamics that impact Reform Judaism. On one hand, the Reform movement has built up impressive congregations and institutions throughout the United States, as well as in other parts of the world. On the other hand, it has faced a great deal of resistance and leaves an ambiguous legacy, even in places such as the United States where it has become the dominant Jewish religious force. Most Jews see the good things that happen, as well as the bad ones, but are seldom able to understand the broader trends that have frequently contributed toward the end result. American Reform Judaism is very much an American religious denomination, and this volume explains the movement in that context.

My third goal is to argue that Reform Judaism's liberal theology—which is attractive to many highly educated, secular-oriented contemporary Americans—makes it difficult to create the type of committed religious community which can perpetuate that commitment from decade to decade and from generation to generation. Therefore, the Reform movement is in the unenviable position of having to constantly "market" itself to its congregants, as well as to the large number of unaffiliated American Jews. This marketing effort is part and parcel of the advertising-based nature of contemporary American society, and there is no reason to believe that the Reform movement will not be able to reinvent itself and to attract and re-attract members, former members, and the unaffiliated and even "unchurched gentiles." And yet the lack of a strong and compelling theology forms the weak under-belly of the movement.

I begin with an overview of the Reform movement from its origins in early nineteenth-century central Europe to our day. I then outline the basic beliefs and practices that make Reform Judaism distinctive, explaining what leading Reform thinkers believed and believe, and how those beliefs are translated into practice. In the third chapter I look at the evolution of Reform theological statements. Theology is of central importance in any religious enterprise. The Reform movement in particular has the flexibility to alter not only its practices, but also its beliefs. It is therefore imperative that we examine how those beliefs have evolved. Many of the theological challenges that the movement faces today have surfaced time and again.

We then move to the contemporary American context. As Ameri-can Jews have become more comfortable in the United States, their need to insist that they are loyal Americans has declined. Over the past thirty years, most American Jews have felt that they are full partici-pants in the American drama. While they were proud when Senator Joseph Lieberman was named to the vice presidential spot on the Democratic ticket in the 2000 elections, they did not need the selec-tion to make them feel "at home in America."[1] Similarly, scandals or crimes involving Jews did not make most American Jews feel insecure. They have become highly acculturated and, in many cases, completely assimilated. This shift has had a major impact on American Jewish life. The Reform synagogue has, like other Jewish institutions, felt the impact of these changes. The movement has begun embracing traditional ritu-als once ignored or rejected. It is not possible to keep doing the "same ol' same ol'." Congregations that have not changed with the times have found that their membership has aged and declined. Fortunately, the movement has responded vigorously to the new challenges that it faces. This "Reform revolution" is led by Eric H. Yoffie, president of the Union of American Hebrew Congregations (UAHC). Speaking in

Orlando at the UAHC's 1999 biennial, Yoffie declared, "We proclaim a new Reform revolution. Like the original Reform revolution, it will be rooted in the conviction that Judaism is a tradition of rebellion, revival, and redefinition."[2]

After giving a broad overview of the state of the American Reform movement, I concentrate on how Yoffie and other UAHC leaders are hoping to transform Reform Jewish life. There is a sense that the movement is undergoing rejuvenation, or as some refer to it with a touch of humor, "re*Jew*venation." Congregations are developing sophisticated approaches to marketing and have targeted singles, seniors, and a variety of other special interest groups. I will argue that the UAHC has been able to plug into social trends and effectively harness a series of strategies to bring in different types of previously alienated potential congregants. This includes, most importantly, interfaith couples. The Reform movement officially accepted patrilineal descent in 1983, provided that the children of Jewish fathers and non-Jewish mothers were raised as Jews. The movement's willingness to invite women to participate equally in ritual and communal life has generated tremendous enthusiasm and innovation. More recently, the Reform movement has enthusiastically embraced gays and lesbians, first welcoming them into congregations and then accepting them into rabbinical and cantorial schools.

Yet all this activity disguises the tremendous vulnerability of the Reform movement. Many American Jews expect the movement to be open, tolerant, pluralistic, and accepting, all characteristics that explain why the movement has grown as fast as it has in recent years. But this openness also makes the Reform movement a loose conglomeration of disparate individuals, many of whom are seeking "services" as religious consumers rather than devoting themselves altruistically to service.

For decades, the movement was dominated by Classical Reform, a form of practice that emphasized the belief in ethical monotheism and rejected most traditional practices. But over the last several decades, this rigorous if nontraditional form of Judaism became, for many, an excuse to do little and care less. The Reform movement had been a "low tension" religious group, which sociologist Rodney Stark explains is a religious body whose beliefs and practices do not dramatically set it apart from its environment. In contrast, a "high tension" religious group has beliefs and practices that conflict with the surrounding ethos.[3] The Reform movement's traditional open-door policy allowed people not only to come in without any concrete expression of commitment, but also to stay without any active participation. This is less true today. In this book, I offer examples of how the movement has begun to reverse its policy of low demands and how this has already shown a great deal of benefit. But the next several years will be crucial. As Rabbi Eric H. Yoffie stated at the 1997 biennial: "This is the single most momentous hour in the history of our movement. We must now decide if our Reform heritage will be permitted to wither, or if it will be handed over to generations to come. We have a few years, a decade at most, to respond to the spiritual emergency that threatens to engulf us."

The movement has set out to meet this challenge, for example, in its handling of recent controversies. I explore a number of these "hot button" issues, including the outreach campaign to intermarried couples; the struggle for religious equality for women, including the role of women rabbis, cantors, and other professionals; the acceptance of Jewish gays and lesbians, including the controversial decision made at the Central Conference of American Rabbis (CCAR) Charlotte, North Carolina, conference in spring 2000 to support rabbinic officiation at same-sex commitment ceremonies; and the controversy over the 1999 CCAR Pittsburgh Platform, which pitted neotraditionalists against Classical Reformers.

These pressing and controversial religious issues are of interest beyond the American Reform community. As the national press has reported, various Protestant denominations have dealt with the same questions. People unaffiliated with religious organizations have probably had to confront some of them in their personal or family lives. This volume tries to put these controversies in the context of the history and sociology of the Reform movement. As members of an international movement, what American Reform Jews decide to do has ramifications for their affiliated organizations in Israel and elsewhere in the world, and therefore the Jewish people. For example, a video made quite a number of years ago in the United States showing a Reform rabbi co-officiating with a Christian clergyman at an interfaith wedding was shown on Israeli TV. The Israeli public was shocked and dismayed, and it has taken the Israel Movement for Progressive Judaism years to rebuild their image along lines that their potential Israeli supporters would find more appealing. On the other hand, the State of Israel's questioning the authenticity of Reform Judaism may lead to increasing American Jewish alienation from the Jewish state. If this process is indeed occurring, it may have extremely serious implications for the future relationship between Israel and the diaspora.

The future of American Judaism is uncertain. The prophets of doom suggest imminent destruction, while the eternal optimists speak of a "golden age." The evidence can support any number of positions, and this book is not going to resolve that debate. What I hope it will do is provide a comprehensive overview and an accurate analysis of the largest and perhaps most important American Jewish religious denomination—where Reform Judaism has come from, where it stands today on the major issues, and where it may be going. I offer this work as a small contribution to the understanding of a vibrant, if controversial, segment of the Jewish religious world today.

Chapter 1   A Historical Overview

*We are children of the nineteenth century, proud of our
mother, and her motto shall be our watchword:
emancipation of the mind, mental culture, redeems the
human family from the misery of existence in all its
forms.*   —ISAAC MAYER WISE, 1884

THE REFORM MOVEMENT was a bold historical response to the dramatic
events of the eighteenth and nineteenth centuries in Europe. Despite
the frequent claim that pluralism has always been a central feature of
Jewish life, the idea that Jews could practice their faith according to the
moral precepts of Judaism but without complete adherence to the code
of Jewish law was a radical one. Jews had been a persecuted minority in
Christian Europe for hundreds of years. Despite or perhaps because of
this, they developed a thriving spiritual and religious life inside their
own community. But the increasing political centralization of the late
eighteenth and early nineteenth centuries undermined the societal
structure that perpetuated this way of life. At the same time, Enlightenment ideas began to influence not only a small group of intellectuals
but also wider circles. The resulting political, economic, and social
changes were profound. From a religious point of view, Jews felt a tension between Jewish tradition and the way they were now leading their
lives.

Many responded to this new situation by observing less and less of
that tradition. As the insular religious society that reinforced such

observance disintegrated, it was easy to fall away from vigilant observance without deliberately breaking with Judaism. Over the course of a few decades, a large percentage of the Jews of central Europe were no longer sure exactly how much of the traditional belief they subscribed to. Some tried to reconcile their religious heritage with their new social surroundings by reforming traditional Judaism to meet their new needs and to express their spiritual yearnings. Gradually these efforts became a movement with a set of religious beliefs, with practices that were considered expected as well as practices regarded as antiquated, and with an identity as a coherent and cohesive modern Jewish religious stream or denomination.

Reform Judaism was the first of the modern responses to the emancipation of the Jews, a political process that occurred over an extended period. Orthodoxy is the branch of Judaism that believes in the literal transmission of both the written and oral Torah from God to Moses at Mount Sinai. It believes that as a consequence of that revelation all Jews must observe halacha, Jewish law, as interpreted by the sages. Orthodoxy saw itself as the direct continuation of medieval Judaism, although the movement formed to protect traditional values from the corrosive effects of modernity. Conservative Judaism, which developed in response to the perception of many that Reform Judaism was going too far, traces its origins to 1845, when Zacharias Frankel protested the majority opinion at a Reform rabbinical conference in Frankfurt am Main that the use of Hebrew in worship was only advisable, not required.

In the United States, the serving of shellfish at the first Hebrew Union College graduation precipitated the organization of those who favored change in the context of traditional observance. Eventually, these dissenters coalesced into what became the Conservative movement. A fourth denomination was Reconstructionism, the only one of the major movements completely indigenous to the United States. Mordecai Kaplan argued the Reconstructionist view that Judaism was an evolving religious civilization, not simply a religion in the narrow sense of the term. Reconstructionism developed out of Conservative Judaism before and after World War II but in recent decades has grown closer to the Reform movement. Nevertheless, Richard Hirsh has argued persuasively that the two movements remain distinct theologically.[1]

Because of its stress on autonomy—both of the individual and of the congregation—Reform Judaism has manifested itself differently in various countries. Nevertheless, Reform communities throughout the world share certain characteristics. Although many Orthodox Jews harbor the stereotyped view that Reform Jews believe nothing about religion, Reform Jews believe that religious change is legitimate and that Judaism has changed over the centuries as society has changed. While in the past this evolutionary process was subconscious and organic, in the modern world it has become deliberate. The guiding principal of the contemporary Reform movement is that it can adapt Jewish religious beliefs and practices to the needs of the Jewish people from generation to generation.

The first Reformers—long identified as "German" Jews but, in fact, Jews from many European countries—were seeking a middle course between halachic Judaism, which they wanted to break away from, and conversion to Christianity, which they wanted to avoid.[2] Looking for a way to remain Jewish while adapting to the prevailing social customs, they hoped that by introducing modern aesthetics and strict decorum, they could make worship services more attractive to the many central European Jews who were drifting away from traditional Judaism but had not become Christians. Most of the early reforms focused on minor cosmetic changes: They abbreviated the liturgy and added a sermon in the vernacular, a mixed choir accompanied by an organ, and German along with Hebrew prayers. From the point of view of Jewish law, reading some additional prayers in German was a relatively minor divergence. But for the congregants eager to create a synagogue service that would look respectable to their neighbors and at the same time feel authentic to themselves, such a change carried great import.

By the early 1840s, a trained Reform rabbinic leadership had emerged in central Europe. Rabbi Abraham Geiger, called to the Breslau Jewish community in 1839, developed into the most distinguished intellectual defender of Reform Judaism in nineteenth-century Europe.[3] Reform rabbinical conferences in Brunswick in 1844, Frankfurt in 1845, and Breslau in 1846 gave rabbis an opportunity to clarify their beliefs and the practices that could follow from them. A debate over the use of Hebrew in the services led Zacharias Frankel to walk out of the 1845 conference, a moment many see as the beginning of the historical school, which advocated positive-historical Judaism. Frankel accepted the evolutionary character of the Jewish religion but insisted that the "positive" dimensions of Jewish tradition needed to be preserved. Although most of the rabbis at these conferences were much less traditional than Frankel, like Frankel they taught in the established Jewish community, the *Einheitsgemeinde*, and therefore had to remain sensitive to and conversant with traditional rituals and observances.

A number of radical Reform rabbis, in particular Samuel Holdheim, made strong anti-traditional statements that shocked many more traditionally inclined. Geiger himself has been quoted as seeming to repudiate the circumcision rite as "a barbaric act." Yet the practice of most German Reform rabbis remained far more traditional than their rhetoric. They worked to remain a part of Klal Israel, the totality of the Jewish people, and did not fully accept the radical Reform groups in Berlin and Frankfort.[4]

Reform Arrives in the United States

The history of Reform Judaism in the United States differs profoundly from that in Europe. Whereas in Europe the movement developed under the shadow of anti-Semitism and the threat of conversion to Christianity, in the United States a much freer and more pluralistic atmosphere prevailed. Over two hundred years, the U.S. Reform movement has changed significantly and has seen substantial regional and even local variation among individual congregations. Nevertheless, it can point to a surprisingly high degree of continuity.[5]

The first attempt at Reform occurred in Charleston, South Carolina, in 1824, when forty-seven members of Congregation Beth Elohim signed a petition requesting that their congregational leadership institute certain ritual reforms, including the introduction of prayers in English. The congregational board rejected the request, and a small group of intellectuals decided to form a new congregation, to be based on enlightened liberal values. On November 21, 1824, the Reformed Society of Israelites came into being, and the group published the first American Reform prayer book, *The Sabbath Service and Miscellaneous Prayers Adopted by the Reformed Society of Israelites*.[6] Although the original group disbanded in 1833, due in part to the relocation and subsequent death of one of its more dynamic leaders, an interesting Sephardic intellectual named Isaac Harby, Mother Congregation Beth Elohim soon began to move toward Reform under the leadership of its *hazzan*, Gustavus Poznanski.[7]

One of the most fascinating episodes in American Jewish history, the Charleston Reform attempt was an isolated phenomenon. Far more important for the development of the Reform movement in the United States was the arrival of large numbers of central European Jews beginning in the 1830s. The Jewish population of the United States jumped from approximately 3,000 in 1820 to 15,000 in 1840 and 150,000 in 1860. Although many scholars have assumed that these immigrants brought Reform Judaism with them from Germany, Leon Jick has argued persuasively that American Reform was not "imported" but rather developed in the United States in response to the American socioreligious environment of the antebellum period.[8] While Jick overstates his argument, his book was a much needed corrective to the earlier historical consensus.[9]

Jewish immigrants settled throughout the United States. As they established businesses and built homes, local Jews began to put more effort into building a community. They consecrated cemeteries and held High Holy Day services, usually in a private home or a hotel meeting room. Eventually, they erected synagogue buildings and, if the community was large enough, engaged a religious leader with training in religious matters in the old country who could read the Hebrew prayers and perform the required rituals. For the congregations in Fort Wayne, Indiana, or Lexington, Kentucky, this was sufficient. As the immigrants gradually acculturated, they wanted their synagogue practice to reflect American norms. They wanted to use English as well as Hebrew in the services and to create an atmosphere to which they could bring Christian neighbors, who would come away impressed with the propriety and nobility of the ritual. Thus they moved their congregations toward Reform, not out of an intellectually based theological commitment, but as a practical response to daily life in the United States. Most of the functionaries went along with that trend. They were not theologically motivated but rather saw the practical benefits of adapting religious practices to the American patterns of living.

But ideologically motivated reformers also existed. One group of liberal religious intellectuals in Baltimore formed a *verein* in 1842, a small religious group that met to discuss theology and conduct services based on that theology, the Har Sinai Verein. In 1845 a similar group founded Emanu-El in New York City, which developed into the largest and most prestigious Reform congregation in the country. These groups, dedicated to Reform Judaism in ideological terms, differed from the vast majority of congregations in the United States, whose members were more concerned with the realities of everyday life in America than with the intricacies of Judaic theological debate.

Isaac Mayer Wise and the Development of the American Reform Movement

As more congregations developed in the antebellum period, the need for strong rabbinic leadership grew. Not all congregations felt this need; many treasured their independence and many local lay leaders enjoyed dominating communal affairs. Despite the difficulties, rabbis carved out a leadership niche for themselves. Numerous immigrant teachers and ritual functionaries were interested in serving in the rabbinate and, in some cases, in assuming leadership roles on a regional or national level. One of the best known was Isaac Leeser of Philadelphia. A traditional-ist minister who published an influential newspaper, *The Occident*, Leeser also promoted many other intellectual, social, and educational projects. But it was Isaac Mayer Wise who had the charisma and deter-mination to develop into a national Jewish religious leader and to actively work to build American Jewish institutions and organizations.[10]

Isaac Mayer Wise arrived from Bohemia in 1846, and although he was advised to become a peddler, Rabbi Max Lilienthal encouraged him to consider the pulpit rabbinate and sent Wise in his stead to ded-icate a number of synagogues. This led to an opportunity for Wise to begin serving as rabbi in Albany, New York.[11] When he was offered a life contract in 1854 to become the rabbi of Congregation B'ne Jeshu-run in Cincinnati, Wise accepted, and the pulpit became his base for building the American Reform movement.[12]

Wise established a newspaper, *The Israelite*—later *The American Israelite*—and edited a siddur called *Minhag Amerika: Tefillot Beney Yeshurun/Daily Prayers*.[13] Credited with establishing or being the driving force behind the founding of all three major institutions of the Reform movement, he inspired one of his lay leaders to establish the Union of American Hebrew Congregations (UAHC) and himself founded the Hebrew Union College (HUC) and the Central Conference of American Rabbis (CCAR).

Although Wise had hoped to build an American Judaism that included all American Israelites rather than just the more liberal elements, a moderate form of Judaism that combined some ritual reforms with traditional elements, this vision proved unworkable. The Reform movement, however, was the first Jewish religious movement in the United States to organize itself on a denominational basis. Reform Judaism includes three types of organizations, each with its own territorial parameters: the congregational organization, today represented nationally by the UAHC; the four campuses of the Hebrew Union College–Jewish Institute of Religion (HUC-JIR); and the rabbinate, represented by the CCAR. The movement pioneered this "tripartite polity," as Lance Sussman refers to it, subsequently adopted by the other major denominations of American Judaism.[14]

In the early 1870s, Wise, who had been trying for many years to create a national association of U.S. congregations, encouraged Moritz Loth, the president of Wise's Congregation Bene Jeshurun, to issue a call to congregations to meet in Cincinnati for the purpose of establishing a Hebrew theological college. In July 1873, representatives from 34 congregations from twenty-eight cities, mostly in the Midwest and the South, came together to found the organization.[15] The following year, 21 additional temples joined. By the end of the decade, 118 congregations belonged to the UAHC, more than half of all identified synagogues in the United States.

The UAHC dealt with congregational issues and strategies for working together as an organized congregational movement. Its first goal was to create a rabbinical school. Wise had been trying to create such a school for many years and had actually opened one shortly after his arrival in Cincinnati in 1855, Zion College, which lasted for only one year. But Wise did not give up on the idea. He was further encouraged when Henry Adler of Lawrenceburg, Indiana, offered a $10,000 gift toward the establishment of an American rabbinical college. With the UAHC's establishment in 1873, Wise saw a new opportunity to build a successful school. That same year, the University of Cincinnati was founded, presenting the possibility for rabbinical students to attend the university simultaneously and graduate from rabbinical school with a university degree as well. At the UAHC annual meeting in July 1874, congregational representatives voted unanimously for such a college to be established, with Wise as president. In 1875 the Hebrew Union College was founded. Wise served as president until his death in 1900. A number of distinguished Reform rabbis followed him in this role: Kaufmann Kohler (1903–1921), Julian Morgenstern (1921–1947), Nelson Glueck (1947–1971), Alfred Gottschalk (1971–1996), Sheldon Zimmerman (1996–2000), and David Ellenson (2001–present). Since its founding, the college has educated the professionals who would assume leadership roles in the congregations, as well as many women who would marry future rabbis. In recent decades, many women have studied to become rabbis themselves.

A long period of tension and conflict between the theologically oriented radical Reformers in the East and the more moderate Reformers in the Midwest had created a great deal of bitterness between the two groups as they attempted to influence the direction of American Judaism. Because of this divisiveness, Wise waited until HUC had graduated a sufficient number of rabbis and only then moved forward with the establishment of a permanent rabbinical association. David Philipson, an early HUC graduate and rabbi at Congregation Bene Israel in Cincinnati, helped Wise issue a call to rabbis planning to attend the 1889 UAHC conference to meet separately to establish their own organization. The rabbis created the Central Conference of American Rabbis, then elected Wise president by unanimous vote; he continued to serve until his death eleven years later.

By 1890 ninety rabbis had affiliated with the CCAR, which dealt with rabbinical issues, including controversial religious questions. Membership was open to any rabbi who was serving or had served a synagogue as spiritual leader. After the first year, membership would be open to those from several categories, not only those with ordination from HUC, but also a wide variety of religious functionaries. As time went on, more and more members were HUC graduates. Today the CCAR has a membership of more than 1,800.[16]

Despite his successful leadership, Wise was considered an uneducated and unworthy colleague by some of the "German" Reform rabbis who arrived in the 1850s and 1860s with doctorates from prestigious central European universities. Primary among them was Rabbi David Einhorn, who immigrated to the United States in 1855. Einhorn wrote a number of scathing attacks on Wise for abrogating Reform theology and turning what he saw as a consistent and principled approach to modern Judaism into a jumble of incoherent beliefs. The issue debated by Wise and Einhorn has remained a relevant theme throughout the history of the Reform movement. Is it more important to be theologically unswerving, or to respond effectively to changing societal trends? Most of the time, the movement has favored pragmatism over theological consistency.

Wise represented a pragmatic approach to American Judaism. Although some scholars have pointed to the numerous inconsistencies in his written positions, he was primarily an institution builder who attempted to use ideology as a tool for compromise and consensus.[17] To take his words at face value and to express shock at the outright contradictions is to miss the brilliance of his activities as an organizational leader. Wise succeeded in building an entire American religious movement from scratch, under very difficult circumstances.

The Classical Reform Period

Classical Reform was the type of Reform Judaism that developed in the late nineteenth century. American Jews, most of whom were of central European background, saw the tremendous influence that liberal religion had on their Protestant neighbors and wanted to develop a form of Judaism equivalent to Episcopalianism, Presbyterianism, and especially Unitarianism. As presented in the 1885 *Declaration of Principles*, known as the 1885 Pittsburgh Platform, Classical Reform Judaism minimized Judaic ritual and emphasized ethics in a universalist context, stressing universalism while reaffirming the Reform movement's commitment to Jewish particularism through the expression of the religious idea of the mission of Israel. The document defined Reform Judaism as a rational and modern form of religion in contrast with traditional Judaism on one hand and universalist ethics on the other.

Motivated by his concern that persuasive personalities were urging American Jews to embrace these alternatives, Kohler, the platform's principal author and a son-in-law of David Einhorn, wanted to present in a formal manner what distinguished Reform Judaism from traditional Judaism, as well as what was Jewish about Reform Judaism. Earlier in 1885, he had debated in a series of public forums with Alexander Kohut, a Hungarian rabbi recently arrived in New York who espoused the traditionalist approach. Their debates had attracted wide attention in the synagogues and the press. That the founder of the Society for Ethical Culture, Felix Adler, was the son of Samuel Adler, the rabbi of Congregation Emanu-El in New York, particularly galled Kohler. The rabbi's son, who had returned from rabbinic studies in Germany advocating a philosophical approach to ethics in a universalistic framework, was attracting to his philosophy and organization many Reform Jews who wanted both to express their conviction that ethics was important and to loosen or break their particularistic ties with Jewish ethnic identity.[18] Adler placed himself on the extreme of the continuum between particularism and universalism, emphasizing the individual's connection with and commitment to humanity as a whole, rather than to any one ethnic or religious grouping.

Kohler chose a middle road, as this excerpt from the *Declaration* indicates: "We hold that all such mosaic and rabbinical laws as regulate diet, priestly purity and dress originated in ages and under the influence of ideas altogether foreign to our present mental and spiritual state. They fail to impress the modern Jew with a spirit of priestly holiness; their observance in our days is apt rather to obstruct than to further modern spiritual elevation."[19]

Reform Judaism has historically emphasized what it interpreted as the central message of the prophets: the need to fight for social justice. The Reformers believed deeply in working with their Christian neighbors to help make the world a place of justice and peace, and this belief was a central part of the religious worldview. The platform emphasized the prophetic mandate to work tirelessly for the rights of the downtrodden, and the term "prophetic Judaism" described the Reform vision of following the dictates of the prophets to create a just society on earth. Coupled with the emphasis on its interpretation of prophetic Judaism, the early Reformers in particular spoke frequently about the mission of Israel, which presented the idea that the prophets of the Bible served as advocates of ethical monotheism.[20] Ethical monotheism combined the

Jewish belief in one God with rational thought and modern innovations in scientific knowledge. The mission of Israel was to stand as an example of the highest standards of ethics and morals and to help bring the world to an awareness of and commitment to ethical monotheism.

American Jews who embraced Reform were greatly influenced by the popular belief in the sovereign self. They started with their own religious feelings and tried to place their personal understanding of what we would today call "spirituality" in a Judaic context. When Rabbi Emil G. Hirsch of Chicago Sinai Congregation in 1925 entitled one of his books My Religion, he was making a statement about the source of his religious inspiration.[21] Still, the Reformers understood that American Judaism could not stand solely on the basis of personal inspiration but needed a connection to Jewish history through a religious concept not "nationalistic" in orientation, but pure and holy.

They believed that the prophets stressed universalism rather than particularism, and therefore the Reformers felt justified in likewise stressing the universal over the particular. At the same time, the concept of the mission of Israel justified the continued existence of the Jewish people by arguing that their ongoing survival as a religious group was essential if the Jews were to bring their universalistic message of ethical monotheism to the world. David Einhorn used a version of this argument to oppose intermarriage with non-Jews, since "the small Jewish race" needed to preserve itself as a separate entity to fulfill their religious mission on earth. Taken to its extreme, the mission of Israel concept helped Reform leaders present Judaism as the ultimate expression of ethical monotheism.

As the purest form of monotheistic religion, Judaism was therefore the strongest theological argument for ethical behavior. As such, it deserved to be taken seriously as a way of thought and a way of life by all individuals committed to finding a true understanding of God and God's place in the world. This allowed Reform leaders such as Wise to declare that Judaism was destined to become the faith of all humankind, or at least of all Americans who held liberal religious beliefs. But this lofty religious rhetoric masked institutional atrophy, the result of individual indifference on the congregational level. Yet if synagogue attendance never measured up to rabbinic expectations, optimism for the future remained widespread. Reform leaders believed that as time passed, humankind would be better able to understand the will of God, and thus society was certain to become a better place. This belief became most pronounced in Classical Reform.

Yet this description of the theology of the Classical Reform rabbis is only part of the story. Yaakov Ariel has argued that historians have portrayed the Reform movement of this period in stereotypical terms taken from eastern European Jewish perceptions of the German Jewish elite. Specifically, such historians have presented the Reform movement as having divorced itself completely from the national as well as the ethnic components of Jewish identity. Ariel argues that there was an "astonishing gap" between the ideals of the Reform movement as expressed by rabbinic leaders, and the attitudes held by the vast majority of members in the congregations: "The Reform movement held a character almost diametrically opposed to its universalistic aspirations. As an ethnically oriented, parochial, and tribal group, Reform Jews were concerned with Jewish matters on local, national, and international levels, and were strongly involved with their non-Reform Jewish brethren."[22]

An example of this startling discrepancy between Reform theological posturing and actual congregational behavior can be seen in a series of letters written by W. E. Todd of Tappahannock, Virginia, to Rabbi Edward Calisch of Richmond in 1896.[23] Todd expresses interest in converting to Judaism and studying at HUC for the Reform rabbinate. Calisch asks a number of prominent figures in the national Reform movement, including Rabbi Emil G. Hirsch and Bernhard Bettmann, president of the Board of Governors of HUC, for direction. Despite their universalistic rhetoric that advocated proselytization and invited non-Jews to join the synagogue, they uniformly responded negatively to Todd's request. Hirsch told Calisch: "My advice to your friend would be to the Unitarian or Liberal Christian ministry . . . [because] it will be impossible for him to procure a position in a Jewish congregation. . . . Theory in our congregations is, as you will know, one thing, practice another. We are liberals, until a non-Jew believes us to be in earnest."[24]

Classical Reform Judaism had developed during a period of heady optimism at the end of the nineteenth century. But as early as 1881, Jews began fleeing to the United States to escape the pogroms of eastern Europe. By the time the Nazi Party rose to power in 1933, it was increasingly difficult to see the world as a place where Jew and gentile could continue to work side-by-side to make the world a better place and to bring justice and peace to all in the spirit of the prophets. The 1930s brought signs that at least some of the Reform movement's leaders felt the need for a return to tradition. Jews increasingly believed that the world was profoundly hostile to them. Rather than universal goals, they yearned for a Jewish homeland that could absorb the hundreds of thousands or even millions of Jews who faced prejudice, persecution, and murder. While no one imagined the enormity of the tragedy that would befall European Jewry, the possibilities were apparent. In response to the changing political environment, the Reform movement began to accept and eventually embrace a more particularistic understanding of Jewish identity, including political Zionism. The Reformers began to accept a definition of Judaism centered on Jewish peoplehood. Nevertheless, Reform rabbis continued to speak of ethical monotheism, which stressed that the Jewish belief in one God would lead to the highest ethical behavior.

The Changing Character of the Reform Movement

The Reform movement changed its direction as a consequence of the increasingly brutal nature of the twentieth century. World War I jumpstarted the process of reexamining the liberal sense that had propelled Reform religious thought until that time. The movement's optimistic view of human progress in collaboration with God underwent further change after the rise of the Nazi movement in Germany and the subsequent murder of six million Jews. In the aftermath of that tragedy, the Reform movement veered away from its universalistic triumphalism toward a more ethnically based cultural identity. But the breakdown of this optimism did not mean the end of either Reform Judaism or the Reform movement. Congregations continued to attract new adherents as sociological patterns shifted. Many Jews found that the Reform temple met their need for a nominal religious identification, while allowing them to join the stew in the American melting pot.

From 1881 until 1920, the Reform movement grew slowly relative to the increase in the American Jewish population, with only ninety-nine congregations consisting of 9,800 members in 1900 and two hundred congregations with 23,000 in 1920. The Reform movement went from being the single most important voice of the American Jewish community to being a small minority. Although the elite nature of many Reform Jews meant they retained a high profile, they were swamped by the eastern European organizations and ideologies.

The eastern European mass immigration increased the American Jewish population from 250,000 in 1880 to 1 million by 1900 and 3.5 million by 1920. The bulk of the immigrants came from Russia, Ukraine, Lithuania, Poland, Romania, and other regions where there had not been full emancipation. Since most of the native population in their home countries had viewed these Jews as an alien presence, they came to America from an insular Jewish background. As a consequence, few joined the Reform movement. The immigrants did not like the Reform service, which they found lacking in traditional Jewish elements. Many Reform Jews maintained a haughty attitude toward the newcomers, preferring not to remember that their own parents or grandparents had arrived in the United States one or two generations earlier under similar circumstances. Indeed, a mythology developed that had the "German" Jews descended from aristocrats. Historically inaccurate, it reflected a widely held perception.

Nevertheless, over the course of time increasing numbers of eastern Europeans joined Reform congregations. Under their influence, the Reform movement inched back toward a more traditional approach to Jewish thought and practice, hastened by world events. By the 1920s and especially the 1930s, with the worldwide rise of anti-Semitism, this direction became clear. Even though the 1885 *Declaration of Principles* had argued that Jews should remain together solely as a religious group to fulfill their mission of bringing ethical monotheism to the world, the rise in anti-Semitism threatened Jewish physical survival, a concern that far outweighed theology or ideology. Policies that had seemed levelheaded just a few decades earlier now appeared naive and foolhardy. As a result, the CCAR adopted the Columbus Platform in 1937, officially named *The Guiding Principles of Reform Judaism*. This new platform embraced Jewish peoplehood and leaned toward support of political Zionism. The culmination of a revolutionary shift in the ideology of the American Reform movement, it encouraged a greater diversity of opinion and a multiplicity of approaches.[25]

By 1945 the Reform movement was well on its way to accepting Zionism and the soon-to-be-created state of Israel. The interwar period saw the rise of two strongly Zionistic Reform rabbis, Stephen S. Wise and Abba Hillel Silver. Wise (no relation to Isaac Mayer Wise) began his rabbinic career in Portland, Oregon, then moved to New York, where he established his own congregation after Temple Emanuel refused to promise him freedom of the pulpit. In 1922, he established the Jewish Institute of Religion (JIR) in New York City to provide a Zionist alternative to Hebrew Union College. Wise believed in both the importance of social justice and the centrality of Jewish people-hood. Like him, Rabbi Abba Hillel Silver was a prominent leader in American and world Jewish affairs as well as a congregational rabbi. After serving as a rabbi in Wheeling, West Virginia, he became rabbi of the temple in Cleveland, Ohio. From this pulpit he worked tirelessly to build up the American Zionist movement in the hope of establishing a Jewish state. With Wise, Silver formed the American Zionist Emergency Council, which lobbied the U.S. Congress on behalf of the Zionist movement. Silver was the leader who announced to the United Nations that Israel had declared itself an independent state. Both men were Classical Reformers devoted to Jewish nationalism, a synthesis that would have been incongruous just a few decades earlier.

Post–World War II Developments

The aftermath of World War II brought a massive suburban construction boom that within American Judaism benefited the Conservative branch most.[26] Conservative Judaism appealed to the now American-ized eastern European immigrants and their children, because it appeared substantially more traditional than Reform but allowed far greater flexibility than Orthodoxy. Nevertheless, Reform Judaism benefited from this suburbanization trend as well: The 265 congregations in 1940, with 59,000 units in the UAHC, grew by 1955 to 520 congregations and 255,000 units.

Many suburban Jews who joined Reform congregations saw the temple mainly as an extracurricular activity for their children. Congregations that moved most rapidly to meet the needs of these new suburbanites thrived. The temple became a social center that substituted to some degree for the loss of the old Jewish neighborhoods, such as those once clustered on the Lower East Side or Brownsville in New York. The Reform leadership faced the challenge of conveying a religious message to congregants who had not joined their synagogues primarily to share a religious vision. Yet the leaders needed to captivate and motivate them to care and to feel that the congregation was helping them fulfill themselves as ethically concerned people.

The Reform movement grew in large part because it benefited from strong leadership. While much of this strength was more perception than reality, it nevertheless inspired many in the rank-and-file. A tremendous amount of private infighting remained largely hidden from public view. Rabbi Maurice N. Eisendrath, who became UAHC executive director in 1943 and president in 1946, moved the national headquarters from Cincinnati to New York, where he constructed an entire building for the organization on Fifth Avenue across the street from Central Park and next to Congregation Emanu-El.[27] He called the new headquarters the "House of Living Judaism," and it remained the operating center of the Reform movement until it was sold under the presidency of Eric H. Yoffie in 1998. Rabbi Nelson Glueck, a world-famous archeologist who had appeared on the cover of *Time*, became president of HUC in 1947. While many viewed him as more interested in his archaeological pursuits than in his administrative responsibilities, his fame brought a great deal of attention to the movement. He oversaw the 1950 merger of HUC with JIR, and under his leadership HUC-JIR established a third U.S. branch in Los Angeles in 1954 and a fourth campus in Jerusalem in 1963.[28] Although this growth may have owed more to the burgeoning of the American Jewish community than to Glueck, the perception grew that the Reform movement had competent and visionary leadership.

The leaders could project this image of a strong, unified movement partly because of the number of pressing causes that could galvanize members of Reform congregations. In the 1960s many Reform Jews became involved in the U.S. civil rights struggle as well as in the movement opposing the war in Vietnam. The Six-Day War of 1967 dramatically increased American Jews' emotional connection and commitment to the state of Israel. As they worried about its ability to survive in the face of Arab promises to destroy the country during the tense three weeks preceding the war, many came to realize how important the Jewish state had become to them. This fear resurfaced in 1973 when Israel's physical survival was in doubt during the early stages of the Yom Kippur War. The cumulative effect was to increase dramatically the Zionist fervor of most American Jews, a sea change felt throughout the movement.

Interest in liturgical issues also increased. Many began to feel that *The Union Prayer Book,* used in Reform congregations since the 1890s, had become outdated; new prayers would better express how people felt in the aftermath of the volatile 1960s. Joseph Glaser, executive vice president of the CCAR, initiated a campaign in 1971 to write and publish new forms of liturgy. A thick blue prayer book, *The Gates of Prayer,* replaced *The Union Prayer Book* in 1975 to a mixed response—great excitement at the numerous options offered, along with horror at the drastic changes. This publication was joined in 1978 by a completely reworked High Holy Day prayer book, *The Gates of Repentance.* Both new prayer books contained a great deal more Hebrew than their predecessors and reintroduced many traditionalist elements deleted from *The Union Prayer Book.* There were ten different Friday night services offered, most of which presented a specific theological approach, as well as services that catered specifically to children or those preparing for bar mitzvah. Synagogues introduced new ceremonies and experimented with various types of innovations. While many congregants embraced these changes, others resisted—some who had ideological objections, some who missed the liturgy they had been using their entire lives. To this day, some congregations, such as Congregation Emanu-El in New York, continue to use *The Union Prayer Book.* Others, such as Temple Sinai in New Orleans, have a Friday-night service once a month that uses *The Union Prayer Book* instead of the more recent liturgical works.[29] The Reform movement's boldness in its liturgical publications matches its brave leadership in the realm of social justice, as well as its willingness to break with traditional belief and practice.

New Approaches to Changing Social Trends

Alexander M. Schindler, who became president of the UAHC in 1973, gained renown for his assertive support of the social action agenda of the Reform movement of the 1970s and 1980s, including civil rights, world peace, nuclear disarmament, a "Marshall Plan" for the poor, feminism, and gay rights, as well as his opposition to the death penalty. Although this advocacy of liberal causes landed Schindler frequently in the pages of the *New York Times*, he nevertheless got along with traditional Jews and Israeli leaders better than had any of his predecessors. Despite a disinterest in administrative issues, Schindler and his German accent became synonymous with Reform Judaism. His leadership inspired not only individuals, but also entire temples, to join the movement. During his presidency, the UAHC grew from 400 congregations in 1973 to about 875 in 1995. Of course, the continuing move to suburbia made much of this growth possible, but Schindler's inspirational leadership on issues meaningful to American Jews disconnected from traditional belief or practice played an important role.

Schindler had to lead the movement nationally while at the same time cultivating the growth of Reform Judaism in hundreds of towns and cities throughout the United States. The percentage of Jews who self-identified as Reform varied from city to city and region to region, and Schindler had to understand the local dynamics so that he could best promote the Reform movement in each locality.[30] Schindler was facing one reality in many Midwestern and southern cities where Reform Judaism had been strong for 150 years and a very different situation in urban areas with a high percentage of first-generation immigrants. In Texas, 47 percent of Jews in Houston and 48 percent in Dallas indicated that they regarded themselves as Reform. Elsewhere, 49 percent in Cleveland and a whopping 60 percent in St. Louis likewise identified themselves as Reform, but only 33 percent in New York and 26 percent in Miami did so.[31] Particularly important were cities such as Denver and Phoenix, to which large numbers of East Coast Jews were relocating. Schindler managed to adjust his rhetoric and his strategies to accommodate each situation.

Schindler is perhaps best remembered for two issues, his outreach to intermarried couples and his advocacy of patrilineal descent. Intermarriage had long been a taboo in the Jewish community, and many parents ostracized children who "married out." Some would even sit shiva for children about to intermarry, as if the child had died. Schindler, who felt strongly that this taboo was counterproductive as well as inappropriate, came to believe that a bold gesture was in order.

At a meeting of the UAHC's Board of Trustees in Houston in December 1978, he issued a public call to the Reform movement to reach out to the non-Jewish spouses in interfaith marriages. Even more surprising, he urged making the Jewish religion available to unchurched gentiles. This controversial call to proselytize those with no connections of blood or marriage to the Jewish community appeared to be a dramatic departure from two thousand years of Jewish religious policy against proselytization. His critics argued that such a move would encourage certain Christian groups to launch opposing campaigns against the Jewish community, using Schindler's call as an excuse for proselytizing unaffiliated Jews. Despite the attention that this suggestion created, little proselytizing of unchurched gentiles has occurred in the succeeding years, whereas many outreach programs to interfaith couples have been developed.

During the Schindler years the Reform movement adopted the patrilineal descent resolution, which stated that the child of one Jewish partner is "under the presumption of Jewish descent."[32] While the document's vague wording led to some difficulties, the patrilineal descent policy insured that if one's father was Jewish and one's mother was not, one would still be regarded as Jewish, provided that one was raised as a Jew. This would supplement rather than replace the traditional matrilineal descent policy, which established that the children of a Jewish mother would be Jewish regardless of their father's faith.

Also during Schindler's presidency, the Reform movement invited women to assume a more central role in the synagogue, a direct consequence of the feminist movement that influenced every aspect of American life. As American women in the 1960s and 1970s took on a far greater role in religious life than those of previous generations, the Reform movement responded quickly and actively to the changing sex-role expectations. Increasing numbers of congregations allowed women to assume responsibility for all aspects of religious and communal life, even the rabbinate. In 1972, Sally J. Priesand became the first woman ordained a Reform rabbi at HUC-JIR, a revolutionary breakthrough. Even though Reform Judaism had been committed to egalitarianism from its origins in the early nineteenth century, it had maintained a male-only policy in the rabbinate. Priesand's ordination moved congregations to look at the role of women in new ways. Since 1972, hundreds

of women have enrolled in HUC. As the changes in the Reform movement paralleled social changes, its character as an American religious
denomination made it popular with an increasingly Americanized Jewish community.

Contemporary Trends

Reform practice today, especially in the synagogue itself, is characterized by the partial restoration of a number of formerly abrogated rites
and rituals. Ritual items eliminated by the Classical Reformers, such as
the yarmulke, tallith, and even tefillin, have been brought back. But
because of the concept of religious autonomy, individual congregations
cannot and do not require congregants to wear any of these traditional
prayer items. Rather, they are offered to those who find them religiously
meaningful or who prefer to wear them as an expression of traditionalist nostalgia. This generates some incongruous and perhaps amusing situations. For example, it is not uncommon to find congregations where
many of the women wear yarmulkes and tallitot, while most of the men
sit bareheaded and bare shouldered. This is the converse of the norm in
traditional synagogues, where all men wear yarmulkes, tallitot, and
tefillin, and women never do. The Orthodox Jew who wanders into a
Reform sanctuary by mistake would either break out laughing or with-
draw in shock and horror.

Another dramatic trend has been the move away from a formal
style of worship and music toward more jubilant and enthusiastic prayer.
Certain particularly progressive congregations, such as the independent
Congregation B'nai Jeshurun on the Upper West Side of New York,
have served as models for most congregations that have been slowly
evolving toward this more informal, exuberant style. The formalized
Classical Reform service, which could uncharitably be called sterile, no
longer impresses many with its dignity and majesty. Younger people
have grown up with a different aesthetic. New types of music incorporate simple Israeli, Hasidic, and folk styles, a style of worship developed
at the UAHC summer camps under the rubric of the North American
Federation of Temple Youth (NFTY) programs.

Eric H. Yoffie, the president of the UAHC since 1996, inherited a
movement that had grown substantially in numbers yet was perceived

as having fundamental problems. Yoffie moved quickly and boldly to address these challenges, taking advantage of the new enthusiasm for spirituality and launching a systematic campaign to rebuild the entire Reform movement. He initiated a Jewish literacy campaign, which encouraged every Reform Jew to read at least four books with Jewish content every year. Recognizing that NFTY, the movement's youth organization, had dwindled in effectiveness, Yoffie proposed a system that would include the appointment of full-time youth coordinators in each of the UAHC's thirteen regions.

Yoffie has only begun the process of reorienting the movement to meet the sociological challenges that Reform Judaism faces in contemporary America. At the same time, the rabbinic leadership has proposed a number of interesting initiatives, most notably Richard Levy's new Pittsburgh Platform. This restating of Reform religious beliefs generated a firestorm of controversy in 1998 and 1999. Although the CCAR at its annual conference in Pittsburgh in May 1999 eventually passed a revised version called A Statement of Principles for Reform Judaism, supporters found it severely watered down, while Classical Reformers viewed it as a betrayal of the Reform legacy in America. Despite extended conflict over this issue, the values that inspired people to join the Reform movement have kept them from splitting off or leaving altogether. Although many traditional Jews remain persuaded that Reform Jews have no strong religious beliefs, the movement has created and propagated a religious vision that remains compelling after two hundred years. It owes its success to its ability and willingness to respond theologically to changing times.

Chapter 2

An Introduction to Reform Jewish Belief

The prophetic declaration of Ethical Monotheism bound
Judaism to the doctrine of responsible human freedom.
So long as there were many gods, conflict was inevitable
and order in human events was unthinkable. Zeus
could, and often did, upset the plans of other deities.
A unique God, the Creator of heaven and earth,
substituted cosmos for chaos, and made possible the free
moral relationship between Himself and man. God and
man are voluntarily covenanted, each possessed of
freedom and responsibility. —LEVI A. OLAN, 1965

FROM ALL OVER the world and with many different backgrounds, most Jews—at least until recently—believed and believe in Judaism as a religion.[1] So while Judaism is not the religion of a single ethnic or racial group, the Jews are a people who have one religion, and that is Judaism. Until the dawn of the modern era, that Judaism was defined in rigid terms that corresponded to the medieval attitudes of the dominant Christians or Muslims, depending on where a Jew lived. Medieval Judaism accepted Jewish law as binding because God had given both the written and oral Torah to the Jewish people at Mount Sinai. Jewish thinkers explained that Judaism believed in God, Torah, and Israel and that these three categories formed the native categories of the religion. God gave the Torah through Moses to Israel, that is, to the Jewish people. As the chosen people, Israel accepted special obligations incorporated into the corpus of halacha, Jewish law. This law included regulations governing all aspects of daily life, not only aspects that we would see as "religious" but also activities ranging from how one should wake up in the morning to what one could eat at dinner. This relatively homogenous medieval Judaic world began to fall apart as Jews were emancipated in European countries and as Enlightenment philosophy influenced more and more people.

Reform Judaism differs from the other streams of Judaism in its view of the Torah's authority, its approach to legal reasoning, its strategies for promoting Judaism, and its view of the world. On a theological level, traditionalists believe that the Torah is God's will, that the commandments in the five books of Moses are binding on all Jews; this belief in divine authority imposes narrow parameters on legitimate legal reasoning.. In contrast, Reform Jewish thinkers accept a wide variety of interpretations concerning how revelation occurred and what it means in today's world. In terms of legal reasoning, Reform Judaism rejects Jewish law as binding. Elements of that law may be practiced, but only if the particular ceremony provides spiritual meaning. The Reform movement believes that the Torah should be interpreted and reinterpreted to meet the needs of the contemporary Jew. The traditionalist vigorously rejects this relativistic approach: The religious structure of Judaism is not simply a modern social construct, but literally the word of God. Reform Judaism sees the Jewish religion as a theological system that can help modern Jews understand the world. Most Reform Jews interpret the essential myths of Judaism as elaborate metaphors designed to help us create and transmit a sense of "cosmos."[2]

God, Torah, and Israel

Judaism, like other Western monotheistic faiths, believes in the existence of one God. According to the tradition, an eternal covenant was made between God and the people of Israel. The Torah, the Hebrew Bible, is the cornerstone of the religious wisdom of the Jewish people. This emphasis on Torah led to a focus on learning that has dominated the Jewish faith for at least two thousand years. God is the transcendent divine being who exists beyond the limits of human knowledge. God is the most powerful force in the universe and the creator of all life. Genesis describes the process of creation and while traditional Jews may not necessarily believe that the world was created in six days, they do believe that God created the world and continues to guide everything that happens on earth.

Reform Jews pride themselves on their commitment to rational thought and therefore accept that science explains how the universe was born. Nevertheless, most Reform Jews believe that God created the world and continues to be involved in an ongoing process of creation. This is not seen as a contradiction, since they believe that the laws of science carry out God's will. They view the biblical account of creation not as a valid and binding scientific theory of the world's origins but as of spiritual value; the Torah is a holy text because it reflects the religious perceptions of the ancient Israelites. Reform Jews believe that human beings are responsible for being God's partners in fulfilling the potential of God's creation.

Most Reform Jews believe that God revealed the Torah to Israel in some form, but they would differ on what form such revelation may have taken. Most would agree that God revealed the divine presence to people not just in a onetime event at Mount Sinai but in stages over a long period of time. Such progressive revelation means that all people have the potential to understand God's will. Maurice Eisendrath, president of the Union of American Hebrew Congregations during the Vietnam War era, explains that "God is a *living* God—not a God who revealed Himself and His word once and for all time at Sinai and speaks no more."[3] Every time a person studies Torah, he or she is continuing the process of bringing God's revelation to human beings. The study of God's ways helps humans to understand the ethical monotheism that is the core belief of Judaic theology.

While the traditional Jewish conception holds that the theophany that occurred at Mount Sinai constitutes the normative and permanent expression of God's will, Reform Judaism does not accept that the written Torah—the five books of Moses—was revealed to Moses, word for word and letter for letter. Reform thinkers believe that humans have far more control over how the religious tradition develops and is practiced. Thus the term "reform" refers not to a particular reform that occurred at a specific point in the past but to a commitment to a continual and ongoing process. That is why the proponents of the movement prefer the term "reform" rather than "reformed." In other parts of the world, many Reform movements prefer the designation "progressive" to emphasize their commitment to continuing revelation and the ongoing nature of divine communication. Nineteenth-century Reformers stressed the importance of ethical monotheism. They believed that the unique ethical and moral message of Judaism derived directly from the presence of one all-good God who was responsible for creating everything in the world. This belief was taught not only by the rabbis in the Talmudic period, but also by the Jewish religious leaders described in the Bible.

Many Classical Reformers believed that the prophets represented the highest and purest stage of ethical monotheism. A few American rabbis, such as Emil G. Hirsch of Chicago Sinai Congregation, went so far as to advocate removing the Torah scrolls from the ark in their synagogues, in the belief that the prophetic works, not the five books of Moses, contained the highest religious message. Hirsch argued that the five books, the Pentateuch, borrowed their ideas and practices from neighboring Near Eastern "tribes and races," while the prophets represent an original religious contribution: "Not sacrifices, not ritual, not holy convocation as such are religious. They are inconsequential, and if urged as final and essential cease to be religious and sufferable. In the stead of the religion that operates with sacrifices and rites, the Prophets taught a religious view of life and world in which the Holy God could only be revered by Holiness on the part of man. And this divine-like holiness of man consisted in 'doing justly, loving mercy, etc.'"

Many Reform rabbis identify the core ethical teaching of Judaism as a passion for just human relations. Jews and all people were admonished to treat their neighbors fairly and respect their rights, their property, and their persons. If people deal justly with each other, truth will triumph and peace will reign. One of the Sages declared in the Mishnah that the world rests on three foundations: justice, truth, and peace. If justice exists in the world, then truth and peace will follow. Such justice applies to all peoples, not only Jews, because God recognizes no distinction among people on the basis of creed, race, gender, class, or handicap. All are equal in God's sight. All people are responsible for one another.

Despite this inherent universalism, Jews have a special obligation to other Jews. In traditional Judaism, this includes the obligation to admonish one's fellow Jew for ritual as well as ethical lapses. All human beings are made in God's image and therefore have an infinite capacity to do good.[4] The Jewish people have a special role to play in helping bring ethical monotheism to the world. Partly because the prophets railed against injustice of any type, many Reform Jews have taken a special interest in social justice. Even today, when most liberal causes fail to generate mass enthusiasm, large numbers of Reform Jews devote substantial volunteer hours to eradicating poverty, working for civil rights and civil liberties, lobbying for environmental protection, and so forth. As an organized body, the Reform movement maintains a well-staffed office in Washington, D.C., dedicated to working for social justice through the political process. Established in 1961 with the backing of Rabbi Maurice Eisendrath, the Religious Action Center of Reform Judaism is recognized as one of the nation's preeminent religious advocacy groups.

After the Exodus stories, the Torah focused primarily on the recitation of technical laws and obscure practices. It describes the erection of the tabernacle in the desert and the sacrificial service offered. Reform rabbis found these themes largely irrelevant to the ethically focused universal religious message they were cultivating. The prophets, on the other hand, emphasized the central role ethics should play in any religious system. Prophets such as Micah, Isaiah, and Hosea emphasized social responsibility and hence fit nicely into the Reform message. The Jews had a prophetic mission to teach the world an ethical vision of society. Reformers interpreted prophetic comments as indicating the prophets' belief that Judaism was based on ethics, not ritual. For example, the prophet Micah (6:68) seems to denigrate the importance of ritual and to elevate the centrality of ethical behavior:

> Wherewith shall I present myself to Adonai?
> And do homage to God on high?
> Shall I present myself with burnt offerings,
> with calves a year old?
> Will Adonai be appeased with thousands of rams,
> with ten thousands rivers of oil?
> Shall I sacrifice my first born for my transgression,
> The fruit of my body for the sin of my soul?
> He has told you old man what is good

and what Adonai requires of you:
Only to do justice
and to love mercy
and to walk humbly before your God.

The prophets thus seemed ideal models for the ethical monotheism the rabbis were preaching. The rabbis cited Torah selectively to reinforce the central themes of the prophetic literature, but they minimized the legal aspects of the Torah and ignored most rabbinic legal interpretations.

The Mission of Israel

The Bible tells of how God selected Abraham to carry out his religious vision and promised Isaac and Jacob that they too would benefit from this unique relationship. This covenant concept developed into the doctrine that the Jews are a people chosen by God to enter into a special covenant and that this relationship determined the course of their history. In traditional Judaism, this idea was tied in with the settling of Eretz Israel, the Holy Land promised by God as an eternal gift to the Jews. To this day traditional Jews aspire to settle in the state of Israel, not necessarily as a nationalistic act but rather as a way of fulfilling their religious ideals.

This covenant idea remained important to the Reformers, although they adapted it to fit their modern conception of religion and their reinterpretation of the meaning of Jewish history. They vehemently opposed any suggestion that they should hold political loyalties other than loyalty to the land of their birth and citizenship. To reinterpret the covenant idea to justify their intent to remain permanently in the Diaspora, early Reform theologians used language from the prophets to declare that the Jews had a special mission to be a light unto the world and thus needed to remain dispersed: God had deliberately scattered the Jews among the nations to bring the ethical monotheistic message of Israel's God to all people.

While theological reflection had its place in traditional Jewish thought, it was secondary to God's charge to the Jews to observe all the commandments, both ritual and ethical; such observance shows their commitment to the covenant. Numerous Talmudic statements argue that perplexed Jews should begin to observe the commandments—the mitzvoth—for this will bring them closer to God. The more mitzvoth the person does, the more mitzvoth the person will do. Similarly, regular sinning will result in more and more sinning. Throughout rabbinic thought, the stress is on what Jews should do rather than on what they should believe. If Jews continue to be faithful to the covenant, then at the end of days God will redeem the Jews and bring them back to the Land of Israel and, at the same time, bring peace to the world. This religious vision was not appropriate for the early Reformers, who could neither subscribe to the emphasis on ritual behavior nor see the return to the promised land as a hoped-for outcome. Yet because they needed a religious justification to continue the Jewish religion and therefore the Jewish people, they adapted the traditional concept of chosenness and referred to it as the mission of Israel.

This mission of Israel was to make God's unity known to people throughout the world, a teaching that would lead Jews and eventually all others to work to make society a better place for all. As early as 1869, at the Philadelphia conference, a gathering of mostly radical Reformers, rabbis argued that Israel's messianic aim was not the restoration of the ancient Jewish state but rather the union of all of God's children in the confession of his unity. Therefore, the destruction of the second Jewish commonwealth by the Romans in 70 C.E. was not a divine punishment, since the dispersion of the Jews throughout the world was necessary for them to fulfill "their high priestly mission, to lead the nations to the true knowledge and worship of God." Kaufmann Kohler, a leading Reform theologian of the late nineteenth and early twentieth centuries, explained it this way:

> The task which the God of history has assigned to us is to unfold and spread the light of the monotheistic truth in its undimmed splendor, ever to be living witnesses, and also to die, if needs be, as martyrs for the Only One and holy God, to strive and battle and also, if needs be, to suffer for the cause of truth, justice and righteousness, and thus to win the nations, the races and creeds, all classes of men by teaching and example, by life of mental and moral endeavor as well as of incessant self-sacrifice and service for Israel's religious and ethical ideals.[5]

This mission of Israel justified the continued existence of the Jews as a separate ethnic as well as religious group.

The Messianic Idea in Reform Judaism

Just as Reform Judaism reinterpreted the mission of Israel, so too did it reinterpret the idea of a Messiah. Traditional Jews believe that at some unknown point in the future, a Messiah will come to redeem the Jewish people. The Messiah will, according to the most accepted viewpoint, be a male descendent of the House of David. While a great many different traditions describe what will happen during this time period, all agree the Messiah will bring the remnants of Israel back to their homeland, rebuild the temple in Jerusalem, and reinstitute the sacrificial cult.

Reformers presented a different eschatology. They rejected the idea of an individual Messiah and instead argued that it was up to human beings to work toward a messianic era, a time of world peace when all suffering due to poverty, plague, war, and so on would be eradicated. The Jews would not be brought back to the land of their ancestors but would fulfill their messianic hopes in their current places of residence. This significant departure from traditional thought reflected Reform Jews' determination to be accepted in their home countries. It is not coincidental that Reform Judaism grew in countries where the emancipation of the Jews had to some degree succeeded. If Jews were treated as outsiders and outcasts, then the basic premise of Reform Judaism would make no sense and few local Jews would be attracted to it as a religious ideology. The social obstacles and anti-Semitism Jews in Western countries faced motivated them all the more to demonstrate their commitment to their countries. Jews felt that they belonged, and they wanted their religion to help integrate rather than isolate them. A messianic belief based upon the return to Eretz Israel, the Land of Israel, would be inconsistent with their contention that, for example, American Jews owed their sole loyalty to the United States.

When congregation Beth Elohim of Charleston, South Carolina, dedicated a new building in 1841, a reporter wrote of Hazzan Gustavus Poznanski's comments: "In dwelling on the plenitude of civil and religious privileges, enjoyed by the House of Israel in this land of liberty and equal rights, he kindled with a noble and generous enthusiasm, and declared, in behalf of himself and all grateful Israel, that 'this synagogue is our *temple*, this city our *Jerusalem*, this happy land our *Palestine*, and as our fathers defended with their lives *that* temple, *that* city and *that* land, so will their sons defend *this* temple, *this* city, and *this* land.' "[6]

Max Lilienthal, an important Reform Rabbi in Cincinnati in the later part of the nineteenth century, echoed this view:

> We Israelites of the present age do not dream any longer about the restoration of Palestine and the Messiah crowned with a diadem of earthly power and glory. America is our Palestine; here is our Zion and Jerusalem: Washington and the signers of the glorious Declaration of Independence—of universal human right, liberty and happiness—are our deliverers, and the time when their doctrines will be recognized and carried into effect is the time so hopefully foretold by our great prophets. When men will live together united in brotherly love, peace, justice and mutual benevolence, then the Messiah has come indeed, and the spirit of the Lord will have been revealed to all his creatures.[7]

Lilienthal understood messianism in distinctly American terms, a shift made possible by the Reformers' willingness to reinterpret core religious beliefs: The Messiah's mission had changed. As a consequence of that reinterpretation, they also felt free to reject Jewish law as a binding system. Reform Jews saw their local religious involvement as paralleling Christian participation in local churches. Jewish religious activities would not only be compatible with being American, but also would make them better Americans.

Rejection of Jewish Law

Traditional Judaism had focused on the observance of the mitzvoth, the commandments given by God and incumbent on every adult Jew. The mitzvoth developed into a system of law referred to as halacha. Traditional Judaism viewed halacha as the core of Judaism, and observing the code of Jewish law was obligatory. The Reformers argued that if the Sages developed specific laws as a response to historical conditions,

then halacha could be changed or even abrogated. The Reform movement thus viewed halacha, Jewish law, as no longer obligatory.

Yet there was never complete agreement over how to relate to ritual observance. This was not a new debate; medieval philosophers had
discussed the relationship between freedom and authority. By the middle
of the nineteenth century, a wide spectrum of opinion existed on the
issue. The historical school, which developed into the Conservative
movement, argued that although halacha might develop over time, it
nevertheless remained binding. The historical school developed innovative religious approaches as well.[8] The main difference—a significant
one—is that the historical school attempted to show that halacha
evolved in order to justify ritual change on the basis of contemporary
needs. The Conservative movement viewed itself as faithful to the
halachic process.

But Reform thinkers understood the historical changes within
Judaism as far more radical. According to a Reform understanding of
the history of Judaism, the religion has evolved in a revolutionary fashion at several key points in its history. These changes were not simply
adaptations of a minor nature, but dramatic developments that marked
huge jumps in both belief and practice. Reform theologians believed
that generations in different time periods fashioned a Judaism that
suited their contemporary religious sensibilities.

But if Jewish law was not obligatory, then what was the purpose of
Judaism? Many nineteenth-century rationalists believed that human
beings possessed an autonomous sense of ethics and morals. Immanuel
Kant had argued that individuals can achieve happiness by using their
autonomous will to choose the ethical option. Kant argued that the full
exercise of human reason could free enlightened people from the
shackles of external authority. People therefore can derive these principles through the use of reason and need no externally imposed set of
laws, no halacha.

The rationalist philosophers argued that religion imposed an externally derived legal system on individuals that prevented them from exer-
cising their autonomous will. Such reasoning could lead one to conclude
that the essence of Judaism is ethics rather than law. That explains why
so much of the early Reform literature stressed abstract ethical lessons
and avoided describing ritual acts. Religious law, the Reformists believed,

was inferior to ethics; Judaism's challenge was to develop along Kantian lines. Revelation became a bit tricky, because one needed autonomy to choose the ethical path. If God made all the decisions and issued all the commands, then the individual would not have autonomous choice. Therefore, Reform thinkers developed the notion of man and God as partners in an unfolding process of continuing revelation.

The rejection of halacha as a legal system meant that every individual practice had to be justified on its own merits, which produced widespread inconsistencies and contradictions. For example, the halacha requires all Jews to fast not only on Yom Kippur, but also on Tisha B'Av, a fast day commemorating the destruction of the first and second temples and other catastrophic events, and four additional minor fast days. But if halacha no longer bound Reform Jews, then they no longer had to abstain from eating even on the holiest fast day of the year. Most pulpit rabbis seem to have chosen to ignore the glaring problem of ritual inconsistency, particularly in the private sphere. While Reform synagogues developed a standard liturgy and a formalized ritual, no corresponding code detailed how Reform Jews should live their lives outside the synagogue; each person had to decide what rituals, if any, remained meaningful. Perhaps the rabbis preferred not to interfere with the private habits of their congregants.

Some theologians, however, tried to provide an ethical justification for specific observances. For example, Moritz Lazarus, a turn-of-the-century German Jewish thinker and author of *The Ethics of Judaism*, argued for fasting on Yom Kippur:

> Satiety, the sense of satisfied hunger, is at once the condition and the sign of complete gratification, bringing about self-complacency that easily passes over into wantonness and arrogance. Fasting means want, deprivation, longing, which lead to humility, and humility produced by the consciousness of sins committed is repentance. Indulgence increases desire, and desire in turn hastens to satisfy itself by indulgence; privation, on the other hand, tends to abstemiousness. In favorable circumstances, the gratification that accompanies satiety may prompt to generosity; self-satisfaction and wantonness, however, are connected with illiberality, but privation and longing attune one to self-devotion.[9]

Most Reform Jews chose to ignore the minor fast days, and so the issue of whether to fast or not arose only once a year, on Yom Kippur. But the question of the food laws came up every day. Most Reformers rejected kashrut, the traditional system of keeping kosher. Although some retained a nostalgic attachment to some elements of kashrut, most were quick to begin eating all sorts of forbidden foods, including shrimp, milk with meat, and even pork. Isaac Mayer Wise, who retained kosher food practices to some degree, derided the traditional concern with following the letter of the law as a narrow and unbalanced approach to religion. Since most Jews who followed the traditional rules spent a great deal of their time on the food laws, he dubbed such an approach "kitchen Judaism."

In recent years, many Reform Jews have come to a new appreciation of the importance of ritual in religious life, which some Orthodox observers misinterpret as a return to halachic observance. Rather, these Reformists find that specific traditional practices provide spiritual meaning for the individual. And that is, at heart, what the Reform movement stands for.

Differentiating Between Biblical and Talmudic Laws

From the beginning, lay leaders who wanted specific practical changes implemented pushed Reform forward. Innovation developed in response to local needs and took into account no overarching theological system or broad religious blueprint. Nevertheless, Reform thinkers had to develop a system for interpreting the tradition. One of their most important concepts was to differentiate between biblical and Talmudic laws.

In traditional Judaism, the Sages differentiated laws that were Midiorita, from the Torah, from laws that were Midirabbanan, from the rabbis. But both types of laws were obligatory to the same degree, and one could not justify nonobservance by pointing out that a given law was "only" Midirabbanan rather than Midiorita. Even restrictions added as a "fence" around the Torah became obligatory. One such fence, for example, related to the biblical commandment not to boil a kid in its mother's milk. This stricture was extrapolated in the oral law to mean that one could not eat any meat and milk together. The Sages included chicken in this prohibition because they worried that some people might not understand that chicken was meat, and if it was permitted to eat chicken with milk, then they might think it permissible to eat meat with milk. Despite its being only a fence to prevent potential violations, this rabbinic law was unconditionally obligatory.

What was important to the Reformers was to develop a religious system that synchronized Jewish belief with contemporary trends yet retained enough particularistic elements to distinguish their religion as a form of Judaism. To this end, they wanted to eliminate laws and practices that would prevent or restrict their social and economic integration into the host society.

Writing in the 1960s and 1970s, American Jewish sociologist Marshall Sklare argued that the Jewish rituals most likely to endure were those capable of being redefined in modern, universal terms. A ritual would command widespread observance only if it did not bring with it social isolation or the adoption of a unique lifestyle. The message of the ritual had both to accord with the religious culture of the larger community and to provide a Jewish alternative to it. These usually focused on children and were performed infrequently so as not to be overly burdensome.[10] Passover and Hanukkah, two holidays that met people's needs well, were therefore widely observed.

Reform Jews were quick to abandon practices such as kashrut that did not meet Sklare's criteria. Although it could be redefined in modern terms, for instance, keeping kosher would still demand a relatively high degree of social isolation as well as the adoption of a unique lifestyle. Nevertheless, some Reform Jews remained observant of the kosher laws, at least to some degree. Late-nineteenth- and early-twentieth-century Reform rabbi Bernhard Felsenthal argued that Reform should retain at least some aspects of the kosher laws. Since he could no longer claim that they should be preserved because they were literally God's commandments, Felsenthal argued that they served an ethical purpose.

> It would be irresponsible and reprehensible to advocate the
> total disregard of the dietary laws. It would prove Reform to be
> very superficial indeed. These laws not only have hygienic but
> also a deeper ethical significance, because they keep us apart

from all that is bestial and crude. They teach us the lovely
virtue of self-discipline and may hereby assist us to become a
holy people, a demand that the Torah relates to these laws. It
is not necessary for a Jew to eat ham and oysters and he need
not listen to the deceptive serpent of a "sausage philosophy"
which says, "Go ahead and eat."[11]

Felsenthal ties the observance of some of the laws of kashrut to the
virtue of self-discipline, which in turn can help Israel fulfill its role as a
holy people. This is the mission of Israel, and Felsenthal hoped that
connecting kashrut with one of the key beliefs of Classical Reform
Judaism would make his argument more persuasive.

But Felsenthal wanted to differentiate between the basic kosher
laws of the Bible and all sorts of supplementary details added much later
by the Talmudists. "On the other hand the simple Mosaic laws have
through later Talmudic casuistry grown into tomes of law. Cautious souls
are careful not to eat a certain meat because they are fearful that the
Shochet might have used a knife which—God forbid—had a nick or
because the meat was not sufficiently kashered [made kosher]. But
groundless laws need no longer be observed. . . . Why should one continue to observe such statutes and others which lack all foundation?"[12]

The rabbi thus differentiated between laws that continued to serve
a religious purpose by teaching valuable ethical lessons and the pursuit
of holiness on one hand, and excessively punctilious rabbinic ordi-
nances that serve only to obscure the original meaning of the commandments on the other. This standard Reform distinction was not
made in the tradition itself.

Reformers emphasized the prophetic ideals of justice and righteousness, arguing that these universalistic values formed the essence of
Judaism. The 1885 Pittsburgh Platform, which differentiated moral
and ritual laws and became the "principle of faith" for Classical
Reform Judaism, stressed that most of the ancient laws were not to be
observed: "To-day we accept as binding only the moral laws, and maintain only such ceremonies as elevate and sanctify our lives, but reject
all such as are not adapted to the views and habits of modern civilization. We hold that all such Mosaic and rabbinical laws as regulate diet,
priestly purity and dress originated in ages and under the influence of

ideas altogether foreign to our present mental and spiritual state. They fail to impress the modern Jew with a spirit of priestly holiness; their observance in our days is apt rather to obstruct than to further modern spiritual elevation."[13]

Classical Reform was not only a system of beliefs, but also an aesthetic approach to religious practice. Although as immigrant Jews Americanized, they wanted their synagogues to reflect American norms, even in Europe many had seen the Orthodox way of worship as disruptive and undignified. Joseph Krauskopf, a dynamic Reform rabbi from Philadelphia, described the traditional service in these terms: "During the reading of the weekly portion from the [Torah] scrolls, the women, who were enclosed behind the latticed galleries, apart from the men, being considered unworthy of worshiping near their fathers and husbands and brothers, gossiped freely; the men conversed and often carried on business transactions undisturbed; the children ran in and out; the uninitiated Christian stranger shook his head in misgiving when told that this constituted the Jewish mode [of] those worshiping God."[14]

The traditional synagogue was in fact not a tightly controlled environment, but noisy and individualistic to the point where German Christian parents admonished their children not to run around the house wildly as if they were in a Judenschul, a synagogue. The implication was that Jews did not know how to behave properly, whereas Christians did. Many of the central European Jews not only believed that houses of worship should be places of propriety but also wanted their synagogue worship to reflect American norms and standards; they borrowed structural and stylistic features from local Protestant churches, copying their architecture, seating arraignments, musical styles, and so forth. Reform Jews also made a number of ritual changes solely on the basis of what they considered the most dignified approach. A Classical Reform aesthetic slowly developed into a compulsory system of ritual that replaced the halachic system.

The Challenge of Unrestricted Autonomy

While Reform Judaism stood for the autonomy of the individual and against the belief that halacha was binding in its entirety, in the post–World War II period, Reformers took a variety of positions on religious authority and how it can be reconciled with individual autonomy. While some argued against all boundaries, others tried to develop a post-halachic justification for some form of Jewish legal authority. Reform thinkers understood that the freedom of action they advocated could result in unintended consequences. If individuals could make their own decisions over what to observe, then what would stop those individuals from observing nothing at all? Indeed, there were those who used the Reform movement to justify apathy and even apostasy. But no obvious solution presented itself.

In 1946, Solomon Freehof of Pittsburgh's Congregation Rodef Sholem urged Reform rabbis to "restudy our relationship to traditional Jewish law." He further urged them to "revive the concept of mitzva, of Torah, and thus attain orderliness and consistency and authority in our Reform Jewish life."[15] Freehof spent the next several decades writing *responsa* literature—rabbinic answers to practical questions that arose in Jewish religious life posed by either rabbis or lay members. Traditional rabbis had written responsa since at least the Gaonic period, and Reform rabbis in both Germany and the United States had adapted the format as well. But Freehof made responsa literature his specialty, writing hundreds of answers, *teshuvot*, over the course of his long career. Particularly striking about his answers was his extensive citing of traditional rabbinic material. He used not only biblical and Talmudic sources, but also medieval and modern rabbinic commentaries seldom referred to by other Reform writers. Freehof frequently traced the development of an idea all the way from biblical sources to the most recent Orthodox *teshuvot*, a bizarre practice, since the Orthodox writers that he cites would have been horrified by his entire approach.

In 1965, Rabbi W. Gunther Plaut recommended to the Central Conference of American Rabbis (CCAR) that a Sabbath manual be written as a beginning toward a comprehensive guide for the Reform Jew. Plaut edited the result, *A Shabbat Manual*, published by the CCAR Press in 1972.[16] The manual went much further than any previous CCAR publication in urging Reform Jews to perform certain mitzvoth—to light Shabbat candles, to recite or chant the kiddush (the blessing over the wine), and to avoid working or performing housework on the Sabbath. This watershed publication led to additional efforts to "return to tradition."

Yet a return to tradition should not be misunderstood as an acceptance of halacha as a binding system. Most Reform Jews believe that religion in general, and Judaism specifically, is very much a human institution. They believe that it is impossible to know with absolute certitude what God wants from us. Certainly, behaving ethically is necessary for people of all faiths. But we cannot know what ritual behavior God expects from us. Eugene B. Borowitz, HUC-JIR theologian, has suggested that "when it comes to ritual, they [Reform thinkers] admit we are dealing largely with what people have wanted to do for God . . . ceremonial [behavior] discloses more of human need and imagination than it does of God's commands"[17] The traditional belief that the mitzvoth are binding because they are God-given is reinterpreted to acknowledge God's indirect inspiration in what is essentially a process of human spiritual expression.

The central beliefs and major theological concerns of Reform Judaism developed not in a void but as a religious response to the social and political changes in Europe in the eighteenth and nineteenth centuries. Jews were emancipated and had far more choice about how they would identify and how they would live their lives. In central Europe, many decided the best solution was to give up their Jewish identities entirely by converting to Christianity. Others remained steadfast in the tradition. Reform Jews were among those who wanted to remain Jewish while modernizing their beliefs and, even more important, their practices.

The Evolution
of American
Chapter 3   Reform Theology

*Today we accept as binding only the moral laws and
maintain only such ceremonies as elevate and sanctify
our lives, but reject all such as are not adapted to the
views and habits of modern civilization. We hold that all
such Mosaic and Rabbinical laws as regulate diet,
priestly purity, and dress originated in ages and under
the influence of ideas altogether foreign to our present
mental and spiritual state.*
                 —*Declaration of Principles, 1885*

ONCE A REFORM rabbinic leadership developed by the 1840s, these
men—and for most of the first two hundred years, males led the movement—felt they must justify their religious positions theologically. The
more intellectually oriented Reform rabbis believed that religious reflection was a process as well as a product. If they could convince their lay
people to put time and energy into theological contemplation, the
Reform movement could live up to its potential. Precisely because that
theology was complex, they needed congregants who could connect
with the religious ideas on a cerebral level. As a result, the leading rabbis were committed to reflecting critically on the way that they and their
congregants lived out their faith. They wanted to study the origins and
the development of Judaism to try to understand how to express and
reshape the tradition to make it relevant in the contemporary world.[1]

Toward this end, Reform leaders wrote and accepted four major
platforms over 115 years, beginning with the original Pittsburgh Plat-

form of 1885. Preceding the adoption of each of the platforms was a period of growing awareness that the Reform movement had changed substantially and needed a written document to reflect its current stance. Some have seen these periods as times of creative gestation; others have argued that they indicated socioreligious crisis.[2]

The Reform movement adopted platforms in 1885, 1937, 1976, and 1999.[3] Earlier statements of principle included an agreement by Reform leader Isaac Mayer Wise and traditionalist Isaac Leeser on two religious principles that would form the basis for a union of traditionalists and moderate Reformers at the Cleveland Conference of 1855. Although both right and left attacked the principles, the result was increasing polarization rather than unification. Another attempt to develop a theologically consistent set of principles for American Reform Jews occurred in Philadelphia in 1869. But the 1885 Pittsburgh Platform became the best-known statement of what Reform Jews believed and what they stood for.

The Pittsburgh Platform of 1885

The Reform movement had been moving toward what became known as Classical Reform since the end of the Civil War. Rabbi Kaufmann Kohler had been involved in a series of debates with Rabbi Alexander Kohut, who had been preaching from his pulpit at Ahavath Chesed in New York not just that American Jews needed "a Judaism of the healthy golden mean," but that "such a reform which seeks to progress without the Mosaic-rabbinical tradition, such a Reform is a Deformity: It is a skeleton of Judaism without flesh and sinew, without spirit and heart."[4]

Kohler began to formulate a response to Kohut's attacks and, during the summer of 1885, used his pulpit at Beth El in New York to present his own series of lectures on the future of Judaism. "Forwards or backwards?" he asked. The way forward was going to be found not by remaining shackled to halacha, but rather by embracing a "living Judaism" that could be both pious and rational. Kohler consulted with Isaac Mayer Wise and Samuel Hirsch about holding a conference to formulate a statement on the meaning and purpose of Judaism in the modern world, then invited "all such American rabbis as advocate reform and progress and are in favor of united action in all matters pertaining to the welfare of American Judaism."

The nineteen rabbis at the 1885 Pittsburgh conference passed a platform, mainly written by Kohler, that included the statement: "Judaism presents the highest conception of the God-idea as taught in our Holy Scriptures and developed and spiritualized by the Jewish teachers in accordance with the moral and philosophical progress of their respective ages."[5] In contrast to the ethical culture movement, which sought to develop an ethical perspective independent of revealed religion, Kohler wanted to show that Reform Judaism was sensitive to universalistic spiritual concerns. The platform specifically acknowledges that the consciousness of God is present in other religions, not only Judaism. "We recognize in every religion an attempt to grasp the Infinite, and in every mode, source or book of revelation held sacred in any religious system, the consciousness of the indwelling of men." One does not need to be a Jew to achieve salvation.

Judaism should not be harnessed forever to Mosaic law, which was "a system of training" that the Jewish people underwent in ancient times when they lived in the land of Israel ("Palestine"). In the contemporary world, only the moral laws remained binding. Reform Jews should "maintain only such ceremonies as elevate and sanctify our lives, but reject all such as are not adapted to the views and habits of modern civilization." This meant that rabbinical and even biblical laws that governed such areas of daily life as diet were no longer obligatory. As the platform put it, such laws "originated in ages and under the influence of ideas altogether foreign to our present mental and spiritual state." If such regulations still held spiritual meaning, then they could continue to be practiced. But this was not the case. Rather, "they fail to impress the modern Jew with a spirit of priestly holiness; their observance in our days is apt rather to obstruct than to further modern spiritual elevation." This Reform criterion for the observance of a given ritual remains to this day, although the popular view has evolved regarding what types of rituals might elevate one spiritually.

The Pittsburgh Platform stresses that Judaism believes in "progressive" revelation, although the word is never used. Jews will not return to the land of Israel nor will the temple sacrificial worship be reinstituted, for the Jews are no longer a nation but solely a religious community. They do retain the duty of fulfilling the mission of Israel. Christianity and Islam likewise "aid in the spreading of monotheistic and moral truth." Jews believe that it is their duty "to participate in the great task of modern times," which is to solve the social problems that cause so much suffering.

Reflecting the optimism abroad between Reconstruction and World War 1, the platform foresees a bright future of peace and justice, the coming of the messianic era spoken of by the prophets of Israel thousands of years earlier. Yet this optimistic document, written by rabbis who believed that their religious vision was swiftly becoming accepted by much of the rest of humanity, needs to be put in context.

That the 1885 Pittsburgh Platform followed a period of socioreligious crisis for the Reform movement may surprise the many people used to thinking of its framers as having tremendous confidence in the movement they had built, and tremendous optimism for both the future of Reform Judaism as a religion and the inevitable forward progress of Western civilization. But serious problems were apparent to any casual observer. While Kaufmann Kohler had confidence in the integrity of his theological approach to Judaism, he was far less sanguine about his congregants lining up behind him.[6] Accounts of the period describe how Kohler called the conference and developed the platform to respond to ideological challenges from the left and right. To the right, Kohler tried to explain the theological premises of Reform Judaism that differentiated it for the better from the much more traditional approach of Alexander Kohut. For the left, Kohler tried to establish the superiority of Reform Judaism over Felix Adler's ethical culture movement. Not usually stressed is Kohler's belief that an endemic religious decline had struck Reform congregations throughout the United States.[7] He had long been concerned with the low level of commitment shown by congregants in the temples he served in Detroit, Chicago, and then New York. He was, in fact, concerned that the logical consequence of radical Reform might in some way be contributing to Jews' apparent increasing apathy toward religious activities. Even social activities in many congregations showed signs of slowing down.

Kohler was upset by the lack of religious fervor. In 1879, he was serving Chicago Sinai Congregation when temple president Morris Selz described what was going on:

> This congregation has during the past year not undertaken or
> accomplished any one thing or act, which could entitle it to
> any special credit or praise at this present meeting. . . . We
> claim to be the principal congregation in the Western country
> and we are thus classed, but we deserve it not. We own a
> temple erected by your liberality in days gone by, today we
> would not build it; we would be unwilling to bring a sacrifice.
> Service is held as stated but we do not attend. . . . We have a
> minister of whom we are justly proud [Kohler], but he preaches
> before empty benches. No doubt we lack inspirations; we are
> indifferent. And our children? Will they follow our examples,
> and if possible improve upon our evil ways, and still we remain
> indifferent. . . . In this manner we have brought religious
> matters to a standstill and have transformed our grand Temple
> in[to] a grand vacuum.[8]

Kohler hoped that the Pittsburgh Platform would function as not only
a theological statement but also a concrete contribution to the revival
of a deep and sincere religiosity.

In Kohler's preconference paper, he draws direct connections between theological principles and practical policies for the building of
the Reform movement in America. A coherent unified theology, combined with what he called a "Jewish mission" to work with Jews, could
reverse the apathy in many Reform congregations. There was an immediate need to increase the religious commitment of the congregants;
any strategy that might achieve this goal was worth consideration and
implementation on a trial basis. But such a strategy had to spring from
a coherent theology.

In the Pittsburgh Platform, Kohler did succeed in building a theologically consistent document that helped the Reform movement
establish standards for ritual as well as for ethical behavior. Drawn from
American Protestant forms rather than traditional Jewish ones, they
were nevertheless based on a coherent theology. But because it repudi-
ated much of traditional practice, the Reform temple of that time had
little in common with an Orthodox shul. For example, the Classical
Reform synagogue prohibited head coverings, allowed men and women
to sit together at services, did not observe kosher laws, and so forth. In
virtually every area of ritual, the Reform movement of this period

reversed traditional practice. Yet Jacob Neusner has argued recently that one of the strengths of Classical Reform Judaism was its theological coherency.

> When Reform Judaism began, its principal theologians did not offer the Jews *a* Judaism—another choice among the equally available and comparable alternatives. Nor did they claim merely to modify an authentic, received Judaism in order to accommodate a less than ideal circumstance. Reform Judaism did not present itself as Brand X, and it did not concede it was a lesser version of a good thing that was authentically realized elsewhere, in Orthodox Judaism, for instance. Reform rabbis did not wear head coverings because they did not believe it was correct to do so, the criterion being established by the Torah. That is to say, Reform Judaism thought of itself as Judaism pure and simple: the Judaism that everyone should practice, all Jews and Gentiles as well.[9]

Most Reform Jews today find the Classical Reform approach to religion formulaic and uninspiring. Traditional Jews often found it appalling, even blasphemous. But for many Reform Jews from central European backgrounds in the late nineteenth and early twentieth centuries, Classical Reform Judaism was Judaism.

The Columbus Platform of 1937

More than fifty years later, the Columbus Platform also was created in part to stimulate an apathetic and possibly alienated constituency. As historian Michael A. Meyer writes, during the interwar period, "Reform Judaism . . . had great difficulty fostering enthusiasm for its cause. For all of its rabbis' efforts to be relevant, for all their pronouncements on social justice, it could not—and some of its adherents would not—shake its image as a genteel, upper-class institution that demanded little from its affiliates. . . . Rabbis spoke repeatedly of anemia, indifference, paralyzing apathy. And except for the most talented among them, they often spoke to half-empty synagogues."[10]

During the economic crisis of the depression years, congregational membership dropped precipitously at many temples. Membership at Congregation Emanu-El in New York City dropped more than most—

44 percent between 1930 and 1942, from 1,652 to 874 units—because of its policy of insisting on the payment of dues. Many other congregations allowed those who had trouble paying to remain members, asking them only to consider making up the difference if and when times improved.[11] But financial difficulties were only part of the picture. Many in the 1930s wanted to avoid social gatherings, among them many Reform Jews who stopped coming to services to avoid people they had known in more prosperous times. Membership fell nationwide.

The national movement too experienced financial turmoil. Hebrew Union College (HUC) had prudently invested its recently raised endowment funds, but the other national organizations had serious difficulties.[12] Furthermore, the sense that there was a uniform practice based on the theology outlined in the Pittsburgh Platform was in the process of breaking down, although some remained devoted to the Classical Reform ways.

The Columbus Platform attempted to reinvigorate the movement by allowing for a degree of religious pluralism. Whereas the 1885 platform had posited only one way to practice Reform Judaism, the 1937 platform began to recognize divergent practices and even different belief systems. This created a new problem: It became very difficult to maintain a consistent theology. If God is commanding a certain way of behaving, that should be reflected in certain behavioral norms. Without behavioral norms, how can one argue that God has a specific set of expectations? At the 1935 Central Conference of American Rabbis (CCAR) conference, Louis Binstock of Temple Sinai in New Orleans argued that it was unacceptable that some Reform congregations had Friday night and Saturday morning services, others had Saturday morning and Sunday morning services, and still others had Friday night and Sunday morning services. Because rabbis were teaching completely different approaches to Sabbath and holiday observances, Reform congregants in different parts of the country would inevitably grow up with dramatically different and even contradictory ideas about religion in general, and Judaic beliefs in particular. Binstock claimed that the increasing diversity of the Reform movement in the interwar period was not a positive factor for the movement but destroyed respect for Judaism as a tradition and as a religion. "I do feel that Reform Judaism must declare itself positively; decree definite dogmas of affirmation or denial . . . furnish a clear chart of religious principles and truths by which we must steer safely and surely in the present storm-tossed sea of religious strife."[13]

In the subsequent debate, HUC theologian Samuel Cohon argued that although he did not want Reform Judaism to accept dogmas per se, he felt a clear formulation of the principles of Judaism to be critical.[14] Then people could understand what Judaism stood for and how they could observe their religion. Cohon called for a "crystallization of thought as to what is primary and what is secondary" among the theological principles of Reform Judaism. When he presented a report of the Commission on the Guiding Principles of Judaism in 1936, he stated: "The time has come for us in this age of chaos to take our Judaism seriously and instruct our people in the way they should follow and the things they should do. We should teach them that we believe in God, in Israel, and in Torah, and show them how to revive prayer, ceremonials, and other observances, whereby we can strengthen our lives."[15]

Cohon believed that Reform congregants needed guidance through the chaos produced by a rapidly changing religious environment and a deteriorating world economic and political situation. If Reform rabbis could provide no firm direction in terms of religious belief and practice, the religious lives of their parishioners would degenerate further—a point similar to Kaufmann Kohler's in 1885 and one of Kohler's reasons for pushing the Pittsburgh Platform. But the Columbus Platform was less successful in creating a document that conveyed a clear and decisive religious vision. Perhaps that was inevitable. Times had changed, and religious agreement was becoming harder to reach within the Reform movement. The platform is today remembered mostly as an affirmation of Jewish peoplehood. The document accepted the notion that the Jews are a people and a nation as well as a religious group. But it failed to unify the entire movement behind a shared religious vision. Nevertheless, the 1937 platform did signal the growing influence of Mordecai Kaplan on Reform Judaism. The focus on Jewish peoplehood and the revival of interest in Jewish "ceremonials" reflect Kaplan's notion of Judaism as a civilization that encompasses the Jewish people and its historical character expressed through its rituals, ceremonies, and other communal practices.

The 1976 San Francisco Centenary Perspective

In his study of the Reform movement, Michael A. Meyer subheads "Malaise" a section on the years preceding the 1976 San Francisco Centenary Perspective: "In the late 1960s severe self-doubt and anxiety about the future displaced the ebullience that had characterized American Reform Judaism since the war. Divided and uncertain of its course, it long remained in a state of crisis."[16] This was particularly upsetting because the Sixties were a time of activism and renewal. HUC theologian Eugene B. Borowitz, the primary author of the Perspective, wrote more circumspectly: "As Reform Judaism entered the 1970s there was a general feeling that the movement needed to rethink its directions. The tremendous enthusiasm generated by the rapid expansion of the number of Reform congregations in the 1950s and '60s had passed. The integration of American Jewry into the society had largely been accomplished, but the style of synagogue life that resulted, which seemed so fresh a few years previous, in the '70s, seemed somewhat stale and in need of invigoration."[17]

While many young people view the Sixties as a time of sex, drugs, and rock 'n 'roll, the social reality also had a dark side. The antiwar movement led to a painful division in American society that has taken decades to heal. The "generation gap" seemed wider than ever before. Men and women died in the Vietnam War abroad, and the Black Power and the women's movements, among others, struggled for recognition at home. The energy required for all these causes seemed to draw Reform Jews away from their synagogues. But independent of the social turmoil, institutional factors also negatively affected the Reform movement. Membership in Reform congregations remained static or even declined, while only a few new congregations joined the Union of American Hebrew Congregations (UAHC) each year. A number of congregations were forced to merge due to declining membership. Religious schools, long the primary recruitment tool for Reform temples, also experienced a decrease in numbers due in part to demographic trends, in part to the refusal of many preteens and teens to participate in the synagogue, an institution that seemed to represent their parents' generation.[18]

The Centenary Perspective was written at a time not only of demographic problems for the Reform movement, but also as the theological currents of the Sixties and early Seventies had made it increasingly difficult to speak about God with confidence. Many American Jews were just beginning to grapple with the theological implications of the Holocaust. Some were influenced by the "death of God" theology and theologian Richard Rubinstein's Judaic interpretation of that theology. When the Perspective refers to "our uncertain historical situation," it alludes to this situation: Theological as well as social assumptions were being questioned, and the confidence that many people had in the future had been weakened if not destroyed. The San Francisco Perspective includes the traditional categories of God, the people Israel, and Torah, and adds sections on religious practice, the state of Israel, the Diaspora, and others. Yet, it is ambiguous about what the Reform movement believes about the Divine.

For instance, the document's statement about belief in God begins, "The affirmation of God has always been essential to our people's will to survive," which says nothing about belief in God but concerns rather the consequence of that belief for the Jewish people. Further, "in our struggle through the centuries to preserve our faith, we have experienced and conceived of God in many ways." Again the stress is on the struggle of the Jewish people to survive, and the text never defines the faith it has preserved. Already a contradiction arises: If the will to survive has depended on affirming a specific conception of God, then how can one say that Jews have seen God in so many ways? It seems highly unlikely that Jews before the Emancipation and the Enlightenment saw God in many ways. Premodern society was homogenous, and one can reasonably assume that before 1800 most Jews held a relatively uniform conception of God.

The 1976 statement was trying very hard to be relevant. Like the 1885 and 1937 platforms, it reached out to people who seemed preoccupied with more pressing issues. It was felt that the statement had to empathize with a widespread religious alienation; thus, "the trials of our own time and the challenges of modern culture have made steady belief and clear understanding difficult for some." The statement attempted to turn this situation into a positive by explaining that "we ground our lives, personally and communally, on God's reality and remain open to new experiences and conceptions of the Divine"—the intentional ambiguity was necessary because there was no consensus on the nature of God. Hoping to appeal to many American Jews looking for a spiritual mooring in an age of rapid change, the statement affirms that "amid the mystery we call life, . . . human beings, created in God's image, share in God's eternality despite the mystery we call death."[19] The strongest that could be made under the circumstances, the statement still was not going to provide the theological direction clear enough to build a strengthened religious commitment throughout the movement.

Defining the Limits of Reform Pluralism

A well-known joke goes that while Orthodox rabbis can get thrown out of their rabbinical association for eating salad in a restaurant, and Conservative rabbis can get suspended from their movement for officiating at an intermarriage ceremony, a Reform rabbi can be ejected from the CCAR for only one thing—refusing to pay dues. While this anecdote inevitably brings smirks to rabbis' faces, the Reform movement is not just a collection of congregations working together for institutional convenience. Although the Reform movement's commitment to pluralism allows rabbis to believe and practice differently, the movement has tried to set limits beyond which congregations cannot go.

The question of whether the movement has theological boundaries was tested in the early nineties when Congregation Beth Adam of Cincinnati applied to join the UAHC. Its founder, Rabbi Robert Barr, had graduated from HUC-JIR; many if not most of its congregants came from Reform backgrounds, including three current or former members of the HUC-JIR Board of Governors. An adherent of Rabbi Sherwin T. Wine's Humanistic Judaism, Barr had founded Beth Adam in 1981. Arguing that it was possible to follow Judaism without believing in God and certainly without a traditional conception of God, Wine had established the small movement in 1963, along with the first Humanistic Jewish congregation, the Birmingham Temple, in Michigan. By 1969, the Society for Humanistic Judaism (SHJ) linked like-minded individuals and groups worldwide. Wine went on to form a number of other small organizations devoted to a similar perspective, including the North American Committee for Humanism and the Humanist Institute, the Leadership Conference of Secular and Human-

istic Jews, the Institute for Secular Humanistic Judaism, the Conference on Liberal Religion, and the Center for New Thinking. Apart
from his best-known book, *Judaism Beyond God*, Wine wrote several
theological and liturgical works, including *Humanistic Judaism, Meditation Services for Humanistic Jews*, and *The Humanist Haggadah*.[20] A member of SHJ, Beth Adam had grown unhappy with the organization, in
particular, as Barr explained, because the group had begun ordaining its
own leaders.[21] After about ten years of belonging to no national organization, Barr and the congregation felt the need to be in closer touch
"with the issues and concerns of the wider Jewish community." The
board of Beth Adam decided to apply to join the UAHC.

UAHC president Alexander Schindler encouraged Beth Adam's
application but took no public stand on what the Union should do,
stating at the 1991 UAHC biennial only that the controversy would
"generate a boon to our community" by opening a debate on what a
Reform congregation must accept, if anything. The debate centered on
the congregation's exclusion of God from its liturgy. Neither the Shema
nor the kaddish was recited, the group's literature explained, because
prayers "which presume a God who intervenes or manipulates the
affairs of this world" would be inconsistent with its religious message.
Beth Adam did not believe that it as a congregation should pray to
God, for "the use of prayer in services would be incompatible" with the
humanistic affirmation of "our right and responsibility to control our
own destiny based upon ethics and morals arising out of the human
condition." The congregation had removed not only the word "God"
from its prayer book, but all synonyms such as "Source of Life." To the
UAHC, Barr described his congregation as "on a religious journey" and
pointed out that it was ludicrous for the UAHC to consider recruiting
irreligious gentiles—a project Schindler had enthusiastically advocated—and exclude a Jewish congregation already organized and willing to join. Despite possible objections to its theology, Barr argued,
Beth Adam was "already making a contribution to the Jewish future."

While some supported Beth Adam's application, the response was
largely negative and even hostile, and in 1990 a majority of the CCAR
Responsa Committee voted against accepting the group. Chairperson
W. Gunther Plaut wrote that its "elision of God" means the congregation "does not admit of Covenant or commandments"; while the

Reform movement can accept individuals who may be agnostic or even atheist, it cannot accept congregations whose declared principals contradict the religious beliefs of Reform Judaism. Three rabbis on the Responsa Committee disagreed with the majority view, arguing that to accept Beth Adam into the UAHC would not necessarily imply that the Reform movement accepts its theological views. Eugene Mihaly argued that article 6 of the UAHC constitution states that the Union must not "interfere in any manner whatsoever" in the internal affairs of any congregation.[22] Gary Zola made a good point, impossible to refute: "Over the years, I have worshiped in literally a dozen 'experimental' NFTY services which differ only marginally" from the Beth Adam services. But the existence of mimeographed North American Federation of Temple Youth group services does not necessarily create a binding precedent. The debate continued through the early 1990s. In March 1994, all four UAHC- affiliated congregations in Cincinnati petitioned the national board to oppose the admission of Beth Adam. Allowing such a congregation to join would "infuse our community and our national movement with divisiveness, discord and disharmony," they claimed.

In June the UAHC Board of Trustees spent an entire day deliberating the matter in Washington, D.C. Among the many presentations the board heard, some supported the congregation. Judith Sherman Asher of Santa Fe, New Mexico, argued that particularly in the light of the many unaffiliated Jews in the United States who turned to all sorts of other spiritual paths, it made sense to accept Beth Adam, even though the congregation might not conform theologically. She also pointed out that most Israelis might hold views very similar to those of the Beth Adam congregation. Doris Finkel-Peltz of Portage, Indiana, said that it was important to accept all Jews and not to exclude: "I don't go around asking, 'What kind of Jew are you?' The Holocaust taught me not to." One can sense the intense emotion the issue stirred up. Finkel-Peltz, then the chairperson of the UAHC's Small Congregations Committee, was used to operating in a community where small memberships lent every member a great deal of weight. Board members from larger Jewish communities had a very different perspective simply because of their greater numbers. For them, issues relating to the creation and maintenance of legitimate theological parameters carried greater importance.[23]

At the end of its deliberations, the board voted 115 to 13 with four abstentions to reject the application.

The Beth Adam decision meant that while congregations still had the right to adopt the prayer book of their choice or write one of their own, there were theological limits on what could legitimately be regarded as Reform liturgy. After the vote, Schindler reiterated that prayers such as the Shema were "the primary mode of our being aware that we are Jews, whatever our ideological divergences." Removing the Shema from the liturgy "is not just a severing of our ideological roots, but also of our historic roots as a people." The vote also reaffirmed that the drive for inclusion did not obligate the Reform movement to accept every group from every background espousing every ideology. John Hirsch of Temple Beth El of Great Neck, New York, who had fought for the inclusion of gay and lesbian Jews, strongly opposed the admission of Beth Adam. It is "Beth Adam that is being exclusionary. It's one thing to come into synagogue and choose not to say a particular prayer, or any prayers, for that matter—or to join and try to change the traditional prayers to better reflect our beliefs, our lives, our identities. Beth Adam does not give Jews the right to make that choice." A number of board members felt hurt by what the Beth Adam congregation had done. As Hirsch pointed out, "I cannot go there and say the Kaddish for my mother. I cannot go there and say the prayer that our ancestors said on their way to the gas chambers."

Schindler argued that the decision was the correct one for the movement. "Some common understanding is necessary to give us the kind of ideological cohesion which a religious movement . . . requires to retain its distinctiveness and to secure its continuity." He expressed the hope that the members of Beth Adam "will come to recognize 'that the genius of Judaism is best expressed in the declaration that only God is God and there is none else,' though God can never be known." The UAHC board chairperson reiterated the Reform movement's committment to believing in God in his summary of what the decision meant: "What has been reaffirmed in this debate is the fact that Reform Judaism is and has always been God-centered, and that the responsibility of the synagogue and its liturgy is to encourage congregants in their search for God."

To an outsider, the parameters of the movement may seem rather arbitrary. But there is a commonly accepted consensus operating that creates a sense of continuity at the same time the movement pushes forward with revolutionary change.

The Search for Spirituality

Despite the lack of consensus on all theological issues, most American Reform Jews, like most other American Jews, say that they "believe in God." What kind of "God" is another question. The religious behavior of most American Jews could lead one to conclude that they are de facto secularists who treat religion as a marginal enterprise.[24] Synagogues no longer are the central institutions of the Jewish community they once were, but rather serve limited functions on Holy Days and at life-cycle events. Yet an irrepressible desire remains among many to embrace something spiritual, and the Reform movement has proved itself adept at adjusting to the trends that have influenced the U.S. religious scene in recent decades.

For the many American Jews searching for a sense of spirituality, particularly those in the baby-boom generation, denominational doctrine is taking a backseat to the experiential elements of religion. Robert Bellah has argued that "utilitarian individualism" is a central feature of American religious life: "Utility replaces duty: self expression unseats authority . . . 'being good' becomes 'feeling good.'"[25] Reform Judaism is ideally situated to take advantage of this new trend. As a non-halachic movement, Reform is amenable to the "pick and choose" approach to faith. Reform services are not wedded to a rigid liturgy and can incorporate disparate elements designed to please "religious seekers." While this approach may cause many problems for a religious movement in the long run, it has allowed the Reform movement to appeal to many American Jews consciously or unconsciously committed to "utilitarian individualism."

In such a scenario, there is a danger that God may no longer be able to command attention, much less obedience. Rather than a presence that is always with us in our thoughts and acts, God can become an intellectualized abstraction who exists only on a theoretical plane. Modern Jews may feel God's presence only at exceptional moments, "signals of the transcendent" that Peter Berger argues are important despite their transient nature. But such episodic interactions cannot form the basis for an ongoing Buberian "I-thou" relationship, only a distant and formal one. This may be one reason many perceive their religious experience growing up in the American synagogue of the 1960s and 1970s as sterile and vapid.

As the traditional sense of community continues to decline, more Americans are looking for substitutes, which are not easy to find. Any real sense of community requires common values and a willingness to make a commitment to a set of obligations. Many younger Reform Jews are finding that the concept of covenant can play a central role in creating a common sense of mission necessary for the creation of community, which in turn forms the basis for an ongoing spiritual life. Some Reform Jews have drawn inspiration from the Hasidim, and in particular the Lubavitch, also known as Chabad (or Habad). Others look to the East, to Buddhism or any one of a number of other Eastern philosophies, religions, or meditative approaches.

It is not only Eastern mystical concepts that have worked their way into segments of the Reform movement. Kabbalah and other types of Jewish mysticism have become increasingly popular, and not only among Jews. Virtually everyone has heard that Madonna studies kabbalah, as do a number of other Hollywood stars; Americans have long shown interest in the subject. As early as 1969, Herbert Weiner of Temple Sharey Tefilo-Israel in South Orange, New Jersey, published the wildly successful *9 1/2 Mystics: The Kabbala Today*.[26] Much of the book focuses on Hasidism rather than kabbalah, but it gave many readers their first chance to view the mystical tradition as a contemporary movement. Authors from across the denominational spectrum have since published numerous such books. Even some written by Orthodox authors have managed to attract a considerable following among Reform readers. Followers of Zalman Schachter-Shalomi and the Jewish Renewal Movement have also written extensively, frequently from a first-person perspective.[27] A number of feminist theologians in search of an affirming, transformative model of God have adopted the kabbalistic concept of the Shechinah as a suitable feminine archetype. On a more popular level, nonscholarly authors have used kabbalistic concepts to show how people can achieve money, power, fame, and romance.

Other popular books argue that the kabbalah is the key to overcoming anger, hatred, and envy and to transforming negativity into joy.[28] In the search for existential meaning, American Jews are increasingly willing to experiment with new ideas, as well as with innovative approaches to ceremonies and rituals.

Some people are attracted to Reform synagogues because of the charisma of local rabbis. For example, Rabbi Steven Lebow, nicknamed the "Rock 'n Roll Rabbi," has tripled the size of his congregation in a decade due at least in part to his outgoing musical ways. Lebow attracts between 400 and 500 worshipers to his suburban Atlanta temple every Friday night. "We always have guitar and drums, and sometimes we play Jewish songs to a rock 'n' roll beat, or include [melodies of] Bob Dylan and the Grateful Dead in the service." One year on Purim, Lebow and Cantor Steven Weiss impersonated the Beach Boys and chanted the Scroll of Esther to the tune of "California Girls." The next Purim they dressed up like the Beatles and chanted to the tune of "Yesterday." Lebow is very aware that the synagogue needs to touch people's emotions. "If you make people feel good, they'll come back." Journalist Heather Robinson writes that the "Rock 'n' Roll Rabbi" has approached his spiritual leadership of Temple Kol Emeth in Marietta, Georgia, with "the zeal and iconoclasm of a modern-day prophet." Lebow also runs radio spots and print ads to attract people from the surrounding area. In 1995, he launched a marketing campaign throughout greater Atlanta with billboards that read "Make Our Home Your Home—Temple Kol Emeth, Marietta." Lebow distinguishes between advertising, which he sees as consonant with traditional Judaism and helpful for both the congregation and the potential congregant, and proselytizing, which he opposes. "I don't believe we should go door-to-door or try to convert anyone who is happy with another religion." But he is interested in connecting with the "many Americans with no religion [who] are seeking some spiritual connection."[29]

Other attempts to develop creative religious responses to the changing social environment have been less successful. In 1997, Ellen Levin, a woman suffering from multiple sclerosis, asked Rabbi David Cohen of Congregation Sinai in Milwaukee to develop a ritual to allow her to thank God for Bucky, her deaf two-year-old dalmatian, who was helping to ease her suffering. Cohen replied that Judaism indeed has much to say about the relationship between humans and animals.

Therefore, if the family was willing to study the relevant sacred texts and understood that the ceremony would be nothing like a conventional bar mitzvah, then he would be willing to help. Unfortunately, the family chose to call the occasion a "Bark Mitzvah," as the *Milwaukee Journal Sentinel* and other local media reported.[30] Highly critical letters to the editor followed, and vicious gossip continued for weeks. Eventually Cohen felt obligated to explain himself in a letter to the *Wisconsin Jewish Chronicle*.[31] When I asked him recently for comment, he wrote, "As you may understand, I am most reluctant to re-live any aspect of the bark mitzvah episode . . . what was intended as a 'mitzvah' for a woman with progressive MS, turned into a nightmare."[32]

Reform Jews are more open to performing mitzvoth than were their predecessors. Yet their social values are often far more liberal. The Reform movement today is thus moving in two directions at the same time. This is possible because Jews perceive Judaism as a religion that has no fixed dogmas or doctrines, that offers a spiritual context in which they can place the daily events of their lives. Judaism provides them with a series of sacred myths and a religious history that helps them articulate their own sense of what they believe and what they see as important.

What some have found effective is to begin from their own life experiences and then move to the collective Jewish religious understanding. Peter Pitzele, who pioneered a methodology of psychodrama that draws on the individual's own experiences to reenact family stories from the Bible, taught his techniques at HUC-JIR in New York, as did Carol Ochs, who developed an approach of "our lives as Torah."[33] Ochs argues that people could develop a personal theology by exploring their own life stories. Through close examination of their own past, they could learn to recognize God at work and then bring that life story into "conversation" with Torah. Ochs's book was advertised as invaluable for helping "us understand who God is for us by exploring love, suffering, work, prayer, community, and experiences with death."[34] The key phrase is understanding who God is "for us."

The Contemporary Reality

Today, Reform Judaism is a pluralistic American religious denomination. No one could possibly argue that one must accept a specific set of theological principles in order to be a Reform Jew in good standing. Yet the movement is thriving. New congregations are joining the UAHC and existing ones are increasing their membership. This popularity has little to do with Reform's specific theological formulations. Rather, the flexibility that has emerged from its theological pluralism has allowed the movement to draw strength from new types of adherents while enthusing substantial numbers of longtime members.

The Reform movement has come a long way from the theological uniformity of the 1885 Pittsburgh Platform. By the 1970s, there was such full acceptance of a wide range of traditions, customs, and practices that it would have been ridiculous to suggest that one official standard was uniformly accepted and required for a Reform service of any type. Behind this diversity of ritual expression lay the acceptance of the idea that there was no one Reform theology, that Reform Judaism represented many different ways of thinking about God and the relationship between God and the Jewish people.

Eugene Borowitz acknowledges this pluralism explicitly in his book *Liberal Judaism*, published by the UAHC in 1984. He asks, "Who is a good Jew?" And he answers, "I consider nothing more fundamental to being a good Jew than belief in God." But he goes on to suggest that there are many different ways of looking at God, and that many of them can be religiously authentic for a believing Jew. "With our religious and communal authority largely replaced by the insistence of modern Jews on thinking for themselves, no one can easily claim the authority to overrule competing views." In discussing how Jews may legitimately view God, Borowitz admits: "With our new appreciation of pluralism, we have also gained greater appreciation of the extraordinary openness with which Judaism has allowed people to talk of God. 'My' good Jew believes in God but not necessarily in my view of God. We have numerous differing interpretations of what God might mean for a contemporary Jew. . . . I am saying that we Jews have been and remain fundamentally a religion, not that we are very dogmatic about it."[35] From a theological point of view, the acceptance of such a broad spectrum of beliefs makes it impossible to present a clear and compelling religious vision that could motivate followers to sacrifice for the sake of God. There are simply too many images of God for the group to agree on any one. On the other hand, this theological diversity allows the Reform movement to reach out to a broad spectrum of people who differ not only in their lifestyles, but also in their religious convictions.

The pluralistic nature of American religion has mushroomed over the past twenty-five years. "Spiritual individualism" has become an important force as congregants became less willing to sit quietly listening to the choir sing and the rabbi sermonize. They expect to participate actively in a common spiritual quest. More and more Americans seek inspiration from their personal life experiences rather than from a doctrine handed down through creedal statements or religious hierarchies. "Spirituality" is becoming more and more detached from traditional religion. In an increasingly therapeutic age, religion will be viewed as just another means of solving or at least coping with emotional and even medical problems.

Despite these trends, the Reform movement would again urge Reform Jews to embrace traditional rituals and to this end would debate and pass yet another theological statement, the 1999 Pittsburgh Platform. But in spite of arguments over its substance among the Classical Reformers and the neo-Reformers, the movement has continued to grow, further proof that Reform thrives because of, not despite, its pluralism.

Chapter 4

The Reform Revolution of the 1990s

This is the single most momentous hour in the history of our movement. We must now decide whether our Reform heritage will be permitted to wither, or if it will be handed over to generations to come. We have a few years, a decade at most, to respond to the spiritual emergency that threatens to engulf us.

—ERIC H. YOFFIE, 1997

IN LIGHT of the Reform movement's failure to develop a coherent theology, that the movement is undergoing a transformation and revitalization may seem surprising. Yet, this is precisely why Reform temples have been able to reinvent themselves to meet the needs of a new generation. During the 1990s, Reform Jews struggled with a variety of social issues, such as how to respond to the increasing numbers of interfaith couples and whether rabbis should officiate at the wedding ceremonies of gays and lesbians. Each debate strengthened the movement by suggesting ways congregations could reach out to new groups and at the same time preserve a clear sense of identity. The movement has prepared new liturgy and is in the process of revamping its educational system. This too has enthused large numbers of Reform Jews throughout the country. Very few such changes depend on theology. Rather, the movement is drawing strength from people who want to situate themselves within a historical religion that allows them to explore a range of spiritual paths not limited by artificial boundaries.

Eric H. Yoffie, a Reform rabbi and the president of the UAHC, is leading the restructuring and revitalization of the Reform movement. Yoffie was the right person at the right time and place to take over the leadership of a movement that had to either make dramatic changes or watch its fortunes fade rapidly. Large numbers in the movement have been receptive to his proposals. New approaches to study, worship, and ritual practice are being implemented. Speaking in front of more than five thousand Reform leaders at the 1999 UAHC biennial assembly in Orlando, Yoffie said: "It is not only the experience of our worship that affects me so deeply; I am also struck by what it suggests about our Movement. Enormous changes are taking place in Reform Judaism, and they are evident here at our Biennial Assembly." He pointed out that a mere ten years earlier, very few people attended weekday services at the biennial, and even the Friday night and Saturday morning services were dull and uninspiring. While the conferences had offered exciting programs, people had not come to biennials to pray. "Today, however, it is spiritual nourishment we seek."[1]

Yoffie then outlined a plan to reform Reform. "I propose, therefore, that at this biennial assembly we proclaim a new Reform revolution. Like the original Reform revolution, it will be rooted in the conviction that Judaism is a tradition of rebellion, revival, and redefinition; and like the original too, this new initiative will make synagogue worship our Movement's foremost concern."[2] Yoffie urged that this "worship revolution" be built on a partnership among rabbis, cantors, and lay people. This was not just rhetoric. As Yoffie well knew, the Reform movement had developed as a democratic collective partnership. It had thrived whenever there was a good balance between professionals and volunteers. Left unspoken was the possibility that the decline in vitality in recent decades had been due in part to rabbinic dominance that choked off congregational initiative.

Yoffie acknowledged that the movement had some serious problems. "Poll after poll tells us that forty percent of Americans attend congregational worship every week, while for Jews, the figure is under ten percent. We joke about two day a year Jews, but we know in our hearts that the fault is not entirely theirs. We need to ask ourselves why so many of these Jews feel religiously unsatisfied in our synagogues." Yoffie added that the low attendance rates were somewhat ironic, given that Jews had written the Psalms, among the most beautiful prayers ever composed. Clearly Jews had once yearned for deep and meaningful prayer. He asked, "How is it then that we are today the least worshipful of peoples in North America?"[3]

A Low-Tension Religious Movement

One of the hoped-for benefits of the new programs is the revitalization of Reform congregational life. Their cumulative impact will increase the demands of membership, the "costs" of being a Reform Jew. If the movement increases these costs, congregational life should become more intense.

Currently, the Reform movement allows people to join at little cost, that is, without meeting any clear and compelling denominational demands. The values of the synagogue mirror those of the general society, and so members feel little conflict between the two. Absent such demands, members tend to approach the synagogue only when they want or need something. They may attend High Holy Day services but rarely appear in the chapel or sanctuary during the rest of the year. They call on the rabbi for help with a funeral but do not feel obligated to attend regular adult education. This lack of commitment is just one of many indications that Reform has been a low-tension religious movement and has a serious free-rider problem.

Many temples have become little more than bar mitzvah factories. Couples join synagogues as their children reach Hebrew school age or as young adults approach bar or bat mitzvah. They want an extracurricular activity that parallels what their children's Christian friends enjoy in their suburban congregations. One study of Jews in Queens and Long Island showed that the affiliation rate increased to as much as 90 percent among families with children between the ages of ten and twelve.[4] Other studies confirm this pattern. The children attend Hebrew school sporadically for a number of years to be eligible for the bar or bat mitzvah ceremony, which is seen primarily in personalistic terms.

On Saturday mornings, sanctuaries often overflow with unfamiliar worshipers visiting the temple to take part in the bar or bat mitzvah. As family and friends gather to pay homage to the young man or woman and to deliver accolades on his or her many accomplishments, the communal religious component gets lost in the excitement. Those few congregants who have made it a practice to come to services on Saturday mornings feel shut out by the fussing relatives and business associates; most simply stop coming on Saturday morning. As Yoffie commented: "For many Reform Jews, the rite of bar mitzvah is the single most significant religious event in their lives, and we should be respectful of its impact. Still, Judaism is a collective enterprise, not a private pursuit, and we must be troubled by the prospect that a family celebration is displacing Shabbat morning communal prayer."

Sociologists of religion have argued that this free-rider problem is inherent in liberal theology and that the Reform movement will not be able to completely overcome this handicap. Yet, much can be done. Despite the idea that making it harder to practice Reform Judaism would seem to make it less appealing to actual and potential congregants, sociologist Rodney Stark points out that high-cost religious demands actually strengthen a denomination by minimizing "free-rider problems," thereby increasing the production of "collective religious commodities," the "religious goods" essential for the continuing vitality of the organization.[5] As a religious group gradually increases its demands on its members, people are sold on the idea that their participation and commitment are wanted and needed. They begin to understand that belonging solely to derive benefit from the organization without contributing one's personal time and energy is not an acceptable arrangement.

American Reform Judaism reduced the tension between itself and the surrounding society to the point where it severely weakened the movement's ability to motivate its members. The current strategy is an attempt to move back toward the middle. The Reform Judaism of the next few decades will be a medium-tension movement, demanding enough to command respect, but flexible enough to attract and retain a diverse and pluralistic membership.

The Need for a New Liturgical Revolution

It was ironic that the Reform movement would find itself apathetic to worship, since it began in Central Europe in the early nineteenth century as a "liturgical revolution." While today most Jews associate

Reform with a commitment to ethics, social justice, and personal autonomy, the earliest Reformers started out by reforming the prayer service. Israel Jacobson, considered the first practical Reformer, instituted changes in the services as early as 1810. The temple—Jacobson followed earlier precedents in that appellation—featured choral singing accompanied by organ music, German as well as Hebrew prayers, sermons in the vernacular, and so forth. The German Jews who began attending such synagogues were impressed by the dignity and solemnity they experienced.

Early Reform, Yoffie has said, "was a reaction to the chaos and mechanical mumbling of the then-dominant forms of Jewish prayer. Worship Reform was the very heart of early Reform Judaism; Classical Reform Jews, then as now, brought a deep earnestness to issues of prayer." Yoffie was making it clear that whatever their faults, many Classical Reform Jews were regulars at services and took their worship experience seriously. Therefore, it would be simplistic to blame the Classical Reformers for all the movement's problems, as many young Reform Jews do. What happened? Yoffie's explanation was that the innovations made in the nineteenth century worked, in one variant or another, until relatively recently. But by the 1970s, these reforms and the approaches based on them had become radically out of sync with the times. Yet most Reform temples remained resistant to change. The regular worshipers wanted to continue to experience the type of worship service they had grown accustomed to when they were growing up. The idea of starting from scratch and developing new approaches to worship was anathema to a large majority.

Yoffie dubbed the disagreement "the worship wars," as verbal battles were fought not only over whether there should be change but also over what should be preserved. While many older members insisted that Classical forms should be retained—although people's memories of the good old days differed—many younger members wanted a warmer, more informal style of prayer.

The pressures of the worship wars have created a turf
consciousness unusual for our Movement. Caught in the
crossfire, rabbis sometimes insist they alone have authority
over worship; cantors sometimes do the same. Lay leaders seem

to alternate between indifference, and the expectation that
their rabbi will be transformed into a guru who will do their
worshipping for them.

And finger-pointing is still too common. Lay leaders
complain to me that their rabbi has introduced too much
Hebrew, or too little Hebrew, or too many changes, or too few
changes; and that their cantor does not let them sing, or sings
music they do not like. Rabbis and cantors tell me how
frequently their members greet every new idea with that well-
worn refrain: "But we've never done it that way before!" Is it a
surprise that even some of our most dynamic congregations
have grown fearful of innovation?

Nevertheless, there was no reason for despair. A collective resolve
was emerging that could overcome what Yoffie described as "this paralyzing fear of change."

The Transmission of Tradition

The tradition, for Reform religion, implies a religious reality that can
be transmitted from generation to generation, based on the covenant
established between God and the children of Israel. Since the covenant
is an obligatory relationship, those who receive the tradition in each
generation must accept the religious responsibilities that accompany it.
The Hebrew word for "tradition," *masorah*, refers explicitly to the process
of transmitting texts over the course of generations. But the typical
American Jew has understood this term as referring mainly to the folk-
ways of their grandparents who came from eastern Europe. As such *Fiddler on the Roof* connections as borsht, chicken soup, and Passover
Seders fade from memory, today's American Jewish community is coming back to a more "traditional" understanding of tradition. What is
written about Judaism then takes on greater importance, because little
folk culture remains to pass on through the generations.

For Reform Jews, the primary practical text for the transmission of
tradition is the prayer book, the siddur. Of course the Torah is vener-
ated, but it is not always read at services, and even then only a small
portion is recited aloud. If it is chanted in Hebrew, most of the congregation will not be able to understand it, and they are usually not sup-

plied with translations. The prayer book has therefore become the most widely referred to Jewish religious text. When Yoffie told the assembled leaders at the 1999 biennial that the revolution he proposed would require "an accurate understanding of what we mean by 'tradition,'" it was natural that he turn to the siddur.

The heart of the worship tradition consists of prayers that have become part of the standard *tefillah* over the past two thousand years, including the Shema, the Amidah, and the Torah service. These elements of the prayer service have remained essentially the same since the second century. The Reform movement has made changes to all of these prayers, dramatically shortening them and altering them—particularly in very recent years—to reflect the move toward inclusivity and gender sensitivity or neutrality. Those changes aside, the standard prayers are a traditional inheritance from the ancestors.

But the aesthetics of the Reform worship service are not part of "the tradition." They reflect the European mentality of the eighteenth and nineteenth centuries and the American mentality of the nineteenth and early twentieth centuries rather than the ancient Jewish past. "We need not be bound by cultural precedents that no longer resonate," Yoffie told his biennial audience. "Eighteenth century Minsk is not our worship ideal. Neither is Berlin of the 1850s, nor suburban America of the 1950s." Although the movement must both innovate and conserve, at this critical juncture in the history of Reform Judaism, it is more important to innovate. Therefore, a plan must be developed that will encourage rabbis, cantors, and lay leaders to feel they have the freedom to experiment with the liturgy. The hope is that this experimentation will produce a number of different types of communal prayer experiences that are "authentically Jewish" and at the same time indigenous to America.

The stress was placed on transforming worship because this is where most American Reform Jews encounter "tradition." While Judaism was long considered a religion lived primarily in the home, this has become less the case. The Reform synagogue therefore needs to pick up the slack and become the primary transmitter of the tradition. If the temple can use the worship service to transmit tradition effectively within a particular social structure, the Reform movement may inspire a new generation to seek continuity with Jewish belief and practice.

But the current situation does not inspire great confidence, as Yoffie admitted in his speech. He told of a hypothetical twenty-seven-year-old newly ordained rabbi who realizes that she is the youngest person, by several decades, regularly attending Friday night services in her new congregation. The UAHC president suggested that many temples might have unwittingly driven young people out of the regular Friday night service by creating a monthly Shabbat family *tefillah*. While the service is spontaneous and energetic and therefore has succeeded in appealing to young families, its monthly nature seems to suggest that other services are for the older adults. Yoffie left unsaid the implication that the formality of those regular services made many younger people and families uncomfortable.

The New Initiatives

The UAHC leadership has prepared a series of initiatives that taken together constitute "a Reform revolution." Many insiders are very hopeful that the coming years will see radical changes that excite Reform Jews and get them involved in concrete religious activities. To bring the synagogue back as a central Jewish institution, Reformers are developing programs that appeal to a much broader range of individuals and client groups.

Much of the success of this effort relies upon how deeply it can touch people's emotions. In his Orlando address Yoffie asked, "What will be the single most important key to the success or failure of our revolution?" And then he answered his own question: "Music." "Ritual music is a deeply sensual experience that touches people in a way that words cannot. Music converts the ordinary into the miraculous, and individuals into a community of prayer. And music enables overly-intellectual Jews to rest their minds and open their hearts."

The written text—the prayer book—needs to be accompanied by a vibrant musical experience. In every case where congregations have successfully revived their worship services, they began by introducing music that was accessible and participatory. Synagogue boards learned that for congregants to feel welcome, accepted, and empowered, they must be invited to sing.

The new programming has occurred not only within the movement itself, but also in related efforts such as the Synagogue 2000 transformation project led by Ron Wolfson and Lawrence Hoffman. As Wolfson put it, "What defines great, spiritual davening experiences is music, music, music."[6] Some cutting-edge congregations like B'nai Jeshurun in Manhattan and Temple Sinai in Los Angeles have become nationally known for implementing vibrant music programs that draw hundreds to their Friday night and Saturday morning services. That neither congregation is affiliated with the Reform movement may not be a coincidence. A vibrant musical experience requires the congregants to actively participate, to sing the songs with passion as well as confidence, and most Reform Jews do not know the words well enough to sing along. Their Hebrew may be poor, and not enough congregants have so far expressed the willingness to put in the time and effort necessary to acquire more advanced Hebraic skills.

The UAHC has inaugurated a number of programs specifically to address this issue, among them a Hebrew literacy campaign called "Aleph Isn't Tough: An Introduction to Hebrew for Adults" launched to "open the gates of prayer" to the average Jew.[7] The UAHC's new Hebrew primers will focus not only on phonetic reading but also on the comprehension of basic prayers and text. The hope is that more and more synagogues will use these or other texts to offer a variety of adult Hebrew classes. The more Hebrew that Reform Jews know, the more accessible is the textual tradition.

Yoffie argues that in the current religious climate, concrete programming designed to get people doing mitzvoth must precede theological formulations. In his closing remarks to the UAHC board of trustees at a meeting in Memphis in December 1998, he spoke to the debate over the 1999 Pittsburgh Platform: "By nature, I am not inclined to be sympathetic to platforms or to principals of the kind that we have before us. I wonder about the effort required for their production, and tend to be skeptical of the impact that they have on our lives. I am reminded of Franz Rosenzweig's remark that German liberal Judaism produced so many wonderful principles and so few actual consequences."[8]

In an exception to the adage that says the more things change, the more they stay the same, it appears that the more things change externally, the more willing people may be to try new approaches internally. Despite the enormous difficulties of launching and successfully implementing a strategy to rebuild and revitalize a large organization of congregations, a broad spectrum of leaders has been galvanized into action by the very real fear that the American Jewish community could dissolve.

The Shortage of Rabbis and Other Jewish Professionals

The future of the Reform rabbinate depends on the ability of Hebrew Union College–Jewish Institute of Religion (HUC-JIR) to train inspiring leaders in sufficient quantity to lead congregations. When enrollment at HUC rose in the late 1980s and early 1990s, many rabbis worried that the field would be flooded by newly ordained rabbis, drastically diminishing their own career prospects. At the height of the enrollment boom, when as many as fifty-five or sixty new rabbis graduated each year, a resolution was proposed at the 1994 Central Conference of American Rabbis (CCAR) conference calling on HUC to limit and reduce enrollment. The resolution that passed called instead only for an examination into "the implications of the increase." Rabbi Charles A. Kroloff, who headed the CCAR's Rabbinic Population Committee, has explained that "we came to the conclusion rather quickly, that there really was not an over population, especially because there was a demand for rabbis in other areas besides pulpits."[9] But many believed an oversupply of rabbis existed, a perception that "produced a diminution of interest in the late 1990s."[10]

Of a number of studies undertaken by HUC-JIR to find ways to save money, many focused on the possibility of closing one of its four campuses. The college was having a great deal of difficulty supporting all four, each of which catered to local and regional Jewish communities. Each also had specialties that would be difficult to replicate if that campus was closed. The Cincinnati campus was the weakest, because the city had a much smaller Jewish population than that of New York or Los Angeles. But Cincinnati had by far the largest campus and included the prestigious American Jewish Archives, which had been founded by Professor Jacob Rader Marcus in 1947. The Jacob Rader Marcus Center of the American Jewish Archives houses more than ten million pages of historical documents and almost eight thousand linear feet of microfilm, photographs, audio-visual material, near print, and genealogical records. Moving such a collection would be incredibly expensive, even if an appropriate building could be found in Manhattan or Los Angeles. Furthermore, the entire Midwestern Reform Jewish population looked to the Cincinnati campus for leadership and guidance. Many Classical Reformers felt that only Cincinnati understood their religious needs.

The campus in Jerusalem was certainly the least critical in terms of practical considerations. The students from the stateside campuses spent their first year studying there, and a relatively small Israeli rabbinic program was housed there. But the Israeli campus had tremendous political importance. The Reform movement was trying to gain acceptability in the Jewish State, and building institutions was a central element in that strategy. Closing the Jerusalem campus would be a catastrophic blow to those efforts. So each time the question came up of whether HUC-JIR could save money by closing a campus, the answer appeared to be that more damage would be done by closing any of the four than by continuing to run a deficit.

Former President Sheldon Zimmerman was able to raise a substantial amount of money, putting an end to the speculation. But when Zimmerman had to resign in 2000 after being suspended by the CCAR for an "ethics violation," morale at the college fell. When Rabbi David Ellenson was selected the following year as the new president, the choice received nearly universal approbation. Originally from Newport News, Virginia, Ellenson was raised in an Orthodox household. Sincerely interested in every person he meets, Ellenson is a noted scholar.[11] Ellenson explains that his goal is to create "a critical mass of more serious liberal Jews," which he hopes to do by promoting a Judaism that is "passionate about texts."[12] Many hope that his charming personality and academic credentials will attract increasing numbers of students to HUC-JIR.

The college has also taken a number of steps to recruit students. In addition to getting the word out more aggressively, it was decided in February 1999 to allow the Los Angeles campus to expand its two-year curriculum into a full rabbinic program leading to ordination, beginning in May 2002.[13] The decision was prompted in part by competition from the Conservative-affiliated University of Judaism as well as the opening of a West Coast branch of the New York–based Academy for Jewish Religion.[14] In spring 2000, forty-five rabbis were ordained in

New York, Cincinnati, and Jerusalem. By spring 2001, HUC had graduated 2,526 rabbis, among them 344 women; 372 cantors, including 139 women; and 24 rabbis in the Israeli program in Jerusalem, including 5 women.[15]

Still, the "rabbi glut" of the early 1990s has given way to a shortage. Many congregations were unable to find a religious leader who had been educated at HUC. Some made do without a rabbi, while others hired a rabbi ordained at the Academy for Jewish Religion or another seminary perceived as inferior in quality to HUC. Zimmerman, then HUC president, wrote to Reform rabbis in April 1999: "I am profoundly disturbed by the proliferation of seminaries throughout North America. Some schools without adequate academic standing and review are 'producing' rabbis, cantors, educators, many of whom are finding positions in our Movement. These schools are increasing in number because demands are fewer and standards lessened." Others were being ordained privately by Reform rabbis or rabbis from other movements. Obviously, both the CCAR and HUC-JIR were unhappy with these developments. Zimmerman wrote of his concern "about the small but growing number of private ordinations. . . . Private ordination lacks the standards and shared commitment to our movement and progressive Judaism that we share. . . . It undercuts our work at the College-Institute to increase standards and improve our education if colleagues (whose friendship and commitment I treasure) go into the 'rabbi-production' or 'cantor-production' business. We shall be the losers ultimately."[16]

All the stateside campuses hired new student recruiters to seek out potential students. Rabbis received letters urging them to encourage young people to consider entering the rabbinate. Yet Roxanne Schneider, the newly appointed director of national admissions for HUC, admits that the institution was slow to respond to the shortage of candidates. "We weren't as forceful in encouraging people to apply, in encouraging our alumni and lay leaders" to look for and encourage promising candidates. "The best recruitment tool is to go up to someone else and say 'Have you ever considered becoming a Jewish professional'"?[17] Exacerbating the problem, only 58 percent of Jewish seminarians planned to go into congregational work. Also, an increasing number of older rabbinic students were entering school, which reduced the number of years they were likely to work. Along with the perception in the early 1990s of a glut of rabbis, the thriving economy influenced many student candidates to go instead into stocks and bonds, Internet start-up companies, and the like.

Meanwhile, many rabbis found work at local federations, as chaplains, and in private foundations, day schools, and all sorts of other institutions. More and more began to work part-time, especially women on the "mommy track." Many of the larger congregations expanded their staffs to meet the more specialized needs of various constituent groups, which, as Charles A. Kroloff remarks, "just gobbles up the rabbinic supply," although "we're used to cycles, and we've seen it over the decades."[18] But the current shortage was particularly severe. As Zimmerman explained in his April 1999 letter, "We are facing so many *empty, unfilled* slots in our ranks in North America alone that it has reached a CRISIS level."

HUC's 2001 class included only twenty-three graduates. Over the next five years an average of forty rabbinic students will graduate each year. While this is not going to be enough, the numbers seem to be moving upward. The class of 2005 included only thirty-two students, but the class of 2006—the largest in ten years—has about fifty. But current recruitment efforts will not help rabbi-less temples in the short run. Many smaller congregations in isolated locations have been looking for a spiritual leader for years, with little hope of finding a suitable candidate. A continuing shortage could stymie efforts to revitalize the movement.

Defining the Religious Goals and Limits of the Movement

Among the most important core values the Reform movement has begun to focus on is the search for holiness, *kedushah*. For Orthodox Jews, kedushah is inherent in performing the mitzvoth. The halacha dictates what mitzvoth to perform at what time, and the Orthodox Jew must comply. Reform Jews by definition would never commit themselves to doing something automatically out of a sense of obligation. They do not believe that God gave a concrete list of commandments at Mount Sinai, and they strongly believe that their own spiritual needs and desires can and should play a central role in any such commitment.

To understand how Reform Jews see their religious acts, it is important to distinguish between the concepts of ceremony and ritual. Following the general use of these terms, this book uses the words interchangeably to indicate any act performed for religious purposes or in a religious context. But Charles S. Liebman, an Israeli sociologist, differentiates the terms in a useful manner. Ritual is stylized repetitive behavior directed toward a particular religious goal and is a mechanism for achieving that goal. It involves intentional bodily engagement and is believed to be efficacious only when done correctly, that is, as God has commanded. It then connects the participant to a transcendent presence—provides a bridge to God. Ceremony is a symbolic representation of how people involved see the social and cosmological order. The ceremony reinforces the individual's awareness that a social order exists and that the person is a part of that order, and it helps to define the person's place in the order. It is therefore a form of ethicism, which places the highest importance on intention, rather than on the way in which an act is performed.[19]

Reform Jews have begun to reembrace ceremony, as have members of all the American denominations. In fact, "ceremonial behavior flourishes."[20] The key point is that they are not moving toward a belief that they must perform certain ritual acts in certain ways at certain times because that is what God commands. Rather, they are choosing from a smorgasbord of ceremonies that they evaluate and then reevaluate. Does this particular ceremony speak to me? Can I incorporate this ceremony into my life and the life of my family? The ceremony is not seen as either obligatory or efficacious, but as helping the individual search for a spirituality that can provide existential meaning.

Holiness thus becomes a paradigm for the human endeavor. It is a transcendent source that connects individuals' yearning and striving for God with the institutions that serve them. The Reform concept of kedushah emphasizes that life is sacred and that Judaism can help provide the context in which to celebrate the passage of time as people journey through life. Kedushah is both person- and God-centered, in that loving, nurturing relationships enhance the sacredness of life. While internal piety without ethical concern is contrary to Torah, ethical behavior alone ignores the central role that the divine plays in the sacred history of life. Shabbat observance is a primary example of this, allowing the Reform Jew to undergo a transforming and renewing experience. The Shabbat can give Reform Jews a sense that they are God's children, separate from the roles they play in their family and profession.[21]

The Reform movement thus speaks the language of the baby-boom generation so hungry for spiritual nourishment. It is ideally placed, at least in theory, to benefit from the remaking of American religion that a generation of seekers has initiated. But for the Reform movement to remain dynamic, it has to insure that its core population remains infused. It will not succeed if it attracts adherents looking for the newest and latest while alienating Reform Jews whose families have been members for generations. This is the challenge the movement faces. The results so far have been encouraging.

The Worship Revolution in the Synagogue

Chapter 5

The synagogue is our best hope for Jewish survival into the coming century. Whereas less than a third of the total Jewish population ever joins any other form of Jewish organization, almost three out of four Jews affiliate with a synagogue. The problem is that those who become members with a particular end in mind leave when that end is served. Imagine instead a synagogue where people stay, finding it driven by spiritual vision and offering more than they ever thought possible.　　—LAWRENCE A. HOFFMAN, 1996

THE MOST concrete indication of a Reform revolution is the dramatic transformation of the worship service. The twice-a-year High Holy Day Jew cannot help but notice the substantial increase of Hebrew in the service over the past few decades. Even more noticeable to the casual observer is the use of *kippot* (head coverings), *tallitot* (prayer shawls), and other ritual items in services. The trend toward traditionalism was rather brusquely pushed front and center when *Reform Judaism*, the Reform movement's official magazine, featured on the winter 1998 cover a photo of Rabbi Richard Levy, whose beard and yarmulke were reminders of his advocacy of greater tradition. Although Levy was not wearing tefillin, many knew that he indeed put them on every morning, and a surprising number of people imagined that the photo did indeed show him with phylacteries on.[1] The cover article discussed the third draft of Levy's proposal for a new set of guiding principles for the

Reform movement, which was generating a great deal of controversy at the time.[2] The photo became the focus of a debate already raging over the proposed principles and in particular the concern of many Classical Reformers that the trend toward tradition represented an abrupt rejection of the great legacy of Reform Judaism.

Hundreds of thousands of Reform Jews had been raised with the *Union Prayer Book* (*UPB*), the "little black book" used in one form or another by most Reform congregations since the 1890s.[3] The *UPB*'s majestic prose and lofty poetry were intended to elevate the worshiper. Its prayers spoke of a transcendent Deity, who invoked "His" majesty and mystery while inspiring awe and reverence. The accompanying grand chorale works added to the formality seen as appropriate for a serious religious setting. Most of the prayers were in English, and the aesthetics of the experience were clearly copied from the mainline Protestant churches. *Driving Miss Daisy*'s Miss Daisy and her generation attended this kind of synagogue weekly, but many younger people found it increasingly out of touch with their religious sensibilities.

By the 1960s, when American society underwent a traumatic series of changes, the Classical Reform style of worship began to seem less relevant to contemporary reality. Nevertheless, many Reform congregations—particularly those with the longest tradition of loyalty to the Reform movement—retained their Classical Reform worship style and its accompanying religious and social mentality. But many others—particularly newer and suburban ones—adapted to the new social norms, rejecting excessive formality and adopting a more relevant format. The 1975 publication of a new prayer book, *Gates of Prayer*, marked the beginning of a twenty-five-year period of intense liturgical activity and publication.[4]

Reform congregations throughout the country would snap up the new prayer books, and numerous Americans outside the Reform movement would study or pray from the new works. On September 11, 1998, just before the House of Representatives was to release independent prosecutor Kenneth Starr's report on President Bill Clinton, the president hosted a national prayer breakfast at the White House during which he read from the *Gates of Repentance*, the new High Holy Day prayer book—from a *machzor* reading that focused on the religious steps necessary for repentance. These steps include first acknowledging that you have done wrong, then apologizing to those who have been wronged, and finally resolving to avoid repeating the transgression. Miami lawyer Ira Leesfield had given the *Gates of Repentance* to Clinton a week earlier with a note suggesting he might benefit from the prayer. The nation heard the president read a Jewish prayer and understood that Judaism had important lessons to teach all Americans, especially those, like Clinton, in desperate need of spiritual guidance.

The Changing Reform Prayer Book

Judaism is a liturgically based faith that developed a set system of prayers in the early centuries of the Common Era. During the medieval period, a number of "minor" prayers such as *Piyutim* (liturgical poems) were added, but the basic rubric remained unchanged. Despite the Talmud's requirement that certain prayers be recited in a specified order for Jews to meet their obligation, it was accepted that prayer could be offered in any language, not just in Hebrew. Nevertheless, the accepted practice was for the synagogue service to be conducted entirely in Hebrew, with the exception of the kaddish in Aramaic. In the modern era, some "enlightened" Orthodox congregations introduced a sermon in the local vernacular and might call out the page numbers and offer a prayer for the government in the local language as well. But the rest of the prayer service remained entirely in Hebrew.

The impetus for the development of the Reform movement in central Europe was a practical need to adapt religious practices to the changing social environment. Liturgical reform was a central component of the program. The movement accepted the principle that the prayer service could be changed—and even changed radically—to accommodate the spiritual needs of congregants. Many early German Reformers felt the worship service needed to be shortened. In particular, they objected to the repetition: A number of sections of the traditional liturgy were first read silently and then repeated out loud by the cantor or congregation. Furthermore, the synagogue had developed a reputation for being full of loud talking and disruptive behavior, and the Reformers wanted to create a dignified alternative, as decorous as the local church services. These local churches often had chorale singing with instrumental accompaniment, and many German Jews attracted by the early

Reform movement hoped to introduce this musical element into the synagogue as well. And like some of their Orthodox coreligionists, they hoped modern preachers could deliver contemporary sermons in the vernacular. Then the people in the pews could better understand the beliefs and practices of Judaism and the reform under way.

The early Reform prayer book not only reflected many of the theological changes that had been made but also introduced new beliefs unacceptable in a traditional religious worldview. For example, the traditional prayer book conveyed the hope that the end of days would see an ingathering of the exiles, with the Davidic dynasty reestablished under the authority of the Messiah who would become the Jewish king. The holy temple in Jerusalem would be rebuilt and animal sacrifices would be restored as in the days of old. This eschatological vision was dramatically at odds with how most German Jews saw their own present and future lives. Their hope was to integrate further into German society; they did not want to ask God to restore them to Palestine. They wanted their liturgy to reflect their desire for full social and political emancipation. The Reform movement made such changes to the traditional liturgy, excising the hope for the speedy ingathering of the exiles from the Diaspora and substituting a prayer for the building of a universal messianic era.

The Reformers were also concerned that the traditional liturgy stressed Jewish distinctiveness. Many German Jews wanted to maintain a form of Jewish identity, but they saw themselves as part of the German nation and wanted other Germans to accept them as full citizens, not temporary resident aliens. They therefore wanted the liturgy to reflect a degree of universalism that would allow them to maintain a cosmopolitan approach at the same time they perpetuated their ancient religious tradition. The emerging Reform movement allowed them to negotiate between these conflicting goals. Since the Reform prayer book could be edited and reedited, it allowed for the flexibility that many nineteenth-century European Jews required.

The earliest liturgical reforms were mostly practical, but by the 1840s a group of Reform theologians began to expand and develop Reform theological discourse. They wanted to incorporate the scholarship of the German biblical critics who had begun to demonstrate that the Torah text was composed of a series of documents redacted together rather than a single text given to Moses by God at Mount Sinai and passed down word for word. In addition, most Reformers rejected the historicity of the miracles described in the Torah. They rejected the existence of Satan as well as angels, who are described in both the Torah and the Talmud. They rejected the traditional belief in the resurrection of the dead, eliminating the prayer that praises God as the one who resurrects the dead.

The Reformers addressed these theological problems in different ways. The new liturgical formulations could simply drop the offensive word or phrase, thereby eliminating what was perceived to be an antiquated belief. The language could be rewritten to give a more modern expression to the traditional prayer. New phrases, sentences, and entire prayers could be added in either Hebrew or German. The vernacular prayers in particular allowed the German rabbis to address the need for a concrete expression of the hopes and dreams of the contemporary worshiper.

The Reformers began what became an ongoing process of creating new liturgies and then revising them. The lay founders of the Hamburg temple compiled their own prayer book as early as 1819 and revised it in 1841. In 1854, Abraham Geiger edited a new prayer book, which he revised in 1870. It was Geiger's siddur that served as the chief model for the *Einheitsgebetbuch—Einheit* means union—officially titled *Tephilloth lekhol hashanah-Gebetbuch für das ganze Jahr* (Prayer book for the whole year), which became the common prayer book for liberal German Jewish communities.[5] In the United States, David Einhorn edited *Olath Tamid*, with Hebrew and German text, published in New York in 1858. This siddur was later used as the model for the Central Conference of American Rabbis's (CCAR) 1894 *Union Prayer Book* (*UPB*).[6] Isaac Mayer Wise edited *Minhag Amerika*, which he plugged at every opportunity, hoping that it would become the established liturgical text for all American Israelites.[7] But when Reform congregations accepted the *UPB* as normative, even Wise reluctantly supported its use throughout the movement. While revised slightly a number of times, the *UPB* remained essentially unchanged (at least in the eyes of the laity) for almost one hundred years. This stability is one of the main reasons the recent flurry of liturgical activity has upset many, who had come to believe that the *UPB* had always been and would always be their prayer book.

The Revival of the Bar Mitzvah Ceremony

The early Reform theoreticians wanted to abolish the bar mitzvah ceremony and substitute the rite of confirmation. This was more consistent with what their Protestant neighbors were doing in the late nineteenth and early twentieth centuries, and it created a vehicle for continuing religious education until age fifteen or sixteen rather than age twelve or thirteen. Furthermore, the bar mitzvah was actually a celebration of a thirteen-year-old boy's being called up to the Torah for the first time in his life. But the Classical Reform temple no longer called up members of the congregation to read or even bless the Torah. Rather, the rabbi performed these functions as part of his ritual duties. The Classical Reform service was a carefully choreographed ritual and only extensively trained religious functionaries normally participated.

HUC president Rabbi Kaufmann Kohler explained in 1907 that there was an additional reason to replace the bar mitzvah with confirmation: "Ceremonies which assign to woman an inferior rank according to Oriental notions are out of place with us. Reform Judaism recognizes woman as man's equal and sees in her deeper emotional nature, which is more responsive to the promptings of the spirit, the real inspiring influence for religious life in the household. Accordingly all the ceremonies in the domestic life today should be Occidental rather than Oriental in form and character."[8]

For decades, the confirmation service became the standard rite of passage for youth growing up in a Reform temple. The students studied together and participated in the confirmation service together. This service was held on Shavuot, the holiday that celebrates the giving of the Torah at Mount Sinai. Many congregations held the confirmation service on the Sunday following Shavuot, to make it more convenient for family and friends to attend. The confirmants frequently developed a strong sense of group identity, and even decades later remember all of the other students in their confirmation class. Photos of each confirmation group were given to each family and displayed prominently in the synagogues.

But as traditional practices made a comeback, more and more Reform congregations reinstated the bar mitzvah ceremony and added a bat mitzvah ceremony for girls that could directly parallel it. By the time that the CCAR produced a new rabbis' manual in 1988, W. Gunther Plaut could write that "bar and bat mitzvahs have become commonplace in our congregations."[9] Confirmation continues to be celebrated, and some congregations require bar and bat mitzvoth to commit in writing to continue their Jewish education through confirmation. The bar mitzvah ceremony has become so ubiquitous that many Reform Jews forget that it was not encouraged in earlier generations. For example, Classical Reform Rabbi Joseph H. Freedman would not permit bar mitzvah celebrations to be held at Congregation B'nai Israel in Albany, Georgia, as late as the early 1970s. Families who wanted their sons to become b'nai mitzvah had to travel to Tallahassee, Florida.[10]

Even many rabbis never became b'nai mitzvah. Rabbi Jack Stern tells of working with a student many years ago who was totally negligent in his bar mitzvah preparations. In frustration, his mother turned to the boy and snapped at him "I am sure Rabbi Stern studied hard for his bar mitzvah, and that's what you should be doing!" Stern writes that he is grateful that the mother made her comment as a statement and not as a question, because he never did become a bar mitzvah. Rather, he studied for confirmation along with about forty other students his age at the Isaac M. Wise Temple in Cincinnati. The confirmation stressed prophetic ethics and justice. Stern recalls:

> To this day I can visualize the striking figure of the Prophet Amos in his peasant cloak barging into the sanctuary in Sumeria and railing against the people. "You sell the poor into slavery, you cheat your customers with false weights and measures, your judges are corrupt because you corrupt them—and then you dare to put on your finest clothes in a show of sumptuous sacrifice with this soaring music and convince yourselves that this is what God wants? Well, let me set you straight. What god wants, in place of all of this, is for 'justice to well up as waters and righteousness like a mighty stream.'"[11]

The temple stressed that God represented everything that was ethically good and morally right. God required all people to live their lives according to the highest personal standards. The confirmation ceremony was a group process precisely because the religious message was one that grew out of the community and the society.

In contrast, the bar and bat mitzvah ceremony was very much an individual affair. The boy or girl stood on the *bimah* alone, reading from the Torah and conducting part of the service. Although they were required to attend Hebrew school, they were prepared for the ceremony privately by a bar or bat mitzvah tutor. Many of the bar and bat mitzvah celebrations tend to be ostentatious affairs glorifying the boy or girl and every materialistic aspiration he or she might hold. Nevertheless, the reinstitution of the bar mitzvah ceremony is one of many manifestations of the "return to tradition" in the Reform movement. Reform Jews are practicing more of the ceremonies familiar to the traditional synagogue and are continually restoring rituals that were eliminated, abbreviated, or replaced long ago. The publication of a series of new prayer books with much Hebrew and traditionalistic concepts is another indication of this trend.

Recent Attempts at Liturgical Reform

In 1975, the CCAR published a new prayer book. It was more than twice the size of the *UPB* and includes multiple different services. Although this new prayer book was not the first publication marking this new phase of liturgical activity, its introduction was such an important event that Lawrence A. Hoffman called it a "Liturgical rebirth."[12] In 1974, the CCAR had published a new Passover *Haggadah*, edited by Herbert Bronstein with illustrations by Leonard Baskin.[13] It was the following year that the CCAR published the *Gates of Prayer (GOP)*, with the Hebrew title *Shaarei Tefillah*. Stanley Dreyfus explained the title on the occasion of the book's dedication: "Our rabbis affirm that the way to God which is prayer can never be permanently obstructed. But for most of us that way is impeded; the gates of prayer have been so long disused that we can hardly lift the latch, push aside the portals. May this book swing open those gates to us; through it may we come to know the solace and the joy of dialogue with the Highest."[14]

Although today it is hard to see this publication as a dramatic break with the past, at the time it created a tremendous stir. For one thing, the *GOP* contained a great deal more Hebrew than had the *UPB*. Furthermore, it used modern colloquial English. The many congregants who had become accustomed to the uplifting formal language of the *UPB* found the new language pedestrian and therefore uninspiring. But the new prayer book reflected a number of changes that had been developing for a decade or longer. The greater amount of Hebrew reflected the "return to tradition," a move that continued to gain momentum. Entire prayers that had been deleted were now restored; phrasing that had been banned was now rehabilitated.

Equally important, the new prayer book reflected the increasingly pluralistic nature of the movement. The GOP offered ten different Friday night service choices. Each rabbi or congregation could choose one or could rotate through several. One of the services was modeled on the *UPB*; another was based in large part on the traditional siddur. Still other services reflected specific theological perspectives or interests: the belief in an omnipotent God who created the world and performs miracles; the concept of God as the still small voice within each individual; the centrality of mystical experience; social justice as a concrete manifestation of Jewish belief and practice. Other services were intended for use with children or bar mitzvoth.

GOP editor Chaim Stern stresses in his introduction to the new prayer book that the Reform movement includes many theological and liturgical perspectives. He writes that although there is disagreement on many issues, "we do not assume that all controversy is harmful." Stern emphasizes that neither he nor anyone else would want to stifle the expression of sincerely held religious views. As a result, the editorial committee "followed the principle that there are many paths to heaven's gates."[15] David Ellenson argues that "pluralism itself becomes enshrined, in both manifest and latent fashion, as [the movement's] . . . single most vital commitment of principle."[16]

Most of the nineteenth-century Reformers would not have tolerated such a variegated prayer book. They strongly believed that Reform Judaism should and did have a consistent theological approach. The GOP, in contrast, was a model of theological diversity. Less charitably, some called it "a theological hodge-podge." HUC professor Jakob J. Petuchowski sardonically noted that only a bookbinder could put so many conflicting ideas within a single volume. While these comments are true, they ignore the point that the purpose of the GOP was precisely to provide a variety of theological expressions for the increasingly diverse clientele of the growing American Reform movement. And that it did quite well.

In 2000, Rabbi Michael P. Sternfield of Chicago Sinai Congregation published an updated version of the *UPB*. *The Union Prayerbook*, Sinai edition, incorporates material reflecting the new trends in the Reform movement while preserving much of what made Classical Reform distinctive. For example, Sternfield includes prayers that show the influence of the women's movement, the gay and lesbian struggle for equality, the participation of intermarried couples, and racial equality. Despite the love many Classical Reformers felt for the formal English language in the *UPB*, Sternfield agreed with the rabbinic consensus that "the *Union Prayerbook*'s use of Elizabethan English, which was common to most English speaking congregations in the past, seemed arcane, and no longer appropriate."[17] The new text, written in more contemporary English, is even gender neutral. Sternfield made exceptions for prayers that had been recited in a specific manner with great devotion. In some cases the Classical Reform language is juxtaposed with a newer translation. For example, the Shema is printed in the contemporary manner: "Hear, O Israel, the Eternal is Our God; The Eternal God is One," alongside the older, nongender neutral language: "Hear, O Israel, the Lord Our God, the Lord is One." A handful of congregations such as the New Reform Temple in Kansas City have adopted this prayer book, but most prefer to use those published by the national movement. Meanwhile, congregations that favor Classical Reform continue to use the old *UPB*.

Between 1992 and 1994, the CCAR published three versions of a gender-sensitive *GOP* to respond to the growing demand to change the exclusively masculine references to the Divine, while forming an ad hoc task force to assess the need for a new prayer book. Daniel Shechter, the only lay member of the task force, arranged for grants from the Lilly Endowment and the Nathan Cummings Foundation. The ad hoc committee pointed to the dissatisfaction with the 1975 *GOP* and suggested that a new single prayer book was essential to maintain a sense of movementwide Reform identity. Peter S. Knobel, the chair of the CCAR Liturgy Committee, writes that the new prayer book will need to reflect two principles that govern the Reform movement today: the equality of women and men, and the inclusion of previously neglected or excluded groups, such as gays and lesbians, Jews by choice, the non-Jewish spouses of congregants, and people who face physical or mental challenges.[18]

When the prayer book was introduced at the May 2001 CCAR convention in Monterey, California, most rabbis were horrified. "Incomprehensible," "incompetent," and "hopeless" were three of the words I heard rabbis present use to describe the draft they were shown (but not allowed to remove from the hotel auditorium). Much editing has been done since then. Frishman acknowledges the problems that the editing process has faced. "The response in Monterey was instructive; some of the changes were too dramatic. Most importantly, members of the editorial committee recognized the need for greater communication and the participation of individual members of the conference." In June 2001, the then-coeditors (Rabbi Judith Abrams later gave up her coeditorship for health reasons) began work on a new manuscript, and this version was piloted at three UAHC biennial weekday services in November 2001. But many will remain dissatisfied.[19]

Rabbi Michael Sternfield expects many more congregations will adapt his *UPB, Revised Edition* after the new siddur appears. "From what I have seen and heard about the new book, it will be so radically different from anything that has preceded it that it will compel congregations to seek alternatives that are more conventional, and ours [the revised UPB] certainly is that."[20] When I showed the sample pages to one outside observer, she remarked that *Mishkan T'filah* appeared "to allow the congregant to tune out the rabbi and read and interpret the prayers as they wish."[21] But others, such as Rabbi Joel Levine of West Palm Beach, Florida, express satisfaction with the final text. "It is a vast improvement over the earlier drafts."[22] The editor of the upcoming prayer book faces a daunting task: to find language that reflects the theological diversity of Reform congregations while at the same time creating a unified liturgical work.

The CCAR also began publishing new prayer books for children. Over the span of a decade the Children's Liturgy Project conceptualized, edited, and produced a series of volumes with age-appropriate liturgies for youth of various ages. The goal was to combine contemporary educational approaches with inspirational interpretations of Reform

Jewish worship. The first two volumes were *Gates of Wonder* and *Gates of Awe*. Written by Rabbi Howard Bogot, Rabbi Robert Orkand, and Joyce Orkand, with illustrations by Neil Waldman, they are intended for the youngest children who do not yet read. The prayer books are designed to be read to young children and provide opportunities for discussing the themes of the prayers in a Sunday school, a children's service, or at home. *Gates of Prayer for Young People* is an ambitious attempt to provide both Shabbat and weekday services for two age levels. Rabbi Roy Walter and Rabbi Kenneth Roseman wrote the text, and Brad Gaber illustrated the book. *Gates of Repentance for Young People* is the latest in the series. This machzor provides High Holy Day services for both younger and older children and stresses the familiar themes of those liturgies. Edited by Rabbi Judith Z. Abrams and Rabbi Paul J. Citrin, the prayer book teaches that "all people, children and adults, sin but that there is a way to make things whole again."[23] The illustrations by Neil Waldman in the younger children's service are particularly beautiful.

The UAHC Worship Initiatives

When the Reform prayer books failed to captivate the typical congregational member, it became clear that the movement needed other ways to attract attention and develop interest in prayer. In a December 18, 1999, letter to congregational leaders, Union of American Hebrew Congregations president Eric Yoffie noted that while some synagogues had been successful, "all of us—rabbis, cantors, lay leaders—seem ready to admit that far too often, our services are tedious, predictable, and dull. Far too often, our members pray without fervor or concentration and feel religiously unsatisfied in our synagogues." He pointed out that "Reform Jews are rediscovering the power and the purpose of prayer. We sense that our Judaism has been a bit too cold and a bit too domesticated. We yearn to sing to God, to let our souls fly free."

At the biennial convention in Orlando the same month, Yoffie proposed a new Reform revolution that would include five specific worship initiatives. As part of the first initiative, he urged congregational boards to devote a substantial amount of time at two board meetings to defining the synagogues' worship agendas. The UAHC, CCAR, and the American Conference of Cantors' Joint Commission on Religious Living had prepared guides for the boards to use for this task. The first session would be titled "Why Worship Matters" and the second, "Getting Unstuck." The second initiative focused on renewing congregational worship committees, which in many cases had become no more than the technical apparatus for distributing High Holy Day tickets. Yoffie argued that, "if we are to realize this revolution, the committee must become the primary venue for rethinking the congregation's worship agenda." This meant bringing in new members to supplement or replace the "dead wood" that had accumulated on many committees. "I urge our congregations to do what many have already begun: reorganizing the worship committee to include the best and brightest congregants."[24]

Worship committees should embark on a serious study of Jewish prayer and undertake in-depth self-evaluation of congregational worship, both tasks facilitated by UAHC guidebooks.[25] As part of the study, an evaluation team should be put together to visit and observe the worship services at other Reform congregations. This team should include not only members of the worship committee and the clergy, but also representative congregants. E-mail discussion lists now made it convenient for members of different congregations to share their experiences. The UAHC created iWorship, an e-mail discussion group that can address issues such as how to develop meaningful Sabbath and daily worship experiences. Yoffie also urged all congregants to study Hebrew, "the great democratic tool of Jewish worship" that "opens the gates of prayer." He argued that "the full participation for which our members yearn is much more difficult without access to the sacred language of the Jewish people."[26]

Yoffie's worship revolution is being fueled only partly by the UAHC. Many activities have sprung up in various parts of the country on their own or have been initiated by independent organizations and even individuals. While congregations on the East and West Coasts and in major urban areas are more likely to have been influenced by these trends, temples throughout the country have begun to alter their patterns of worship.

Restructuring Synagogue Services

At the dawn of the 1990s, the synagogue service was in trouble. The 1990 National Jewish Population Survey (NJPS) reported that 8 percent of Conservative Jews and only 2.5 percent of Reform Jews attended synagogue at least once a month. While one can imagine the alarm bells going off in the headquarters of both movements, these figures came as no surprise to anyone who had traveled around the country visiting synagogues. For the vast majority of members, worship ranked relatively low on the list of reasons for joining a temple. Nevertheless, there are signs of a revival of interest in worship as a central Jewish activity. Jeffrey Summit, the Hillel director at Tufts University, explains: "There has been a real shift from performance to participation in worship. The concept of participation has changed to where the physical act of singing—being involved in body and breath and song—has become very important."[27]

This shift frequently requires altering the synagogue setting itself. In some cases, the congregation can move out of its large imposing sanctuary into a smaller, more intimate chapel. Alternatively, a renovated main sacred space can facilitate a very different worship dynamic than that envisioned when the synagogue was built. Temple Israel in Boston, for example, moved one Friday night service out of the sanctuary and into a hall. The service is held in an atrium; congregants sit on folding chairs. Summit explains that "they needed a space that was more flexible, movable, and more informal . . . where they can look at each other rather than up at the *bimah*." In the case of Temple Israel, "in order to create worship that feels meaningful, they literally leave their home."[28]

Suburban synagogues expanded family and children services with increasing success. They also tapped into the search for spirituality by offering meditative and healing services. Particularly in extremely large synagogues in major cities, congregations have drawn in many newcomers by offering "synaplex"-style services on Friday nights (a play on "cineplex"), several different types of services intended for different types of worshippers, all on the same evening.[29]

Congregation Emanu-El of San Francisco offers as many as seven separate prayer services in what Senior Rabbi Stephen S. Pearce refers to as "synaplex-multiple worship opportunities." Emanu-El's services include a "traditional" Reform service led by the cantor in the main sanctuary following the Classical Reform model; a service of "peace and comfort" that the congregation calls "a healing, spiritual service for those in need of extra support at difficult times in their lives"; and a Shabbat La'am, which is "an informal worship experience with an emphasis on contemporary liturgy and music." Two small *havurot* meet at the congregation monthly, informal social and worship groups that decide how and when they are going to pray and what they will do at the prayer service. A "family sharing Shabbat" features birthday and family celebrations. The children and their parents who attend a Tot Shabbat are thrilled with a worship experience that not only allows the children to crawl around and make as much noise as they want, but also respects their attention spans.

A monthly Young Adult Shabbat for those in their twenties and thirties that began two years ago with about forty people, Rabbi Pearce wrote me July 7, 2002, is "now consistently getting 1000+ worshippers with all kinds of spin-off activities and several weddings." The service features a young rabbi and a song leader. Very few of the people who attend were members of Emanu-El, although Pearce reports that "a good number of them have joined the congregation and feel a real sense of appreciation for and connection with the congregation." The congregation has also initiated a series of Jewish Journey groups that meet not for worship but for a wide variety of special interests including yoga, cooking, and walking tours. Plans are in the works for a new "lay-led minyan." Congregation Kehillath Israel, a Conservative synagogue in Brookline, Massachusetts, has four separate services every Saturday morning. The Young Israel of Staten Island, an Orthodox synagogue, has as many as seven. These congregations are trying to respond to the American desire for salad-bar religion, where the opportunity to select from an array of choices meets the individualistic need felt by so many congregants. It also provides the option of greater participation.

Sociologist Samuel Heilman explains why this synaplex concept, which started in a number of major metropolitan areas in the early 1980s, has now spread to the suburbs: "Large congregations are not satisfying to this generation of Jewish worshippers in America. The boutique or super market synagogue, where you can mix or match services depending on the hour or point of view, represents a creative solution."[30] Another reason is a byproduct of the anti-establishment feeling of the post–Vietnam War era. Many professional and lay leaders of the contemporary synagogue grew up in the 1960s with an aversion to the formal, hierarchical "high church" decorum of that period's Reform worship style.[31] Many young Reform Jews wanted to get away from the Classical Reform structure and move toward an arrangement that would allow different types of people to worship in different contexts. As Neil Cooper of Temple Beth Hillel-Beth El, a Conservative synagogue in Pennsylvania that has three separate services every Saturday morning, puts it: "It may be stating the obvious, but different people have different spiritual needs. If I had more space to start more *minyanim*, I would start them. We could have five different *davening* groups going on here [simultaneously]."[32]

While the "usual" Reform service is centered on the rabbi and cantor, an alternative service can allow the participants to lead and run the entire worship service, an attractive possibility for the Orthodox synagogue as well. Adam Mintz, an Orthodox rabbi at Lincoln Square Synagogue on the Upper West Side of Manhattan, argues that in today's America, where so many are used to participating fully in their professional world, people do not like being told that in the synagogue they must remain spectators. "At my synagogue, Lincoln Square Synagogue, for example, there are three regular Shabbat Services, at 7:45, 8:45, 9:45. This gives more people an opportunity to participate. Over the course of the year, most men get at least a few speaking parts. We also have a fourth service, expressly for those with little or no background. In this beginner's service, while there is a leader, there is no *Hazzan*. Everybody participates. Everybody sings. Questions are welcome. People deliver *divrei Torah* on a rotating basis. There is truly a sense of participation."[33]

Lincoln Square Synagogue has a number of significant advantages. It is located in a high-density Jewish area, with a large number of singles interested in meeting one another. Furthermore, it is Orthodox and therefore has a high-intensity feel to it, the opposite of many Classical Reform services. But as the Reform movement moves toward more traditional approaches, the Orthodox style can serve as an alternative model for how the multiple-service concept could work in a Reform context. Many Orthodox synagogues have what is called a Hashkamah (early riser) prayer service that attracts men who want to pray early and quickly during the work week. On the Sabbath, many of these same men also prefer to come to services earlier. This means that not only can they complete their prayer obligation by 9:15 or 9:30 instead of being in synagogue until about noon, but also they can participate in a service without excessive cantorial solos or a long sermon. After their services end, they can join a Talmud study group, go home to their families, or do whatever they please. At the same time, the Orthodox synagogue has seen an increased demand for a separate service designed primarily for young couples. While these services are being conducted in smaller chapels or converted halls, the main service can continue to operate as before in the main sanctuary.

Despite these apparent benefits, some see serious drawbacks in the multiservice approach. Many worry that such a system can result in the "balkanization" of the congregation, a problem already apparent in some Orthodox synagogues that have conducted different prayer services simultaneously for two decades or longer. Pesach Lerner, the executive vice president of the National Council of Young Israel, freely admits that in some Orthodox congregations with multiple prayer groups, "loyalty to the institution suffers. If I'm in the main synagogue, I have allegiances to the institution. But if people [pray] in the [early] *minyan*, very often they don't consider themselves part of the entire community; they feel they're just borrowing space." Members of the alternative minyanim may never see or hear the congregational rabbi or cantor. They may never worship with the bulk of the congregational membership. Heilman points out that the existence of these various prayer groups in an Orthodox setting can not only result in a social division between different types of congregants, but can also hurt fundraising. "The whole philanthropic pipeline is hurt. The fundraisers can't give the same pitch. It's easier for people to say, 'I gave at the other *minyan*.' There is not that critical mass."[34]

Despite the potential pitfalls, Reform congregations in most cases will not experience the problems that certain Orthodox congregations have faced. The high-intensity religious commitment of the Orthodox makes an alternative worship fellowship more likely to develop into a full-blown congregational group. In the Reform context, the level of participation of most worshippers will not be sufficient to generate the necessary momentum for a split. Elements marginal in an Orthodox context, such as the newsletter, have a much greater symbolic importance in a Reform temple. Finally, Reform synagogues usually require a great deal of money and a large number of people to make a new congregational entity a viable one. This alone is probably enough to prevent any separate service group from going off on its own.

Furthermore, strategies are available that can preserve and even enhance the sense of community in a synaplex congregation. For example, the Conservative Beth Hillel–Beth El offers one large kiddush after the three services, which enables all the worshippers who have prayed separately to come together to bless the Sabbath and drink *lechaim* together and reinforces the sense that the congregation is a single community. All life-cycle events are held in the main sanctuary rather than in the particular minyan a family may attend. This reinforces the loyalty of the families to the institution as a whole yet allows each prayer group to retain its distinctive character. Other activities, such as adult education and social events, are likewise planned together and done together.

The significant number of Reform congregations successfully using a synaplex model is just one indication of the increasing vitality of many congregations in the movement. Enough temples are being energized to make it clear that the Reform movement of the twenty-first century is far different than what it was just a few decades ago. A far wider spectrum of activities and viewpoints are now accepted and even embraced. The homogeneity of an earlier time is gone, replaced by a broad pluralism.

Innovative Approaches: Westchester Reform Temple's Congregation Education Project

The UAHC has been proactive in trying to evaluate how to apply on a broader scale the innovations of a number of cutting-edge congregations, mostly in urban areas such as New York, Los Angeles, and San Francisco. Working with other Jewish communal agencies as well as on its own, the movement has developed a number of programs to help congregations respond to the rapidly changing religious landscape.

The most significant change in the synagogue is the move toward greater spirituality. Lawrence Hoffman, codirector of the Synagogue 2000 project, explains the vision: "Imagine our synagogues as places where eternal Jewish values such as caring for the stranger and believing in the power of human beings to change the world are represented in every temple board decision. Envision a spiritual home where every single congregant, not just the social action committee, is performing 'ma'asim tovim' [good deeds] in the larger community. Consider the attractiveness of a synagogue where Shabbat services are so participatory and compelling that you cannot help but be moved by the reality of God's presence."[35]

Dramatic changes have been introduced with relatively little opposition because they were so overdue. Even many rabbis admit that the Reform Judaism they observed no longer touched them the way that it perhaps touched their parents or grandparents. Richard Jacobs, the senior rabbi of Westchester Reform Temple in Scarsdale, New York, describes how he felt in the late 1970s: "To tell you the truth, the Judaism I had experienced as a youth growing up in a large suburban Reform synagogue seemed shallow and uninspiring. The dreary services lacked passion and relevance. Our religious education was woefully inadequate. So when I was ordained eighteen years ago at HUC-JIR, I didn't want to be a congregational rabbi. How, in a good conscience, could I take a leadership role in an institution in which I had so little faith?"[36] This particularly blunt comment from a Reform rabbi appeared in *Reform Judaism*, the official organ of the UAHC, its publication justified by Jacobs's conclusion, which fits the official party line: He decided to become a pulpit rabbi and has remained in the pulpit because he believes that the American Reform synagogue can and should be transformed.

Jacobs's criticisms become even more praiseworthy from the UAHC's point of view when he cites them as justification for his decision to participate in the Experiment in Congregational Education Project (ECE). When he first became a rabbi, Jacobs believed that if he could just articulate a compelling vision of what the temple could become, then the members would surely listen to him, and they could all work together to immediately transform the synagogue. But to his disappointment, Jacobs found that although a few modest changes were implemented, the prevailing pattern remained untouched. At that point, Sara Lee, the director of HUC-JIR's Rhea Hirsch School of Education in Los Angeles, invited the Westchester Reform Temple to be one of the pilot congregations in an experimental effort at synagogue transformation. At first the leadership was very hesitant, concerned that the "experts" from Los Angeles were going to dictate how they should run their congregation. But as they became convinced that the purpose of the program was to give congregational leaders the tools to make needed changes, they bought into the concept. Along with six others—in Los Altos Hills, San Diego, St. Louis, Los Angeles, Atlanta, and Newton, Massachusetts—the Westchester Reform Temple became an original ECE congregation. Each was assigned an advisor who would help them through the entire process; Rhea Hirsch faculty and ECE advisors led retreats.

Not everything went smoothly. Many lay participants were at first concerned by the ECE approach, Jacobs reports: "If any of us thought the retreats would be a shopping trip for new programmatic ideas, we were wrong. The ECE staff encouraged us to spend the first year developing a bold education decision that would be the basis of deep, systematic change. The visioning work frustrated some members of our task force, who wanted to solve problems and implement changes, not discuss the many limiting assumptions that inhibit real transformation." Yet the retreats helped the groups develop their own thinking about a model for family and congregational education that could lead to sustainable spiritual growth.

Within a few months, the Westchester Reform Temple invited a group of about forty congregants to join an ECE task force that would spend a year studying and reflecting on what their temple might be "at its very best." Each meeting consisted of text study and experimental learning that included trying new rituals and new approaches to religious practices. The task force attended the ECE retreats, made field trips to cutting-edge congregations, and visited other Jewish educational institutions—summer camps, Hillel Foundations, and even Jewish museums.

Over the same period, a group of trustees began creating a congregational mission statement that would reflect their newly evolving conceptions of what Judaism could mean to them. After batting various ideas around, the trustees wrote up what they believed were five central pillars of their temple's sacred work: Talmud Torah, "lifelong and life enhancing Jewish learning"; *avodah*, "personal and communal religious practices, including worship that fills our lives with spiritual depth"; *chavurah*, "a welcoming, inclusive, and sacred community that embraces each of us with support, care, and wisdom"; Tikkun Olam, "ongoing involvement in bringing healing and justice to the brokenness in our world"; and Klal Yisrael, "strengthening our bonds to Israel and the Jewish people in all lands and building commonality among the various streams of Judaism."

About a year into the ECE program, the task force prepared a series of "community conversations" to discuss with as many members of the congregation as possible the work it had been doing. Just under half of the one thousand families who belong to the congregation participated. These evenings not only helped the task force explain its work, but also generated new ideas, including what became known as "sharing Shabbat." This special service, intended for families with children in kindergarten through fifth grade, is a "spirited" participatory service that "engages worshippers of all ages." Almost one-third of the eligible religious-school families came to the service regularly on Saturday morning. As one can imagine, the service got virtually everyone involved in one way or another. Even parts of the service traditionally viewed as requiring special expertise were now assigned to participants. For example, each week a different family took responsibility for leading the Torah service. After kiddush, the adults and children went off to study in separate classrooms. Jacobs has been impressed with the program's results. "This community has shared the joy of welcoming newborn children and the pain of mourning the passing of loved ones." It is difficult to evaluate how deep this communal feeling runs and too early to judge its long-term impact. But ECE appears to be a significant move toward making the Reform movement a medium-tension religious system rather than an excessively lax one. And that is a solid step in the right direction.

In addition to building a sense of community at Westchester, the program also stressed the centrality of Judaic study and incorporated that study into all activities the group undertakes, including the least formal ones. This decision too appears to be having some impact. As the ECE program began to take hold in the congregation, the leadership realized that the temple needed a different kind of space. Rather than another institutional building filled with classrooms and offices, the congregation wanted smaller, more intimate rooms. In these "sacred spaces" they could create "spiritual support groups," which ranged from alternative prayer services to study sessions to support groups and so forth. The Westchester congregation bought an old house adjacent to the synagogue building and named the renovated mansion the Center for Jewish Life. Here was a retreat-like center right on the grounds of their synagogue. Host to a wide variety of congregational activities, it proved of tremendous value in creating an atmosphere of warmth and intimacy. Whatever the activity, the principle was the same—individuals can connect to their religious tradition through the creation of a community in which the tradition's values are not only taught but also lived. In a sense, this conclusion justifies what the most traditional Jewish element has been doing all along.

"In the struggle for the soul of American Jewry, the Orthodox model has triumphed," writes Samuel G. Freedman in his recent bestseller, *Jew vs. Jew*.[37] Freedman does not mean that the Orthodox alone will survive, but rather that future Jewish communities will base their identity on a firm religious commitment that follows much of the structure the Orthodox have pioneered. And one of the aspects of Orthodoxy that has been most successful has been its ability to create warm and vibrant synagogues in which worship plays a central role.

But that is not the only lesson of the ECE experiment. The congregations found what many others in the Jewish community have been observing—that informal Jewish experiences such as summer camp activities, youth group involvement, and summer trips to Israel are among the most powerful ways to connect young Jews to Judaism. The Westchester Reform Temple hired a special youth rabbi who expanded the programming offered to children and especially to teens. The standard youth group and confirmation programs gave way to a multiplicity of programs specifically designed for modern teens, including healing services, Shabbat dinners, a theatre program, and a *chavurah*—a small spiritual study and prayer group—for informal Torah study. The youth rabbi was charged not only with developing and running these programs, but also with getting to know the young people on a personal basis while providing Jewish spiritual direction for them in a number of different settings. A close personal relationship with a positive Jewish role model can have a remarkable lifelong impact on a teen.

The ECE task force recommended creating a permanent education council that would bring together everyone involved in learning, to coordinate as well as rethink the synagogue's educational programs. The hope was that such a council might help the congregation clarify its goals and values. At one of the education council meetings, the leadership realized that because various committee meetings were being held on the same nights as religious and cultural programs, synagogue leaders were attending committee meetings and skipping virtually all the "content" that supposedly constituted the very reason for the synagogue's existence. As a consequence of the program, many congregants wanted to realign the activity calendar to better reflect the synagogue's core values and religious mission. They decided to move most of their committee meetings to Tuesday nights so that everyone could attend Jewish arts programs on Mondays, adult learning programs on Wednesdays, and healing services or support groups on Thursdays.

Only after four years of ECE-guided change did the task force and the congregation feel ready to begin transforming the worship service, which Jacobs identified as "perhaps the most delicate area of synagogue life." A rapid increase in the amount of Hebrew, for example, could alienate Classical Reformers. Too much guitar playing and other folksy activities might turn off the more formally inclined. Other changes risked upsetting all sorts of other special interest groups. The congregation determined to bring together about thirty-five people to study the prayer curriculum developed by the Synagogue 2000 project. The working group was intended to develop into a spiritual gathering of its own rather than to be simply a businesslike association that discussed an agenda and made decisions. As they continued to grow together, they shared "spiritual journeys" through guided reflections, while engaging on a regular basis in the study of Jewish prayer. They experimented with different modalities of worship, trying first Classical Reform and then Neo-Reform. They also looked at more avant garde approaches using meditation and guided imagery and experimented with traditional prayer by learning how to "daven." Such freedom to experiment can provide the impetus so necessary for generating innovations that will compete successfully in the American "religious economy."

The Westchester congregation decided to offer two separate Friday night services, a 6:15 Kabbalat Shabbat and an 8:15 Classical Reform service. The early service, mostly music and singing with a gentle guitar accompaniment, met in a chapel in an intimate prayer atmosphere. The later service retained most longtime characteristics of the temple's worship. But even here the congregation decided to make certain changes. For example, the late service begins not in the sanctuary but in the social hall with everyone gathered around a large Shabbat table. The congregants are encouraged to join in an opening *nigun* followed by participatory candle lighting, kiddush, and warm greetings.

By intensely studying the options and looking anew at the entire spectrum of religious possibilities, the Westchester congregation has learned a great deal about human spirituality and how it might go about fulfilling people's needs. There is no guarantee that they will actually do that, but their effort goes a long way toward addressing the hollowness that existed in so many Reform temples in the 1970s and even more recently. The point here is not so much what this one congregation decided to do, but rather the process that it undertook.

Jacobs himself acknowledges that the decisions reached were not necessarily the most effective ones. Nevertheless, he believes strongly that his congregation will benefit enormously from its willingness to experiment. "The double Friday night services might turn out to have been a bad idea, or they may continue to grow in popularity. We won't know unless we are willing to experiment and then honestly assess our successes and failures. I am convinced that we are on the right path because we are not afraid to make mistakes as we slowly transform our synagogue. Our members have learned to trust the process that leads to changes, and they know that their input will be welcomed as we continue to evolve."[38]

And that is exactly what American Judaism must do—continue to evolve. Having survived internal migrations, suburbanization, and all the other realities of the post–World War II world, the Reform movement is going to have to continue to meet the rapidly changing interests and needs of a highly mobile population. As boundaries of all types

fade, if not disappear, the resulting openness accelerates the assimilatory process that is both blessing and curse for the movement. American Jews love this sense of inclusivity and will do nothing that might
jeopardize their full membership in American life. And yet a completely open society poses questions of identity that need to be
answered in new, creative ways. For the foreseeable future, that means
reimagining the American synagogue as a spiritual home.

Building on Traditional Strengths
While Considering New Approaches

The new Reform synagogue must create an atmosphere in which people
feel wanted and needed. At the same time, it must build on its traditional strengths. This means finding new ways to connect Reform Jews
to social justice concepts and social action projects. Organizations such
as the Religious Action Center of Reform Judaism in Washington,
D.C., will continue to play a strong role in helping Reform Jews connect their faith to concrete action. Just as Orthodox Jews tie their religious identity to the observance of mitzvoth, Reform Jews directly
associate the prophetic imperative to do good with their religious affiliation. At the same time, the movement is now urging its membership
to consider new ways of being a Reform Jew. Many of these innovations
are connected to the worship service itself, certainly the most visible
arena of change. But Yoffie's "Reform revolution" goes far beyond prayer.
As the movement institutionalizes more and more programs that affect
how Reform Jews study, think, and live, the result may be to shift a low-
intensity denomination to one of medium tension, which would
encourage some marginal members to leave completely. But it also may
reenergize many hundreds of thousands of previously less active Reform
temple members.

People need a religious structure that makes demands on them.
They also need a religious system responsive to their emotional and
psychological needs. The Reform movement of the 1970s and early
1980s was in great danger of becoming a shell of large temple structures
with little spirit inside. The restructuring in process has already shown
that mainline congregations can ask more of their members and in
return give more. In their latest book, Rodney Stark and Roger Finke

cite Reform Judaism as an example of an American denomination that has successfully reversed the sect-to-church process. Put simply, churches and sects can be seen as the endpoints of a continuum made up of the degree of tension, or difference, between a religious group and its social environment.[39] Churches are religious bodies in a low state of tension with their social environment, whereas sects are in a relatively high state of tension.[40]

H. Richard Niebuhr, who argued that only the lower classes want high-tension faiths, while the more affluent prefer lower-tension religious patterns, took it for granted that sects could become churches but not the other way around. Stark and Finke argue that transformation can occur in the opposite direction as well. They argue that Reform Judaism "became progressively more liberal, until it came to be regarded as a religion virtually devoid of conceptions of the sacred or of the supernatural—more philosophy than faith." In the process, "as we have come to expect of the lowest-tension faiths, Reform Jews came to display a pronounced lack of commitment: declining membership, poor attendance, waning contributions."[41]

But Stark and Finke present the new Reform movement as one of their poster children for low-tension denominations that have successfully reversed themselves and undergone a significant church-to-sect transformation.[42] This is confirmed by data from the 1990 NJPS study, which indicate that Reform Jews under the age of thirty observe far more Jewish ceremonies than average, and those over fifty observe by far the least.[43] This is the reverse of the process that one sees when a religious group is moving from a sect to a church. Thus, Reform Jews can take satisfaction in knowing that they are moving in the direction most likely to result in a vibrant religious movement. Worship services will be one beneficiary, but not the only one.

At the same time the Reform movement progresses toward a higher level of religious commitment, it is moving forcefully toward institutionalizing liberal social and political positions. Outreach to previously marginalized groups has become a central element in virtually every congregation, and Reform temples are now filled with interfaith couples and their children. More and more members who were not born Jews and have not formally converted are serving on boards and in other leadership positions. As boundaries fade, American Jews in general and

Reform Jews in particular are perceiving their Jewish identities and American values as not just consistent with each other but identical.

A new term, "coalescence," describes how the "texts" of the Jewish religion and American society are merged into such a unified whole that its various elements are not perceived as belonging to one or the other, writes Sylvia Barack Fishman; rather, American Jews see their new value system and culture as a "unified text."[44] This may help explain how great numbers of Reform Jews see nothing odd about embracing so many previously discarded traditions while advocating vigorously for gay and lesbian marriage and similar ideas. Orthodox Jews may look at what is happening in the Reform movement and shudder. They may wonder whether the Reform movement will move to the right or to the left. But the path the Reform movement is on cannot be defined in those terms. It is a process of adapting to a substratum of American society that is rapidly producing an indigenous religious movement that has far more in common with some of the American Protestant groups than with Israeli Orthodoxy. This Americanness is reflected in the emerging Reform worship experience.

The Decline of the Social Justice Imperative

In the 1980s, numbers of Reform Jews began to criticize what they perceived to be an excessive emphasis on social action projects at the expense of more purely "religious" activities. At the same time, many began moving toward a greater degree of "tradition." The Reform system of ritual incorporated increasing numbers of traditional practices such as the use of yarmulkes, the observance of the second day of Rosh Hashanah, and even the wearing of tefillin. This process culminated in the 1999 *Statement of Principles for Reform Judaism*, viewed by its opponents as an attempt by neo-Reformers to push the movement to the right. Simultaneously, the movement has drawn back from a commitment to social justice projects and embraced traditional ritual practice. The two trends are by no means contradictory, but over time there has been a clear tendency to favor one or the other.

Many believe that the increased interest in ritual is responsible for the decreasing concern for social justice. One longtime congregational employee told me in 1998: "This temple used to be hopping with all sorts of social action programs. We had a regular exchange with a neighboring black church, we housed Central American refugees right here in this building, we organized civil rights marches . . . we were constantly involved in several causes simultaneously. But about fifteen years ago the stream of activities started slowing up considerably and then ground almost to a halt."[45] Many other congregations have reported similar declines.

The challenge facing the Reform movement today is how to integrate a commitment to social justice into the congregational setting. With so many couples working full-time jobs, there are far fewer volunteers, and these are able to donate far less time. Yet, a synagogue with no serious social justice program is a self-oriented religious institution. The right balance between ritual and righteousness can be achieved, but only with a great deal of effort and commitment.

Whether social justice programming is in fact declining remains a question. The Religious Action Center (RAC) led by Rabbi David Saperstein has been working to ensure that social justice issues remain front and center. Founded in 1961 by Reform leaders at the peak of the civil rights movement, the RAC was designed to provide Washington policymakers with a progressive Jewish voice on dozens of social justice issues. The RAC today has seventeen staff members, including seven legislative assistants, usually recent college graduates. Many have gone on to become Reform rabbis and Jewish professionals, an achievement of which Saperstein is justifiably proud. Among the many legislative assistants who have "graduated" from the program is Evan Moffic, who enjoyed "representing the Reform movement in coalitions with other public advocacy organizations, serving as a resource for rabbis and Jewish activists seeking a liberal Jewish viewpoint on social issues, and working with the Reform movement leadership and its Commission on Social Action to formulate resolutions on pressing social and political debates." Collaborating closely with rabbis and Jewish activists from across the country "confirmed my desire to enter the Reform rabbinate by showing me the incredible work that can be done. It made me proud to be part of a movement that holds up the unrelenting pursuit of social justice as central to the understanding of what it means to be a Jew." Moffic went on to study at HUC-JIR in Cincinnati, partly as a result of his RAC experiences.[46]

The RAC also presents programs to help keep Reform Jews informed on the Washington political system. Its highly successful L'Taken program for high school students brings more than 1,200 Reform Jewish teens to Washington each year for four intense days of learning and lobbying. The RAC seeks to train future social activists and organizes groups that can lobby for liberal social, economic, and political issues. Among these is the preservation of the separation of church and state, a principle of great importance to most non-Orthodox Jews. The RAC has also lobbied for Jewish causes, such as legislation designed to help the "refuseniks" not allowed to emigrate by the former Soviet government and for U.S. support of the Ethiopian Jewish evacuation to Israel.

Known for its ability to organize groups with widely divergent ideologies around issues of importance to Reform Jews, the RAC has also lobbied for measures designed to make the United States a more equitable society, such as the Civil Rights Act of 1964 and the Voting Rights Act of 1965. The group supported the passage of the Americans with Disabilities Act and continues to lobby for abortion rights. Internationally, the RAC supported measures designed to bring apartheid to an end in South Africa and to ensure a stable transition to democracy in Eastern Europe. The RAC deserves its reputation as "the nerve center for the struggle for social justice in America today," as Benjamin Hooks of the NAACP describes it.[47]

Working closely with the RAC in advocating for social justice, the Commission on Social Action of Reform Judaism (CSA) is a UAHC committee led by Robert Heller. A recommendation from the CSA, which proposes policy positions to both the UAHC and the CCAR, is usually but not always a slam-dunk. For instance, when the CSA recommended that the UAHC adopt a resolution calling for an end to the economic embargo on Cuba, the UAHC "ran out of time" at the 1999 Orlando biennial and then voted the resolution down at its board meeting in Kansas City in spring 2000. Although most of the activists believed ending the embargo was the right thing to do, some were swayed by the impassioned pleas of South Florida Reform leaders who were worried about the impact of such a resolution on their congregations.

Both the RAC and the CSA are identified with strong personalities. David Saperstein has led the RAC since 1974, while until recently

Leonard Fein headed the CSA. Saperstein studied at HUC-JIR and then became assistant rabbi at Rodef Sholom Congregation in Manhattan. When he took the job at the RAC, "there was just me, a secretary, and a phone." He worked diligently to make the RAC a center of political activism. In 1976, when he invited candidates running in the presidential primaries to speak at RAC headquarters on Embassy Row, it marked Jimmy Carter's first address to a group of national Jewish leaders. George Wallace, already crippled from an assassination attempt, stunned his listeners by apologizing for some of his policies and actions on racial issues as governor of Alabama, noting that his rhetoric had threatened not only African Americans but also southern Jews. One of the key Reform leaders working with the African American community, Saperstein is the only Jew on the board of the NAACP and is a strong supporter of Kweisi Mfume and Julian Bond. With his ability to work effectively with a wide variety of African American representatives, he has, as Jesse Jackson put it, "integrity and the strong sense of racial reconciliation and healing. He's been a great bridge builder."[48] The CSA's Leonard Fein taught at Brandeis University before leaving to establish *Moment* magazine. Alternately charming and abrasive, he has been a writer and editor as well as a social activist.[49] Most recently, he has helped found Amos: The National Jewish Partnership for Social Justice.

Some have suggested that the liberal rhetoric spouted by certain leaders is an aberration and that the Jewish community has always had conservative values. For a community that has undergone so many traumas, it is understandable that members would turn inward. As more and more Reform Jews perform rituals and study Jewish texts, there is naturally going to be less attention placed on social action projects. Fein vigorously disagrees with these assumptions. On the widespread perception that ritual has been replacing social action in the synagogue, Fein commented in 2001: "For some time now, the conventional wisdom has held that Jews have been moving away from their traditional commitment to social justice. We've become not merely too rich, but also too comfortable. We're far from the cities, where American injustice is most manifest."[50] Yet the maxim that the political and economic interests of a group dictate their policy views does not hold true for Jews, long identified as a group with a socioeconomic profile similar to that of Episcopalians that votes like Hispanics.

According to Fein, "One can not responsibly worry about 'Jewish community' without asking how strong and visible is our community's regard for social justice."[51] He warns that if the commonly held perception that the Reform movement is abandoning social justice intensifies, those for whom social justice is central will begin to look elsewhere.

Indeed, social, political, and economic views are an integral part of the Reform movement's religious perspective. The Reform movement, for example, has long opposed the death penalty; most American Jews oppose capital punishment. Although the Torah supports the death penalty in principle, it placed restrictions on when it could be imposed. The Sages of the Talmud put further restrictions on executions. As early as 1959 the UAHC adopted a resolution that affirmed: "We believe that there is no crime for which the taking of human life by society is justified and we call upon our congregations and all who cherish God's mercy and love to join in efforts to eliminate this practice which lies as a stain upon civilization and our religious conscience."[52]

Women of Reform Judaism, the Federation of Temple Sisterhoods (then called the National Federation of Temple Sisterhoods, or NFTS), adopted a resolution in the same year that stated: "We believe there is no crime, however horrendous, for which society has the right through its judicial processes to order the taking of human life. Rather, it is the obligation of society to evolve other more effective and more humane methods in dealing with crime. We pledge ourselves to try to prevent crimes by removal of their causes, and to foster modern methods of rehabilitation of the wrongdoer in the spirit of the Jewish tradition of teshuvah [repentance]. . . . This practice is a stain upon an entire penal system and brutalizes the human spirit." Al Vorspan of the CSA remembers that in the early 1960s, "Our opposition to the death penalty was so firm that we appealed to Israel not to set aside its deeply held commitment to the death penalty even in the case of Adolph Eichmann." The CCAR passed resolutions opposing capital punishment in 1958, 1960, and 1979. The 1979 resolution argued that "no evidence has been marshaled to indicate with any persuasiveness that capital punishment serves as a deterrent to crime. . . . We oppose capital punishment under all circumstances."[53]

Advocates for social justice have argued that social action work is a highly effective way to promote Jewish continuity, as surveys show that most American Jews see a commitment to social justice as a central component of their Jewish identities. The experience of a prominent lay leader in the UAHC, Evely Laser Shlensky, for example, suggests that social justice projects can excite the religious imagination. "One of my most cherished memories is of the night our temple board voted to become a sanctuary congregation, joining the Sanctuary Movement which was protecting refugees fleeing peril in El Salvador and Guatemala in the 1980s. That night we chose to side with the victims of violence, to assert our duty to protect human rights, to call on our Jewish experience with fight and flight."[54]

As Terry Bookman of Temple Beth Am in Miami explains in his book *God 101*, "Every action we take to repair the brokenness of our world, to make it a better place in which to live, frees another spark or lights it within another human being. Every time we volunteer at the soup kitchen, or work for justice legislation, or demonstrate on behalf of a righteous cause, or help make peace between individuals or nations, we are participating in the act of tikkun olam."[55]

Some social action projects continue to attract large numbers of congregants. The most popular by far is Mitzvah Day, an entire day, usually a Sunday, devoted to multiple good-works projects. At Congregation Rodef Sholom of San Rafael in Northern California, Mitzvah Day in November 2000 brought out eight hundred people. Members of Saint Raphael's Catholic Church joined the congregation, making the social justice project an interfaith experience. Looking for projects suitable for groups of volunteers in all age brackets, planners had called virtually every charitable agency in Marin County and offered assistance. Eight and ninth graders raised money for the AIDS Interfaith Network by washing cars. Confirmation class members picked up trash on Angel Island. Others worked to organize a party for the residents of the New Beginnings homeless shelter.[56] Most Reform congregations have such a program once a year. Whether this is a token activity or a significant investment of time and energy is a matter of perception.

Many synagogues still have very active social action committees that are involved in projects throughout the year. Synagogue 2000 director Lawrence Hoffman argues that this is not enough: Good deeds need to be the center of every synagogue activity. He believes that this is practical because of the innate human desire to want to do things that matter. Even busy people are often willing to devote time and energy to a project they believe will make a difference in someone's life. The synagogue needs to function as a center for volunteerism for the entire community. Hoffman suggests that social action be the responsibility not of a single committee but of multiple small groups working on specific short-term tasks designed to make a concrete improvement in the life of the community—efforts to alleviate homelessness, a public awareness campaign about the importance of early breast cancer detection, and so forth.[57]

Creating Religious Meaning in a Materialistic Society

Virtually every writer on the topic has agreed that the synagogue is the most important Jewish institution in America today. For that reason alone, its success or failure has huge implications for the future of Jews and Judaism in the United States. As memories of the Old World become history, American Jews need more than a residual ethnic identity to maintain a vibrant communal structure. The synagogue is the primary vehicle for providing the American Jew with existential meaning. And this is a difficult task. Studies have repeatedly found that American Jews are less involved with and committed to their religion than the general U.S. population. "Religion is a relatively low priority for American Jews who lag well behind the general population in membership in a congregation, worship attendances, and the importance they place on religion in their lives," George Gallup points out; only 44 percent of American Jews said that they were members of a synagogue in 1989, when 69 percent of the general population claimed to be members of a religious congregation of some sort. Gallup explains that "to some degree this reflects the fact that 'Jewish' represents an ethnic as well as a religious group, and not all ethnic Jews are religious."[58] This is certainly one of the reasons why Jewish religious affiliation rates are relatively low. How to successfully respond to this challenge remains a mystery.

Reform congregations are charged with transmitting Jewish tradition from generation to generation. But this does not mean the same thing that it would in an Orthodox congregation. Classical Reform Judaism focused exclusively on Judaism as a form of religious expression rather than as a comprehensive way of life. Reform temples therefore provided religious services and religious education and did not necessarily see themselves as mandated to provide comprehensive lifestyle programming. In recent years, however, scholars have begun to recognize that the early Reform temple did much more than just teach "religion." The Classical Reformers saw themselves as part of a "religious community," a subtle but significant distinction.[59]

Furthermore, the Reform movement is avowedly non-halachic, that is, not bound by Talmudic law. Therefore, the norms of form and style in more traditional synagogues are relatively absent from the Reform environment. The movement has always faced the task of staying on top of people's current mentality in order to remain relevant and therefore to be able to keep them involved in synagogue activities. This has been a challenge for every generation, and the leadership has periodically tried to reformulate its theological orientation and rethink its practical implications. It is frequently an uphill battle.

The Struggle for Recognition in the State of Israel

Chapter 6

If Progressive Judaism can develop and thrive only in a non-Jewish environment, if we cannot succeed in impacting on the lives and values of Jews living in the Jewish state, then the charges of our critics may be substantiated. Therefore, the ultimate test of Jewish authenticity for Progressive Judaism lies in our efforts in Israel. If we succeed in Israel, we pass the test. If we fail in Israel, then doubt is cast on the authenticity of our Diaspora movement. —RICHARD HIRSCH, 1999

IT IS EASY to forget that while Reform Judaism is most influential in the United States, it exists in many other parts of the world, including Israel. The international umbrella organization for Reform, Liberal, and Progressive Jews is the World Union for Progressive Judaism (WUPJ), founded in London in 1926 to maintain and strengthen existing Progressive movements and to initiate efforts to build new ones whenever possible. The WUPJ currently has affiliates in about forty countries on six continents, including North America; the Union of American Hebrew Congregations is by far the largest of about forty constituent groups. Although the WUPJ does what it can to build the Reform movement in Europe, South America, and elsewhere, a greater or lesser degree of success in those areas is not going to make a historic difference. The crucial battleground for the movement is the State of Israel, where the Reform movement is fighting the entrenched, institutionalized Orthodox establishment, as well as widely held negative perceptions about the Reform movement.

Because of the central position the State of Israel holds in the Jewish world, building a strong Reform movement there is the highest priority for the World Union. Israel is the world center of Judaism and Jewish tradition. While some see it as virtually identical with the Jewish people, others see it as representing the Jews all over the world. Radical Zionists tend to view the Jewish Diaspora as transitory, of little consequence other than as a source of new citizens for the state. Regardless of the importance that one places on the Diaspora, it is clear to all that what happens in the State of Israel has great significance. Despite the prediction of David Ben Gurion, the first Israeli prime minister, that the Orthodox in Israel would fade away if left alone, that has not come to pass. Religion has become more important in Israeli politics rather than less.

In the Israeli context, Jewish religion has meant Orthodoxy, the only type of Judaism the Israeli population has been exposed to from the Ottoman period, through the British mandate, and since the establishment of the state in 1948. Orthodoxy is linked directly to the state through a number of important institutions, including the chief rabbinate, the rabbinical courts, the state religious educational system—the Mamlachti Dati—and the local religious councils. In addition, an Israeli civil religion has emerged that accepts Orthodoxy as an integral part of the identity of the state, so that even most "secular" Israelis accept Orthodox Jews and Orthodox Judaism as representing the Jewish religion.

While this scenario has begun to change a little, the ability of the Reform movement to establish itself as a legitimate player in the Israeli Jewish religious world will have tremendous implications for the future of Reform Judaism. If Reform is unable to fight its way into the Israeli societal structure, it will always be perceived by Jews in Israel and throughout the Jewish world outside North America as a passing fad popular only in the United States.

The Development of the World Union

The first attempt to establish an international movement came in 1914, when the German Liberal movement invited representatives from England, France, and the United States to participate in their annual conference. The outbreak of World War I disrupted their plans, and subsequent political and economic events severely weakened the various European movements. Not until 1926 was the British Liberal movement able to host a founding conference; delegates called the new organization World Union for Progressive Judaism. Claude Montefiore as president and Lily Montagu as honorary secretary worked tirelessly to build up the Progressive movement throughout the world.

Many Reform Jews were concerned that should the WUPJ be seen as pushing Progressive Judaism, social relations with the local Orthodox could be harmed. This could have negative ramifications in places where the Orthodox represented the vast majority of the Jewish community and Jews relied on each other for business and social connections. As a result, the WUPJ leadership took care only to respond to indigenous requests for assistance rather than to plant foreign representatives in countries with no Reform constituency. In 1959 Solomon Freehof of Pittsburgh became the new president; in 1960, the organization moved from London to New York, and in 1973, from New York to Jerusalem, reflecting the increasingly central role that the State of Israel was coming to play for Diaspora Jews, as well as for the development of a Progressive movement. The branch of WUPJ that remained in New York has recently merged with the American Reform Zionists of America under the leadership of Ammiel Hirsch.

The Progressive movement faces serious obstacles in virtually every country outside of North America. The State of Israel's failure to fully recognize non-Orthodox religious movements is one reason that relatively few Jews in Australia, South Africa, France, and so forth have chosen to join Reform congregations. But there are also profound psychological factors at play. Daniel Elazar and Rela Mintz Geffen argue that most Jews outside the United States "practice their Judaism like Conservative Jews . . . [but] have not wanted to formally identify with the group that actually says that it changes Halakhah and makes things easier (for that is how it is perceived in their minds) and does not simply close its eyes to individual practice while maintaining a certain public standard of observance."[1] This attitude reflects a very different approach to life. Americans take pride in being pragmatic and want to connect ideals to reality to avoid hypocrisy. Optimists by nature, Americans are convinced that abstract ideals and concrete reality can be synthesized successfully. According to Elazar and Geffen, people in most of the rest of the world are more pessimistic about human nature and have lower expectations of reality. Therefore, they see it as natural to believe that ideals will differ from how life is actually lived.

This general attitude carries over to the religious sphere. Many non-Americans consider it perfectly proper to view a strict form of religion as the ideal, even if they fall far short of its standards and may have no intention of becoming more devout. The public recognition of these standards provides them and their children with an ideal to which they can aspire, a public standard for behavior, and the norm for communal events. Orthodoxy thus should be and must remain the public standard for Jewish attitudes and behavior, although this conviction does not obligate them to personally believe in or practice such a Judaism. As a consequence, the Progressive movement has found it difficult to attract increasing numbers, even in countries where it has been able to establish a foothold.

Jewish communities in countries with an official religious denomination have tended to regard the Orthodox establishment as their alternative "establishment church." Most Jews belong to Orthodox synagogues, although they do not necessarily observe Jewish traditional practices in a strict halachic manner. Some governments, the State of Israel's among them, fund Orthodox synagogues exclusively, thus putting alternative movements at a tremendous disadvantage. The perception that Orthodox Judaism is authentic is thus reinforced by government recognition and in some cases by federal funding of the Orthodox.

Most American Reform Jews have become increasingly and painfully aware that the State of Israel—the country they look to as their spiritual homeland—discriminates against their religious movement. Many are not only expressing their anger toward this state of affairs but donating money directly to Reform synagogues and educational institutions in Israel rather than to general Israeli charities. They are also coupling their strong support for the State of Israel politically with a determination to lobby for changes in the religious status quo.

The Reform Movement's Concern with the State of Israel

The degree to which the Israeli Progressive movement is accepted will have an impact on the perceived legitimacy of the Reform movement throughout the world.[2] While most American Jews have little interest in what happens in Jewish communities outside North America, caring mainly about how their congregation is doing and what that means for their families, what happens in the State of Israel has an important impact on their religious identity. "While the personal identity of many Reform Jews on the micro level may not be affected by developments in Israel, Reform Judaism on a macro level is under attack," warns Israeli sociologist Ephraim Tabory.[3] That attack is not only political. Anat Hoffman, the new executive director of the Israel Religious Action Center (IRAC), located on the Jerusalem campus of HUC-JIR, argues that "the incitement against us has reached such a fever pitch that if a Reform synagogue were to be blown up tomorrow I would not know whether an Orthodox Jew or a Palestinian perpetuated the act." She says there is "an ocean of hatred" against Reform Judaism in the Jewish state.[4]

Israelis range in their religious practices from punctilious to nonobservant, just as American Jews do. About 20 percent regard themselves as *dati*, religious. While Israelis in this category can display a great deal of diversity, they can be divided institutionally into the *dati leumi*, or national religious, and the *haredi*, or ultra-Orthodox. The national religious generally dress in modern clothes, participate in modern society, serve in the Israeli army, and differ from "secular Israelis" primarily in their religious practices. The ultra-Orthodox generally dress in black and white, live in segregated communities, and live qualitatively different lives in almost every way from other Israelis. Sons generally study in yeshiva for several years after their eighteenth birthday and therefore receive deferrals from army service. Daughters are kept out of the army for fear they might become sexually active in the unsupervised atmosphere of the base. Neither sons nor daughters should be exposed to the potentially corrupting influences of secular society.

The rest of the Israeli population ranges from *masorti*, traditional, to *hiloni*, secular. The traditional Israelis, many of whom originate from Sephardic countries, observe a wide range of traditional practices, such as keeping kosher and going to synagogue (Orthodox, of course), but do not see themselves as bound to follow halacha as a system of law. Many masorti sports fans will go to synagogue on Saturday morning, then rush out to the stadium to cheer on their favorite soccer team in the afternoon. In contrast, many antireligious Israelis would not be caught dead in a synagogue. Such *hilonim* express a great deal of hostility toward not only the institution of the Israeli chief rabbinate and the Israeli Orthodox rabbinate, but also the concept of religion generally. But far more numerous are the *hilonim* who, while defining themselves as secular, practice a considerable amount of Jewish ceremony. Most have Passover Seders and celebrate Hanukkah. Many perform rituals that would be seen by an outsider as religious.

Israelis differ from American Jews in both how they perceive their Jewishness and how they live their daily lives. Much of this has to do with the political situation in the Middle East, in particular the ongoing conflict between the Israelis and the Palestinians. The perpetual hostility between the two population groups wedged together so tightly is a major factor in making Israelis appear tense, pushy, and arrogant. It has also provided the justification for the country to avoid any serious reconsideration of the role of religion in Israeli society. But the differences go beyond the political. American Jews live as an ethnic and religious minority in a pluralistic, multicultural society. Israeli Jews live as a majority, with Arab Muslims forming the only other major ethnic and religious group. Charles S. Liebman and Steven M. Cohen have argued that the two groups even view the world in different ways. Israelis "spiritualize and mystify categories of thought," while Americans tend to be much more pragmatic.[5] According to this generalization, Israelis view historical and political events in symbolic formulations. Depending on their religious beliefs and political associations, they may see current events as replays of ancient history, scenes in a divine screenplay leading toward a predestined end. What they do today thus may have tremendous cosmological importance, not only in the short run, but also for eternity. While this generalization is true only of some, it does give a sense of the Israeli mentality that transcends attitudes toward pluralistic Judaism, but nevertheless has an impact on that subject.

On the other hand, both Israelis and American Jews see themselves from the common perspective of what Liebman and Cohen call "historical familism." Familism is the ability and willingness to see oneself as part of an extended family. A family is that group into which a person is born and is composed of one's blood relatives. But the Jewish understanding of "familism" broadens the term to include the entire

Jewish people. The Jewish people, who have endured a common experience through four thousand years, are seen as sharing a common fate.

Even here, the two groups understand familism differently. American Jews mediate their familism through their need to display a degree of universalism expected in the United States. While they publicly affirm a strong connection with other Jews in the United States and throughout the world, they stress that their religious heritage leads them to a universalized commitment to fight against all manifestations of evil. American Jews can affirm their particularity, but it has to be balanced with an equal or greater degree of concern for the universal. For the Israeli, no such balancing act is required. Indeed, the political environment encourages just the opposite. This dynamic has obvious implications for the manifestation of religious belief in general and each group's receptiveness to pluralistic expressions of Jewish religious identity.

As a result of these contrasting viewpoints, the Israeli Progressive movement is very different from American Reform Judaism, and the American Reform leadership accepts this as natural. Eric H. Yoffie states; "We don't expect or even want the Israeli Reform Movement to be the same as in the U.S. or Europe. Unless the Israeli movement roots itself into Israel, it won't be considered authentic by the average Israeli—or by ourselves. Reform Jews everywhere are bonded by a shared religious outlook and a fundamental commitment to Reform principles, but to succeed in each country, a movement must be indigenous."[6]

The American Reform movement has shown its commitment to Zionism and the State of Israel. In addition to allocating funds for the support of the Israeli Progressive movement, the UAHC and CCAR sponsor frequent missions to the Jewish State. Reform leaders meet with Israeli politicians and travel to important sites to get a firsthand look at what is going on. In June 1997, the CCAR adopted a platform devoted to discussing the commitment of the Reform movement to Zionism. The process had begun in 1989 when the Association of Reform Zionists of America initiated a series of three think tanks. Discussions continued, and in 1994 the CCAR joined with the UAHC and HUC-JIR to draft a centenary platform on Reform Zionism to coincide with the hundredth anniversary of Zionism and the fiftieth anniversary of the creation of Israel.[7]

The resulting Zionist platform was voted on at the 1997 CCAR conference held in Miami. The platform states that the State of Israel and Jewish communities around the world are interdependent. They are responsible for one another in the shaping of Jewish destiny. The Sinai covenant demands that the Jewish people accept a distinct religious mission. Therefore, the State of Israel has an obligation to strive toward the highest ethical and moral ideals. Although the platform was soon forgotten by most Reform Jews, it further reinforced the commitment of the Reform movement to the State of Israel. While individual Reform Jews might show little interest in the events transpiring in the State of Israel, the Reform Movement had reaffirmed its intimate involvement.[8]

Problems Facing the Reform Movement in Israel

With such a diverse population expressing such a multiplicity of views and practicing religion in so many different ways, one might expect the Reform Movement to find a ready niche in the Israeli religious marketplace. This has not proven to be the case. Since Israel's rabbinate controls all issues of personal status, non-Orthodox rabbis in that country are not able to perform legally binding marriage ceremonies, divorces, or even most burials. Reform and Conservative conversions are accepted by the Jewish Agency, thus allowing such individuals to immigrate to Israel under the Law of Return. Such converts, however, will not be recognized as Jews by the chief rabbinate and may therefore have problems once they settle in the country.

Complex and multifaceted problems face the Reform movement in Israel. The early Jewish settlers came from countries that lacked the pluralistic religious environment that would have allowed alternative forms of religious expression to develop. The settlers arrived in a Palestine ruled by the Turks, who likewise did not encourage Western liberal cultural or intellectual developments. The early Zionist pioneers included few Western immigrants, and most of those who did settle in Israel adapted themselves to the prevailing social and religious norms. While former UAHC leader Rabbi Maurice Eisendrath had argued in favor of the creation of an Israeli Reform movement as early as 1953, not until the late 1950s did the WUPJ develop an Israeli movement, and not until 1968 did the group hold a biennial conference in that country.

Over the past three decades, the World Union has devoted much effort to building up the Israel Movement for Progressive Judaism (IMPJ), which was incorporated under Israeli law in 1971. The Israeli leaders chose to refer to themselves as the movement for Yahadut Mitkademet, Progressive Judaism, avoiding the use of the term "Reform." By doing so they hoped to minimize the negative associations that many Israelis have of the American Reform movement. Particularly damaging was a video replayed on Israeli TV a number of years ago of an American Reform rabbi and a Christian minister co-officiating at a wedding ceremony, a sight many Israelis, including many secularists, found shocking and offensive. The 2000 Greensboro, North Carolina, CCAR resolution sanctioning same-sex unions has also attracted a great deal of attention and criticism.

Israeli Orthodox leaders, including prominent politicians, argue that the Reform movement has encouraged assimilation and has proven itself a destructive force. Periodically, distinguished Israeli Orthodox rabbis have attacked Reform Judaism and its adherents, sometimes in the vilest of terms. Nevertheless, Israeli-born Reform leaders such as Uri Regev, founder of the Israel Religious Action Center and now executive director of the WUPJ, have become well-known personalities interviewed frequently by TV news crews. Regev has made a great deal of progress in pushing for greater rights through the court system. Each time he has petitioned the Israeli Supreme Court, Israeli news media interview him on the importance of his petition and his understanding of why it was necessary to attempt to change the religious status quo, further positive publicity for the Progressive effort. As director of the WUPJ, Regev is now leading the effort to expand Progressive Judaism, not only in Israel but also throughout the world.

Many non-Orthodox Israelis have been positively impressed. A few years ago, a number of leading Israeli writers and intellectuals called on the Israeli public to join the Reform movement to protest the Orthodox monopoly on life-cycle ceremonies. The Orthodox in turn renewed their attacks on the Reform movement. Orthodox spokesmen

continued to lambaste Reform Judaism, and unknown individuals sus-
pected to be from the ultra-Orthodox community vandalized buildings
associated with Reform institutions.

Orthodox hostility is only one facet of the problem. Many secular
Israelis harbor resentment toward what they see as the religious coercion of the Orthodox. But the coalition agreements between the Labor
and Likud Parties and one or more Orthodox parties have insured that
the status quo is maintained in religious matters. An Orthodox rabbi
must certify weddings between Jews. In the past, a few sympathetic
Orthodox rabbis have signed for non-Orthodox rabbinical officiants.
But the Orthodox rabbinate has worked vigorously to clamp down on
those who helped circumvent the system. Most Jews who marry in a
Reform ceremony in Israel then go to Cyprus to receive a civil marriage
license, as the Israeli Ministry of Interior will accept any marriage certificate issued by an official government. Thus, the Israeli government
recognizes a marriage certificate signed by a Cypriot judge but not one
signed by an Israeli Reform rabbi.

There have been some encouraging developments. As part of a
series of public relations campaigns, the IMPJ launched a $350,000
media blitz right before the High Holy Days of 1999, to encourage
Israelis to attend a Progressive or Masorti (Conservative) synagogue.
Billboards, posters on buses, and newspaper supplements featured the
slogan "There is more than one way to be Jewish." The accompanying
radio campaign became immersed in controversy after the government-
owned Israeli state radio tried to cancel the advertisements, claiming
the wording would offend Orthodox Jews. The Supreme Court issued a
show-cause order, and the campaign was allowed to proceed after IMPJ
and Masorti leaders agreed to change the slogan on the radio to "This is
our way—you just have to choose." The IMPJ reported that an esti-
mated twenty thousand Israelis filled twenty-seven synagogues and
additional facilities rented for the High Holy Days. Many congregations doubled the number of attendees from just a year earlier. The
IMPJ received many phone inquiries about membership and even a few
requests for information on how to form congregations.[9]

In March 2000, the IMPJ worked together with Israel's Masorti
movement to promote non-Orthodox marriage ceremonies. The campaign ran full-page advertisements in the weekend editions of the

major Israeli newspapers and four hundred radio ads featuring couples who had been married in either Progressive or Masorti ceremonies. The ads emphasized the egalitarian nature of the non-Orthodox wedding ceremony, as well as the lack of the intrusive questions Orthodox rabbis usually ask. The campaign also stated clearly that under current Israeli law, the couple would need to marry a second time in a civil ceremony abroad for their marriage to be recognized by the Interior Ministry.

The IMPJ is also continuing efforts to reach Russian-speaking immigrants. In February 2000, Michael Brodsky and a number of other Russian speakers published their first edition of the revised *Rodnik* (The source). Originally geared toward Jews in the Former Soviet Union (FSU), the magazine had shifted its focus to Russian immigrants in Israel. Brodsky, previously spokesperson for the Yisrael B'Aliya political party, now serves as the IMPJ's liaison with Russian-language media outlets. The IMPJ is also working with a number of Russian-language groups in Haifa, Nahariya, Netanya, and Ra'anana. In August 2000, a congregation for immigrants from the FSU was founded in Ashdod. The group began meeting for havdalah services on Saturday nights and expanded to Friday night services led by HUC rabbinical students from the Jerusalem campus. The IMPJ hired a paraprofessional community organizer for the group and has hired similar community workers for the other Russian-language groups in Israel.

The IMPJ has recently formed a number of new congregations. Yozma in Modi'in, between Tel Aviv and Jerusalem, already has established four kindergarten classes as well as a first grade. Sulam Ya'akov was established in Zichron Ya'akov, between Tel Aviv and Haifa. Gusti Yehoshua-Braverman, the director of community development for the Israeli Progressive movement, states: "We must establish new congregations. However, we must also rejuvenate those that already exist but are struggling because they lack a rabbi or are in the periphery."[10] Some long-standing congregations have expanded their programming, including Achvat Yisrael in Rishon Lezion near Tel Aviv, which has also recently hired a community coordinator. The congregation has a growing Jewish study group that regularly brings in well-known guest lecturers and was recently given a city-owned building for its exclusive use. The structure is a former kindergarten in a quiet leafy neighborhood in the city. According to congregational chairperson Shai Eitan, it will need to be extensively renovated but offers "tremendous potential."[11] In Nahariya, Emet Ve'shalom offers a lecture and field trip program for about 150 new immigrants. The IMPJ also caters to those with special needs. The movement offers special Shabbat activities for the residents of Kishor, a community of about seventy people with learning, functioning, and adaptive disabilities—a candle-lighting ceremony, kiddush, Kabbalat Shabbat, and other religious programming three times a month. Joint activities with the IMPJ-affiliated Har Halutz settlement and the IMPJ's Young Adult Leadership Forum are also undertaken.

But the Reform movement has put its greatest energy into establishing a physical presence in Israel. The movement has built an impressive complex on King David Street in Jerusalem; it includes the Israeli campus of the HUC-JIR and Mercaz Shimshon, the WUPJ's cultural center. Designed by world-famous architect Moshe Safdie, the $15 million facility was built adjacent to Beit Shmuel, the WUPJ headquarters. Both centers offer panoramic views of Jaffa Gate, David's Citadel, and the walls of the Old City.

While the movement faced a great deal of resistance, land has been designated for Progressive congregational building projects in a number of municipalities. Affluent families are enthusiastic about holding their children's bar and bat mitzvah ceremonies in the new Beit Daniel in North Tel Aviv. At services, the families seem to adjust without any problem to the mixed seating and the use of *Ha-Avodah She-Balev* (The service of the heart), the Israeli Progressive prayer book. Rabbi Meir Azari explains: "Beit Daniel stands in the middle of a thoroughly Yuppie neighborhood. And the place is hopping! Hundreds of people come here every week—300 for Friday night services alone." Azari states that the congregation has succeeded in drawing in different types of people for different types of programming. "Russian Israelis come here on weekday evenings to study Judaism. Dozens of Israeli-born singles in their 20s attend Shabbat services, together with young Israeli families and older immigrants who grew up in the Movement abroad. We hold around 200 bar and bat mitzvahs here every year and 120 weddings. Our kindergartens are full and 40 different schools came to us for religious programs." Nevertheless, Azari admits, few have joined the congregation. "As far as membership goes, only 300 families are signed up. But in Israel, the synagogue plays a different role: people don't need membership to show they're Jewish or to get a Jewish burial plot."[12] There are now approximately thirty Progressive congregations in the country. Those with their own buildings and full-time rabbis attract a clientele looking for bar mitzvah celebrations, High Holy Day services, and so forth.

Yoffie acknowledges that the Reform movement has learned a great deal through trial and error. "Bringing the Movement to Israel has been a learning process for all of us. For example, 20 years ago, people thought that building synagogues in Israel was not the way to go. Today, we recognize that synagogues are a significant part of the Israeli movement; we've learned that if you provide an appropriate facility and put a talented rabbi at the head of it, you can create a thriving religious community center to which people are delighted to come." Yoffie adds that other strategies have proven effective as well. "Broad-based educational institutions are clearly another important part of what we do. We have more than 30 kindergartens so far, as well as two schools, and a range of evening courses, seminars and study days. And, while our current thrust is to make our presence felt in Israel's urban community, we're also very proud of our settlements—two kibbutzim in the Negev and Har Halutz in the Galilee."[13]

The Reform movement has poured effort and money into building up the Progressive presence in the State of Israel, yet the fear remains that the government would move quickly to pass new laws to bypass any legal gains achieved through future rulings by the High Court of Justice, the Israeli supreme court. Shas and other ultra-Orthodox political parties have already indicated their intention to do just that, if the need should arise. Rabbi Richard Hirsch, who served for many years as the executive director of the WUPJ, states: "The Orthodox monopoly in Israel is an underlying reality. It's a factor to the extent government policies prevent our being allocated resources. But in the final analysis, religious life is about meeting fundamental religious needs, about education, and worship, and creating community. So the fight for rights must be seen in perspective. It's not the sole issue. Without a Movement, there would be no one to exercise those rights."[14] Nevertheless, until the movement can achieve official recognition and equal legal status with the Orthodox, it will remain a small, struggling, barely tolerated denomination on the fringes of Israeli life. The marginalization of the Israeli Progressive movement threatens to undermine the legitimacy of the Reform movement in the United States and throughout the world.

The Waning of the American Jewish Love Affair with Israel

The Reform movement is struggling with the political powers in the State of Israel at a time when the relationship of American Jews to Israel is undergoing fundamental changes. "Clearly there is a distancing taking place among American Jews," said Jerome Epstein, executive vice president of the United Synagogue of Conservative Judaism. "It is manifested by a lack of outward support for Israel—fewer synagogue programs for Israel, fewer Yom Ha'Atzmaut celebrations. And look at the number of synagogue tours canceled, the lack of rallies, the lack of letters to the editors of newspapers, the lack of American tourism."[15] University of Hartford professor Steven Rosenthal agrees that the American Jewish community has shifted its attention away from the State of Israel and toward its own concerns at home. Many American Jews are interested in the personalistic aspects of the Jewish spiritual message, while others are focusing on how to combat assimilation and fuel an American Jewish renaissance. Very few American Jews are interested in making aliyah, moving to Israel.[16] Thus, both those who remain committed to Jewish identity and those who no longer care share a decreasing interest in what is happening in Israel.

A community consensus had developed in the aftermath of the Holocaust, an event that transformed the attitudes of American Jews to Zionism. As the horror of the Nazi murder of six million Jews became known, most American Jews felt an obligation to support the newly founded State of Israel, to partly compensate for their relative passivity during the war years. The United Jewish Appeal slogan "We Are One" expressed the prevailing sentiment that identification with Israel was the prime means of expressing one's Jewishness. One could deny the existence of God, refuse to practice even the most basic Jewish rituals, and never set foot in a synagogue; what was important was supporting the State of Israel. "Instead of identifying Judaism with rituals or attitudes that seemed increasingly alien and a barrier to assimilation, how much more convenient to redefine one's Jewishness as loyalty to a progressive, courageous, modern state and a staunch American ally to boot."[17]

Yet most remained unaware of what was actually going on in the State of Israel. Despite their near obsession with the country, "the Jewish state has had relatively little effect on the religious and cultural life of American Jews."[18] Jews have related to Zionism and Israel as a part of their American Jewish identity. For decades their support for Israel and their identity needs coincided. But today that connection shows signs of severe strain, the result in part of events over the past twenty years: the Israeli invasion of Lebanon, the Jonathan Pollard spy case, the Palestinian Intifada, the "Who is a Jew?" controversy, and the recent Palestinian-Israeli violence. American social and religious trends have also contributed to the increasingly distant relations. American Jews no longer look for the sort of nationalistic expression that so invigorated them in the 1960s and 1970s.

The political situation in Israel can also be divisive. The American Reform rabbinate as a whole has moved to the center or even the right on the Israeli political spectrum, in large measure because of the repeated Palestinian terrorist attacks on Israeli civilians. CCAR president Martin Weiner of San Francisco typifies this trend. In a March 2002 speech at the CCAR's annual convention in Jerusalem, which attracted a great deal of attention because of his position, Weiner explained: "I think many of those who supported the Oslo peace accords have now come to the conclusion there may not be a partner for peace among the Palestinians, and Arafat's possible goal all along was not to make peace but to destroy Israel. . . . From being one who supported peace talks ten or fifteen years ago, back when some people were calling us traitors, I now have serious concerns about the intentions of the Palestinians."[19] Weiner had first expressed his change of heart in a Yom Kippur sermon delivered at his congregation, Sherith Israel, discussing his disillusionment with the peace process in the aftermath of what he described as Yasser Arafat's rejection of Ehud Barak's "incredibly generous offer" in the summer of 2000 at Camp David. "They rejected it—and not only rejected it, but began this campaign of terror, bloodshed."[20]

Weiner's position marked a sharp move to the right for the Reform leadership, which had positioned itself as left of center for decades.

Alexander Schindler had certainly taken liberal positions consistent with those of the Israeli Labor Party throughout the 1970s and 1980s, although he had earned the respect of all, including then–prime minister Menachem Begin. Eric H. Yoffie had also been forthright in his criticism of right-wing policies he saw as foolhardy. For example, in a December 13, 1996, speech before the annual meeting of UAHC's board of trustees in Los Angeles, Yoffie accused then–prime minister Binyamin Netanyahu with the failure of leadership that had exacerbated existing differences between the American Jewish community and Israel. Yoffie accused Netanyahu of bringing Judaism into contempt for the benefit of "relentless and aggressive secularism," and of increasing political tensions in the Middle East. "What Israel's government has given us are inflammatory statements by the prime minister and expansion of settlements. Is also has given us uncertain relations with the United States and growing tension with the most moderate elements in the Arab world, including King Hussein, a traditional Netanyahu ally."[21]

Yoffie spoke out against Netanyahu's settlement policies as well as his refusal to support religious pluralism in the Jewish State. Yoffie accused Netanyahu of ignoring the threats to Judaism posed by ultra-Orthodoxy on one hand and secularism on the other. He attacked the Israeli government for surrendering to the blackmail of the "utterly fanatic" Orthodox political parties. "The greatest tragedy of all is that the ultra-Orthodox have caused an entire generation of Israelis to view Judaism with contempt. Religious coercion . . . compromises Israel's appeal to the idealism of young Jews everywhere." Particularly upsetting to Yoffie was the Orthodox rabbinate's refusal to marry or bury the more than 100,000 Israeli citizens from the former Soviet Union who could not meet the rabbinate's stringent requirements. Yoffie also condemned the Israeli Orthodox rabbinate for preventing nearly 10,000 Israeli women from divorcing because the Israeli rabbinate requires the husband to issue the *get*, the writ of divorce. Yet Netanyahu refused to do anything to limit the power of the Orthodox rabbinate in Israel. "Even if he could do nothing practical for us, an enlightened voice from Israel's highest-ranking elected official would have set the tone for tolerance and the possibility of change."[22]

On August 7, 2002, Rabbi Paul Menitoff, the executive vice president of the CCAR, sent an open letter to President George W. Bush urging the administration to "exercise its capacity to intervene even more boldly than it has in the past by placing on the table a peace plan and demanding that it be presented to both Israeli citizens and the Palestinian population as a referendum in a supervised vote." Menitoff urged the United States to cut off all "diplomatic, military and financial support" to any Palestinian leadership or Israeli government refusing to hold an internationally supervised referendum on a final peace treaty based on the 2000 Taba discussions. Menitoff thus became the first major American Jewish leader to advocate threatening Israel with economic, political, and military sanctions. He also urged President Bush to introduce U.S. military into the region. "These troops must remain through the referendum process. If the respective populations vote to accept the peace plan, the US troops must stay until Israel and the newly elected Palestinian government agree on other military forces or the discontinuation of an outside military presence." Menitoff made it clear he was writing in a personal capacity, although he began the letter by identifying himself as the executive vice president of the CCAR.[23] Rabbi Martin Weiner, the CCAR president and Menitoff's supervisor, told the *Forward* that he had seen Menitoff's letter before it was sent and did not object. "I am a strong believer in the freedom of the pulpit. [Menitoff] made it clear he was only speaking for himself." Rabbi Clifford Librach of Temple Sinai in Sharon, Massachusetts, responded sadly: "I regret that someone in so sensitive a position would call for the use of American muscle against Israel in the midst of a struggle for her survival. And the further suggestion of American military occupation is breathtaking."

Some rabbis remain committed to leftist positions; others simply believe that it is important for American Jews to hear the entire spectrum of Israeli political opinion rather then be force-fed a single official viewpoint. For example, when Stephen Pearce of Congregation Emanu-El of San Francisco invited an extreme left-wing Israeli attorney to speak, the event caused conflict and criticism. Joe Alouf, an Israeli-born member of the congregation, was shocked when the invitation to the event came in the mail. "I can't believe I'm reading this. I can't believe my temple, with my dues, is inviting this guy." The attorney, Shamai Leibowitz, the grandson of controversial philosopher Yeshayahu Leibowitz, said that for the Palestinians to negotiate while being occupied by Israel is similar to "a rape victim being asked to negotiate with her attacker."[24] But Pearce defended his decision in the Emanu-El bulletin; it was important to offer a view that differed from "the official party line that defends the actions of the Sharon government," he wrote. He acknowledged that the crisis in Israel is a highly emotional subject for all American Jews and that for some, "any view that differs from the official position of the Jewish community is seen to be betrayal in some way"; nevertheless, the American Jewish community needs to hear different positions on this and other issues.

According to the *Jewish Bulletin of Northern California*, a group of congregants even discussed trying to fire Pearce, who wrote me that the story was in fact "a tempest in a teapot. I have received well over 100 emails, phone calls, and letters defending my invitation to Shammai. But one member who is mentioned in the JBNC has called for my resignation and that of the entire board. Almost everyone just shrugs their shoulders and thinks she is so far off base that she has discredited herself."[25] Alouf agreed that replacing the rabbi was not the solution. "I don't need him to be fired. I [just] want the largest congregation in the Pacific Northwest to open their eyes and say a temple like this that represents Reform Judaism is not a place where extreme political views should be given a platform, especially when we have innocent Israelis dying every single day."

And yet the State of Israel remains the most important territory for the Reform movement's development. Home to the second-largest Jewish population in the world, it could confer religious legitimacy upon the movement that is absolutely essential. In August 1999, a survey conducted by the Shiluv-Konso research group indicated that more than 90 percent of the Israeli public knew that the Israeli Progressive movement existed. When asked which movement they most identified with, 36 percent answered Progressive, while only 24 percent responded that they identified most with Orthodoxy. But translating the relatively high degree of support into concrete political advances is difficult. The Reform movement must achieve recognition as both legitimate and authentic. The leaders remain optimistic, at least in their public statements. Yoffie argues: "There's been a dramatic growth in interest in Reform Judaism in Israel in the past 15 years. We've learned what works in Israel, what's appropriate, and we've created a pattern in which there is room for the totality of the Jewish people. Once we ordain more Israeli rabbis and educators—and the role of our academic arm, Hebrew Union College, in Jerusalem is crucial here—change will come faster. In fact, I would even go so far as to say that with 50 Israeli rabbis we could change Israel in two generations!"[26]

A strong Israeli Reform Judaism would bring significant cultural benefits for the entire movement. Israelis are the only Jews in the world who speak Hebrew as their first language and the only ones who live in the Promised Land. The Progressive Judaism that they develop can therefore have a creative cultural impact on Reform Jews throughout the world. Regardless of political success or failure in the short term, the Reform movement will continue to invest in building up the Progressive movement in Israel. Achieving recognition in the Jewish State has enormous importance for Reform's long-term health.

New Challenges
in Reform
Chapter 7   Jewish Education

*Jewish education is not limited to the classroom by any
manner or means. It must penetrate every other room
and activity of the temple's life. In the sanctuary, prayer
and study must be intertwined . . . all temple
activities—from committee meetings to conversation
within the temple's halls, from social events to the letters
and bulletins we send out—should be seen and seized as
means to further the Jewish educative process.*

         —ALEXANDER M. SCHINDLER, 1988

I<small>N</small> THE post–World War II period, Emanuel Gamoran served as director
of the Reform movement's Joint Commission on Jewish Education and is
credited with transforming the approach of the Union of American
Hebrew Congregations (UAHC) to teaching Judaism in religious
schools. Shocked that tots were being taught abstract theological principles they had no hope of understanding, he urged the movement to
focus on concrete expressions of Jewishness that could create tangible
memories of religious living. He believed that learning must be based on
experience. In 1952, Gamoran summarized what he saw as the most
important goals of Jewish education: "We include as a minimum a rich
series of Jewish experiences such as holiday celebrations, music, dancing,
arts and crafts." Influenced by Mordecai Kaplan, Gamoran hoped that
children would come away from the Sunday school experience feeling
connected to the Jewish home, the Jewish school, the synagogue, and the
Jewish community. They should have an appreciation of Jewish spiritual,

cultural, and aesthetic values and be equipped to develop "creative Jewish personalities" that could help mold future American Jewish life.[1]

Gamoran was not the first to express high hopes for Reform Jewish education. Since the early nineteenth century, Reformers have debated how to teach their children effectively about Judaism while avoiding chauvinism and ghettoization. Because enthusiastic Jewish commitment developed most readily among those raised in an all-encompassing Jewish environment, the task of Reform Jewish education would prove challenging.

What is an educated Reform Jew? How can we judge the success or failure of a particular Sunday school or of the entire movement? Michael A. Meyer argues that "within the sphere of Jewish education Reform Judaism sets for itself a task that is both unique and exceedingly difficult." What makes it difficult is that the movement is committed to personal autonomy, and therefore educators do not see themselves as teaching a revealed religion that requires absolute obedience. Neither is there a normative body of laws that are taught as binding in their entirety. On the other hand, Reform Jewish education cannot simply teach historical information. That may create a generation with knowledge but without commitment. Rather, Reform Jewish education must influence the choices that the younger generation will make by teaching "core Jewish values." But what those values should be and how they should be manifested is a difficult question. Meyer argues that the movement must aim to create "Jewish religious lives that stand under the authority of an obligating God."[2]

Reform Jewish education must create, Meyer believes, "a strong sense of the Jewish self securely grounded within the Jewish community and within the Jewish religious tradition." This requires emphasizing Jewish particularity. Children have to be raised to see themselves as part of an ethnic group and of the Jewish people. Only then can Jewish education help the student to "reach outward to the human community and forward to the universal goal." Particularism and universalism can peacefully coexist, creating an educated Reform Jew "knowledgeable in the past and of the present Jewish people and immersed in its spiritual life."[3] The sentiment is beautiful, but the reality is jarring. Assimilatory pressures "dumb down" Reform afternoon schools, and educators face many challenges.

An Uphill Battle

Jews face an uphill battle raising their children in the Jewish heritage while participating fully in an increasingly diverse and pluralistic American society. The passing on of the Jewish religious tradition from generation to generation has become a difficult and uncertain process. Whereas in previous generations continuity was assumed, today even deeply committed Jewish parents cannot be sure that their offspring will follow their paths. Most American Jews are not strictly observant; they rely upon social mechanisms to reinforce their Jewish identities and those of their children.

Loyalty to community has formed a key component in the Jewish survival strategy, as Jonathan S. Woocher has described in his 1986 book *Sacred Survival*. The Jewish version of American civil religion stressed nontheological tenets that emerged organically from the historical events the older generations had lived through, the Holocaust and the creation of the State of Israel; they felt it natural to affirm the Jewish people's responsibility for each other. In a threatening world, Jews should work for their survival in the Diaspora while also working (or donating money) to strengthen the State of Israel.[4] But much has changed in recent years, as Woocher himself has acknowledged.[5] The trend toward individualism, personal choice, and "self-realization" has made it much harder to talk about the obligation of group solidarity.

Many believe that there is no need to perpetuate Jewish identity. The new generation does not experience the nostalgic sentiment, the yearnings, and especially the "Jewish guilt" that characterized an earlier generation. Jews today live in a post-assimilatory state in which they are no longer struggling to shed their intrinsic Jewishness, but rather are born, grow up, and live as Americans. They don't have to spend their whole lives hiding, rejecting, or wrestling with their Jewish identity; it simply is not that important to them or to others. If they are not religious and feel no claims (or chains) of Jewish history to obligate them, there may be no reason to worry about the issue at all. Even many who care feel that the cause is hopeless. A Jewish man from Philadelphia bluntly told interviewers Sara Bershtel and Allen Graubard: "Look, if the whooping crane ain't gonna make it, the whooping crane ain't gonna make it. No hatcheries are going to do it.

That's what these rabbis are trying to do, make hatcheries for whooping cranes."[6] He had married a Japanese woman whom he had met in the service and was presumably raising a non-Jewish family. What makes this man unusual is his ability to discuss with equanimity what he believes to be the likely disappearance of the Jewish people. Otherwise, he is typical. Not having experienced the radical change of culture and society that formed the core experience for his parents, he and the rest of the generation of seekers may be looking for a sense of spirituality, but it is not something they were raised with and seek to recover.[7]

The Reform movement has had to formulate an educational strategy that takes into account a pervasive apathy. As a movement that has always defined itself in religious terms, it has had to find ways to appeal to many essentially secular assimilated American Jews. Yet if the "Reform revolution" is to succeed, the temple must help the next generation know more about Judaism and care deeply about perpetuating Jewish scholarship and religiosity.

Contemporary Challenges

Parents are the main agents for transferring religious beliefs and practices to their children.[8] Children are socialized in the family context by observing everything that goes on around them. As time goes on, they acquire the motivation and skills that will enable them to conform to the expectations of their parents. Presumably those expectations will match what they find in school and other social settings. But the Reform pattern of child rearing creates a fair degree of dissonance. The parents rarely are capable of conveying, or willing to convey, Reform Jewish beliefs; most practice little of the traditional ritual. The children go to public school, where they are not exposed to any religious practice. Only at the religious or Hebrew school, which meets once or twice a week for just a few hours, do they get any exposure whatsoever. Children quickly grasp that the subject matter occupies a low priority for adults as well as for the other children.

More than one cynical graduate has remarked that Hebrew school was the place where they did not learn Hebrew. Michael Lerner, the founder of *Tikkun* magazine, describes his Hebrew school experience in the 1950s:

Twice a week after "regular" school, and once a week on
Saturday mornings, I would spend two hours trying to learn
something about Judaism, Jewish history, and Hebrew. There
were 125 of us who graduated Hebrew school the year of my
bar mitzvah, but only five of us continued through Hebrew
high school and graduated that four-hour-per-week program
four years later. Very few of the original 125 felt any particular
connection to Jewish tradition by the time they reached their
twenties. Most of them looked back on Hebrew school as an
ordeal that they went through to please their parents, and once
they were free to make choices of their own, they ran from the
Jewish world as fast as they could.[9]

Lerner is not referring specifically to a Reform afternoon school, but his
comments will strike a familiar chord with many who did attend Sunday school at a Reform temple.

Despite these problems, attendance at a religious school provides a
degree of exposure to both Jewish subjects and Jewish society. The children begin to develop a self-identity, their private version of their patterns of traits, that includes a Jewish component.[10] Yet they live mostly
in a non-Jewish environment, a contrast that creates internal conflict,
which makes the Jewish socialization process of Reform children a difficult task fraught with obstacles.

Ideally, the Jewish home passes on the religious tradition in terms
of a strong self-identity, and the school teaches Jewish history and culture as well as practical synagogue skills. In practice, neither institution
fulfills its role effectively, which creates a dire need for alternative programming that can at least in part fill the void. The North American
Federation of Temple Youth (NFTY) and the Reform movement's summer camps play a critical role in enabling children from Reform synagogues to build strong, positive Jewish experiences that can motivate
them to continue their involvement after their bar or bat mitzvah or
confirmation.

The importance of Jewish youth programming for the future of the
American Jewish community has led all the religious movements as
well as numerous other communal institutions to develop new and
innovative approaches. Plans for a "Jewish Renaissance" have been
drawn up, and a number of large private foundations have agreed to

fund various organizations and programs designed to increase interest in Judaism and encourage the serious study of religion. The Birthright Israel program has the ambitious goal of sending every American Jewish youth on a free trip to Israel over the next five years, hoping that many will subsequently manifest a strong commitment to Judaism. The sponsors behind this program—which was funded with $210 million—believe it can connect the "great silent majority" of diaspora Jews to their history and culture. This in turn may halt or at least retard the assimilatory process by "selling Jewishness to Jews."[11] The outbreak of a new round of violence in Israel has obviously made it much harder to recruit participants. Nevertheless, thousands of young people have already been sent, and many more are scheduled to go. While neither the substance of the follow-up nor the short- and long-term influence of the program are yet clear, many are hopeful that the impact will be substantial.

The intent of such programs is to generate enthusiasm for Judaism among the younger generation. Older people grew up in a time when Jews were much more segregated than they are today, and their parents' admonitions to marry someone Jewish and maintain an affiliation with the Jewish community made logical sense. But today's parents find it harder to convey to their children what their parents transmitted to them, partly because the message was never a clearly thought out religious commitment but an emotionally based, visceral expression of ethnicity. Fear of anti-Semitism likewise kept Jews together. As ethnic identity and anti-Semitism have declined significantly, it has become clear that more Jewish education is essential. Parents need to be able to explain to their children, for example, why the Federation of Temple Youth should be important to them.

Educational Problems Facing the Reform Religious School

The vehicle for transmitting Judaic knowledge has been the afternoon Hebrew school and the Sunday religious school. Until recently, few Reform Jews sent their children to Jewish day schools, and most afternoon schools taught little. Afternoon Hebrew school programs in the Reform movement have on the whole had unclear educational goals.

Rarely was there a clearly defined curriculum with specific expectations. With no consensus about what students should learn, schools tended to repeat much of the same material year after year, further alienating the students, who saw the repetitive subject matter as yet another indication that Hebrew school was of little value. Most students arrived at class exhausted after their public school day or on Sunday morning, when they wanted to sleep late. And there was simply not enough time to educate them. Michael Zeldin of HUC-JIR in Los Angeles admits that it is impossible in just a few hours a week to teach children what they need to know about Judaism or "even the most rudimentary knowledge of Hebrew, an understanding of Jewish ideas, or a sense of their identities as Jews."[12] Because of the unfocused educational goals, the repetitive material, the shortness and lateness of the hour, and the lack of standards, most of the children simply were not receiving enough Judaic knowledge to grow up as Jewishly educated adults.

The educational problems are a direct consequence of the low priority many Reform families attach to Judaism in general. Many parents, non-practicing Jews themselves, hope their children will absorb an abstract sense of Jewish identity rather than learn how to practice their religion in a serious manner.

Janet Marder, the senior rabbi of Congregation Beth Am in Los Altos Hills, California, recalls that she was told that the afternoon school is "the castor oil of Jewish life," a burden passed from parent to child with a sometimes unspoken admonition: "I hated it, you'll hate it; after your bar mitzvah you can quit."[13] The rather distasteful experience of afternoon Hebrew School will be good for the child in the long run. Jonathan Woocher suggests that parents send children to Jewish afternoon schools in the hope that they will be "inoculated" against assimilation later in life. Like other vaccinations, the religious school experience, while passive and somewhat painful, will on the positive side be brief and administered by experts.[14] Marder quotes former Hebrew school students whose recollections unfortunately may be typical: "I remember sitting on uncomfortable chairs and daydreaming a lot"; "The teaching materials were terrible; it was really corny stuff"; "It was a wild scene, the kids were running around the whole time. You could tell that they didn't want to be there and didn't take it seriously." One summarized the prevailing sentiment: "I hated it, it was boring, a real turn-off."[15]

Despite the negative experiences reported by graduates, many parents send their children to religious school simply as part of the suburban experience, just as their neighbors send their children to Sunday school at a church. Further, afternoon religious school meets the needs of parents who want to make only a nominal commitment of time and energy. For the suburban family juggling multiple tasks on a tight timetable, the religious school has to fit cleanly into the carpool schedule. And once that minimal amount of time is allocated, no additional parent participation should be expected. But this is not how traditional Judaism worked, and it is not how Reform Judaism was envisioned either.

Parents who dump their children at religious school and then go play tennis are free riders. They are exactly the kind of people Michael Hechter had in mind when he wrote that "truly rational actors will not join a group to pursue common ends when, without participating, they can reap the benefit of other people's activity in attaining them. If every member of the relevant group can share in the benefits, . . . then the rational thing is to free ride . . . rather than to help attain the corporate interest."[16] These free-riding parents let a small group of devoted temple members run the congregation and organize religious, cultural, and social activities. If their synagogue does not require them to participate actively, most will stay away. No religion can be an influential force for good under such circumstances.

Jan Katzew, the director of the UAHC Department of Jewish Education, argues that the only way to rectify the situation is for families to change their priorities. The Torah commands that "you yourselves shall teach your children; a parent must teach his child." The Babylonian Talmud states that the reason schools came into existence in that Jewish community 1,500 or more years ago was because some parents could not fulfill their obligation to teach their own children. From this perspective, parents need to shoulder the primary responsibility for religious education and acknowledge that all Jewish schools are supplementary. If parents are unable to teach their children how to live a Jewish life, the two to six hours a week that the afternoon school meets is likewise inadequate for the successful transmission of Jewish knowledge and commitment. Katzew argues that "if we expect a secondary institution to serve a primary function, we will be disillusioned." And that, Katzew explains, is exactly what has happened.[17]

Yet afternoon schools need to be more effective, because that is where most Jewish families choose to send their children. To the many educators who believe that the answer is the Jewish day school, Katzew replies, "Rather than see supplementary schools as part of the problem of Jewish learning we should learn to recognize them as part of the solution." These schools can be part of the solution if they supplement values and practices deeply entrenched in the children's homes, the primary educational institution, where parents are the bearers of religious values. But "when the Judaism they live with at home is dissonant with the Judaism students are supposed to learn at school, home wins, and consequently—too frequently—Judaism loses." Although "Jewish learning may be necessary for Jewish living, . . . learning itself is insufficient. The success of Jewish schooling is not only how much the graduates know, or even how much they are able to do, but also how they choose to live."[18] The supplementary school needs to work as effectively as possible in conjunction with home and congregation.

Isa Aron argues that the Reform movement needs to build programs that can "break the mold and create, in some way or another, something that is more community based, more involving, more active learning," and that family-based education is the key to success.[19] He and most other Reform educators today believe that involving the parents can reverse the apathetic attitude that negatively affects their children's commitment to Judaism. The Rhea Hirsch School of Education at HUC-JIR in Los Angeles has been working with fourteen pilot religious schools across the country to help them develop new approaches. Some congregations send cassettes home so parents can play lectures in their cars that correspond with what their children are learning in afternoon school. Other congregations offer special classes for children and parents to attend together. As both parents and children enjoy this experience tremendously, it turns what could be a negative experience into a positive one.

One of the most promising approaches is using informal educational techniques to involve the entire family in activities together. This approach appeals to parents looking to the synagogue school to reinforce their children's educational and social development. Family educator Heidi Eichaker ran a series of programs at Congregation Emanu-El B'ne Jeshurun in Milwaukee called Family Involvement

Time (FIT), whose very name plays on the desire of parents to find constructive activities to do as a family. FIT brings together the families of students in kindergarten through fifth grade for special events that corresponded with their school curriculum as well as the Jewish calendar. Both parents and children actively participate not only in the program itself but in the planning of the event as well. The special program fits into their religious school curriculum, as well as reinforcing the public school educational process. As one example, FIT offers a reading program in which parents and students write their own Jewish children's books together and share them with the group. The second-grade program has families construct a prayer box together that they can fill with prayers and ritual objects, such as a havdalah candle, for celebrating Shabbat in their home. This creative activity encourages family observance. Both parents and children want to make use of the ritual objects they have made with their own hands.

The need to innovate is particularly crucial in the language arts aspect of the afternoon school curriculum. One of the most problematic aspects of Hebrew school is the learning of Hebrew. Any foreign-language teacher knows it is virtually impossible to teach a language in just a few hours a week in an after-school format, particularly when many other subjects are taught simultaneously and the students are tired and cranky. Educators have urged experimenting with alternative approaches, such as teaching Israeli culture and Jewish literature in an interactive manner while avoiding the teaching of Hebrew grammar that can so bore the students. Alternatively, students could be immersed in a Hebrew environment, an intense Hebrew language program that would show students they can learn a substantial amount of Hebrew in a relatively short time. As in the case of congregational dynamics as a whole, the point here is not to find easy solutions that can transform the afternoon school overnight but to try innovative ideas. By experimenting, religious schools can begin to adapt themselves to the contemporary student.

At the same time, Reform is moving in a direction no one ever thought it would take—day school education. Until recently, the Orthodox ran most Jewish day schools in the United States, including some that had mixed student populations. Today the non-Orthodox Jewish day school movement has grown exponentially, due in large measure to general disappointment with the afternoon school as an effective means of transforming Jewish identity. Some reasons for the upswing in interest in Jewish day schools have nothing to do with interest in Judaism. Changing neighborhoods and declining public school systems, as well as a number of other social and political factors, have influenced the traditional Reform position on day schools—that they would segregate Jewish students from the American mainstream and should therefore be opposed. In fact, before 1970 there was not a single Reform Jewish day school in the United States. Over the subsequent twenty-five years, about twenty such schools were founded with a combined enrollment of about four thousand students. This still relatively small number does not include the much larger number of students in community day schools. There has indeed been a revolution in thinking on this topic.

Despite the changing attitudes, the Reform movement opposes vouchers, even though such a system could help parents pay day school tuition. The American Jewish community has a long tradition of supporting the public school system, which was felt to be critical for helping Jews integrate into U.S. society and was a central pillar in giving all citizens equal rights and equal opportunities. The Reform movement has argued that school voucher programs threaten the future of public education by siphoning off both money and students. Speaking at the UAHC biennial in Boston in December 2001, UAHC president Eric Yoffie said that "the people who engineer voucher proposals are almost always those with no interest in maintaining the public schools and whose real aim is to secure funding for their own schools." Yoffie singled out the traditionalist elements that have compromised "the most fundamental values of the broader Jewish community" by endorsing government-financed voucher programs that could help support Orthodox and Conservative day schools. "The public schools were the ladder we used to climb from poverty to affluence in American life. How dare we deny it to others." Yoffie expressed deep concern that the political campaign for vouchers supported by conservatives could undermine the basis upon which our society was built. "I tremble for our nation when I hear the constant drum beat of attack on our public school system. The public schools take the poor and the handicapped, the abused and the foster children, the Christian and the Muslim, the Roman Catholic and the Jew. They do more of God's work in a day than most institutions do in a lifetime. If our public schools are broken, then let's fix them, but let's not destroy them in the name of a highfalutin' principle that is often nothing more than naked self-interest dressed up as caring." Yoffie praised the day school movement but pointed out that "day schools will never reach more than a small percentage of non-Orthodox children in North America."[20]

Both Orthodox and Reform day schools teach Judaic studies. But the Jewish studies curriculum in the Reform day school puts less emphasis on Jewish law and teaches values that reflect a liberal orientation. This orientation, which allows for a great deal of flexibility and tolerance, can be taken to an extreme. In May 2001, a number of national newspapers attacked the Rodeph Sholom Day School in Manhattan for its decision to eliminate Mother's Day and Father's Day in-class programs. Citing the "different family make ups" of the student body, the school stated that the emotional well-being of the students would be best served by not putting them in potentially uncomfortable situations. Cindi Samson, the elementary school's director, wrote to parents that "holidays that serve no educational purpose and are not vital to the children's education need to be evaluated in terms of their importance in a school setting."[21]

The *New York Post* reported that the ban was instituted in response to a male couple who had adopted a son. Similarly, the *London Daily Telegraph* ran an article under the headline "School Bans Mother's Day to Appease Gays." School officials denied these reports, stating that administrators had begun thinking about the emotional impact of Mother's Day on children after one child's mother had died from breast cancer the previous year. Many were not convinced. The *New York Post* called the policy "fuzzy headed." The *Chicago Tribune* referred to it as an "enormous leap into silliness." The *Denver Post* asked, "What's next? Dump Thanksgiving because some people . . . don't like turkey?" Jay Leno on the *Tonight Show* joked that it would be easy to find children who could meet the school's sensitivity requirements in Beverly Hills, because all children there have parents who are both gay and divorced. While the public ridicule upset many parents, Rodeph Sholom's decision was interpreted by many as being one of a number of indications that Reform day schools actively engage the secular world rather than separate from it.

Day schools are at best a partial solution to the problem of Jewish education in the Reform movement. Unlike the Orthodox, for whom day school education is virtually universal, most Reform parents are still ambivalent about the idea. This attitude is changing as the day school becomes more respectable and more popular in non-Orthodox circles. But what may prove more influential for a much larger number of children are the informal educational programs—the temple youth groups, summer camps, trips to Israel, and weekend retreats.

Reform's Informal Youth Education Programs

Temple youth groups are the entry points for many young people into congregational life, and over the last several years, the Reform movement has set out aggressively to nurture the development of teen leaders not only for youth groups but also for congregations as a whole. For example, a training assembly program for temple youth group leaders has been developed to try to build on the tremendous enthusiasm at the UAHC biennials. This assembly aims to give promising present and future leaders an understanding of the Reform movement, how it operates, and the key role that congregations play in the big picture. The leaders' assembly brings together youth group presidents and other youth group leaders to help broaden and strengthen congregational services. It also helps the teenage participants learn how to interact effectively with adult congregational leaders. Young people have usually been dismissed as too immature to play a significant role in congregational decision making. But since the decisions will affect that age group and may have a decisive impact on retention rates, youth must have a say. In a number of cases, this approach has been enormously effective, facilitating the teens' keen desire to contribute to the development of not only youth programs but also the congregation as a whole.[22]

Innovation is urgently needed to revive the movement's youth programs. Eric Yoffie acknowledged in December 1998 that the youth arm of the UAHC, the North American Federation of Temple Youth, was "a shadow of its former self."[23] NFTY was founded in 1939 to foster commitment to the ideals and values of Reform Judaism among the younger generation. Its framework emphasizes the development of personal and leadership skills in a "wholesome" Jewish environment. In addition to Jewish educational activities, the movement organized Tikkun Olam programs to enable youth to do "whatever we can to address the social ills of our time, and thus, to answer the prophetic call to pursue justice everywhere." The youth movement encourages its members to involve themselves in synagogue activities: "NFTY does not exist in a vacuum. As part of a congregational movement, we are committed to encouraging NFTYites to be full and active participants in all aspects of the life of their own temples."[24]

Once a dynamic and successful organization, NFTY failed to keep up as society changed in the 1980s and the 1990s. As a consequence, more and more youth found NFTY no longer as nifty as it had once been, and they voted with their feet, particularly after their bar and bat mitzvahs. Other youth organizations that had experienced similar problems had taken steps to remake their images and reformat their activity offerings, including the Girl Scouts, as Fox News reported in November 2000. "We're no longer about baking cookies and toasting marshmallows around the fire," one Girl Scout leader told a news crew. "We now offer young women the chance to get advanced computer training, learn marketing skills, and network widely."

Yoffie himself called the teen dropout rate in the Reform movement "appallingly high."[25] While many Reform teenagers appear to be uninterested in Reform Judaism and drop out for that reason, others claim that they would love to continue to be involved but are simply not the youth-group type. In response, Yoffie suggested revamping NFTY. To build a structure that could more effectively keep youth involved throughout their high school years, he announced that each UAHC region would hire a full-time professional to organize and develop youth programming in that region. The hope was that this decentralization would allow the UAHC regional directors to have more impact on youth programming, a far more effective approach than trying to run everything out of New York. Yoffie has further committed the entire movement to developing a range of new programs for teenagers who want alternatives to the standard youth group activities. His ideas include a summer travel program focusing on social action projects and a summer study program that combines SAT preparation and college visits with Judaica.

NFTY's own summer programs in Israel have proved remarkably popular, although registration dropped off precipitously as a consequence of the renewed tensions between Palestinians and Israelis. Eric Yoffie set off a controversy when he cancelled Reform youth trips to Israel at the height of the violence, arguing that it was not fair to use other people's children to make political points. He deserves credit for being honest, but internal critics argue that it would have been more astute politically to blame the trip cancellation on the lack of enrollment. In any case, the movement quickly reestablished its Zionist credentials. New trips were publicized, but it remains difficult to recruit teenagers willing to go or parents willing to allow their children to go. At its height, the summer program sent more than a dozen groups for six-week trips that incorporated touring, educational programs, and leadership training. The Israel trips were inspirational because they immersed the participant not only in the NFTY experience twenty-four hours a day, but also in the Israeli context. Most participants came back transformed, although it remains unclear how much of that "transformation" endured. But rabbis and educators feel convinced that a trip to Israel is one of the most significant experiences a family can give teenagers. Rabbi Lee Bycel of the Brandeis-Bardin Institute tells parents that a NFTY trip to Israel allows the youngsters "to see and experience firsthand what it feels like to be in a state where Jews are the majority. These trips change lives and facilitate bonds with Judaism which can last a lifetime."[26]

Despite problems with retaining those on the periphery, the core leadership of NFTY is extremely dedicated. One has only to attend a NFTY convention to see the tremendous enthusiasm. For example, at the 1999 NFTY conference at the Westin LAX Hotel in Los Angeles, more than 1,500 teenagers came together for discussion and debate and for the opportunity to learn about subjects ranging from Judaism on the Internet to congressional laws relating to freedom of religion, packing the grand ballroom for the keynote addresses and the workshops in numerous meeting rooms. One of the hopes is that the representatives will be so excited by their convention experience that they will transmit their enthusiasm to the other members of their youth group back home.

An entirely different style of informal education is available at the Reform movement's summer camps, where generations of youngsters have had some of their most positive Jewish experiences. These regional camps, such as Camp Eisner in Massachusetts, provide "a joyous, invigorating and uplifting few weeks of total immersion in Judaism, with memories powerful enough to last the entire year."[27]

The camps combine a rich Jewish atmosphere, positive development experiences, and a natural setting, as Rabbi Lee Bycel, formerly of Anshe Chesed Fairmount Temple, explained in a synagogue bulletin.

> No matter how much we do here at Fairmount Temple, it is hard to convey the depth and feeling of Judaism in just a few hours each week. At a Jewish summer camp, our young people are immersed in a total Jewish environment. Shabbat is a natural part of the week, which emerges from all they have learned and experienced during camp. For many years, I have spent time in our movement's summer camps. I love watching the faces on our young people as they gather for Shabbat— eager, joyful, immersed in the moment, understanding of the beauty of Shabbat, truly a sight to be seen.

Further, "Jewish summer camps can play an important role in building self-esteem. It is important for our young people to be in a healthy and safe environment, away from parents, where they can learn more about themselves and their own abilities and skills. They gain a lot by having to be responsible for themselves—and it is amazing what they can manage to do without our help." Finally, "hiking, sleeping out under the stars, having the time to see the beauty around them without a car or movies, or video games—teaches some of the most important lessons in life."[28]

The first UAHC camp in North America, Olin-Sang-Ruby Union Institute (OSRUI) in Oconomowoc, Wisconsin, creates "methods of learning that make Judaism come alive" for more than one thousand youngsters every summer.[29] OSRUI has its roots in a series of weekend retreats for Chicago-area youth in the late 1940s at a Wisconsin campsite. Greta Lee Splansky, whose father, Ernst Lorge, was one of several rabbis who organized the early activities, recalls: "He loved the opportunity to be with the kids, to teach them Zionist songs, teach them Hebrew. They all had the idea that this was the way to really educate Reform Jewish youth, to further the aims of the Reform movement.

And it worked. The rabbis were the youth leaders in the early years, and that was the heart of the thing."[30] Lorge and others began to discuss establishing a permanent camp for Reform Jewish youth. When Herman Schaalman became director of the Chicago Federation of the UAHC in 1949, the project was set to move forward. The rabbis found three philanthropists willing to provide the purchase money for a neglected plot of about two hundred acres in Oconomowoc. In the summer of 1951, thirty-nine campers showed up for the first session of what was then called the Union Institute Camp.

OSRUI sessions vary from two to seven weeks, with six programs to choose from. Each session has a different Jewish theme, chosen by the campers, who also participate in the usual summertime activities—sports, song sessions, drama, dance, horseback riding, creative writing, photography, boating, and a challenge-climbing program. More than two-thirds of the counselors grew up as OSRUI campers and have a deep sense of what a Reform camping experience should be. In addition to the counselors, more than forty rabbis, cantors, and professional educators spend at least two weeks each at the camp teaching "Torah in its broadest sense." They work with all age levels and in all the programs, helping shape informal as well as formal educational experiences. Specialty programs target student interests: Maccabiah for campers with a special interest in sports and fitness; the Tiferet program for students with a strong interest in drama, visual arts, dance, and vocal music; Chalutzim for tenth graders interested in living for seven weeks in an intensive Hebrew-speaking environment. Accredited by the Chicago Community Foundation for Jewish Education, the Chalutzim program is designed to increase the campers' Hebrew language skill dramatically over the course of just one summer. They not only learn Hebrew, but also work cooperatively with Jewish communal leaders to assume real responsibility for the development of the program. Special opportunities are promised to those who invest themselves in peer leadership and mature learning.

A source of inspiration for those who attend, the camps have also served as a testing ground for new approaches to ritual. While many of the most creative Shabbat services were written or edited at a camp, the camps more importantly have nurtured the development of a new style of Reform song. When OSRUI began, the music consisted largely of folk songs and, later, of civil rights movement chants "considered to have religious significance in that they embodied Reform principles." The folk music was slowly supplemented by traditional Jewish music and a new American Jewish folk music. OSRUI hired Debbie Friedman as a song leader in 1970 as "a new genre of music was coming to the fore. It was a Reform Jewish genre of music, songs that were mainly liturgical, written by [camp] song leaders. She brought her tunes and her compositions to the camp and helped to empower a whole generation in this region."[31] This music continues to inspire many Reform Jews.

Friedman began song leading for her synagogue youth group in 1968, then attended a song leader workshop at the Kutz Camp Institute in Warwick, New York, and soon began writing her own music. "I taught it to a group of kids who were doing a creative service with James Taylor, Joan Baez, and Judy Collins music. Not only did they sing the V'ahavta, they stood arm in arm. They were moved; they were crying. Here was something in a genre to which they could relate."[32] In 1972 she recorded *Sing unto God*, an album of Sabbath songs that featured a high school choir. "I had planned [only] to make a demo tape, but when I found out it would cost only $500 more to make 1,000 LPs, I thought, why not? They sold like hot cakes at camp. That's how it started. It was a fluke." Friedman moved to Chicago, where she began leading services and continued her youth work. Later she took a position as a cantorial soloist in California, began performing more frequently, and recorded additional albums. Soon people began using her melodies in their synagogue services. Perhaps her most famous creation is "Mi Sheberach," composed for a *simcha chachma*, a celebration of wisdom, to honor a friend on her sixtieth birthday. The prayer offers the hope of healing for those suffering. "My friend was having a very difficult time in her life and a number of her friends were also struggling. Yet she had arrived at this age and was determined to embrace it." Introduced at the UAHC biennial in San Francisco in 1993, the tune has become the most popular adopted liturgical melody in recent decades.

A New Focus on Adult Education

Because study is not solely a youth concern, the UAHC leadership has committed itself to creating a "synagogue of the future" that will provide a place of serious learning for all ages. In traditional Jewish thought, God spoke to individuals through their study of sacred texts. But few in the Reform movement could read Hebrew well enough to study the texts in the original, and most of the few English translations were not suitable for adult education programs. For example, a Sonsino translation of the Talmud was extremely difficult for the novice to understand and of little use in a classroom setting. This has now changed. Random House has launched a multiyear project to translate Adin Steinsaltz's Talmud commentary into English, and the UAHC Press, revamped under Rabbi Hara Person, is producing new textbooks for the adult learner and adult Jewish educational programs.

One indication of the UAHC's commitment is a resolution on Torah study adopted at the 1997 biennial conference in Dallas: "We recognize that North American Jews face a Jewish literacy crisis. While we are the best-educated generation of Jews that has ever lived, we are often woefully ignorant of our own Jewish heritage. At the same time, we are witnessing a renewed enthusiasm for Jewish learning throughout the Reform movement. Those of us who have had the opportunity to study and taste the richness of Torah have discovered that learning is a source of inspiration and great adventure."[33]

Adults throughout the Jewish community are finding their way back to serious textual study. Kenneth Cohen, a founding executive of the software giant Oracle, became involved in Lehrhaus, a Berkeley, California, adult education program named after Freies Jüdisches Lehrhaus (Free Jewish study center), the pioneer program developed by Martin Buber, Franz Rosenzweig and a number of other German Jewish intellectuals in Frankfurt during the interwar period. Cohen said of his motivation for studying: "It's just inevitable that you say to yourself, 'What do I want to pass on to this kid [his child] other than my stock certificates?' I had to have a higher goal." He found that "doing and receiving Jewish education is a remarkable, rewarding thing. It's passing on not the latest hot computer chip, which will be obsolete next year, but taking the accumulated knowledge of humankind and perpetuating that, passing it on to new generations and pass[ing] it on [further]."[34]

In almost every major city today, nondenominational independent institutions offer intensive Jewish adult education. The Florence Melton

Adult Mini-School Program offers a two-year, 120-hour course of study to several groups of students at a time in thirty-four cities. Most students in all of these programs are middle-aged baby boomers searching for meaning. "It's an awakening," says Paul Flexner of the Jewish Education Services of North America.[35] Many had stopped their Jewish education immediately after their bar or bat mitzvah two, three, or four decades earlier. They now feel an acute awareness of how much they have missed and how much they don't know. Many feel their textual illiteracy prevents them from passing on to their children a meaningful Judaism that goes beyond superficial ethnic foods and accents.

The UAHC recognizes the challenge that the movement faces: instilling the current generation with a love of Jewish learning in order to create knowledgeable and literate Jews. Most adult education programs reach only a small percentage of the congregants; frequently the same people enroll, fall and spring, year after year. The UAHC has thus called on the individual congregations to develop programs for synagogue leaders and other adult members that can provide them with a rich and rewarding communal environment, including perhaps year-long courses in which they read significant Jewish books. If undertaken by congregational boards, the discussion of these books could be incorporated into the regular board meetings. The UAHC has urged congregations to make Torah study and discussion a regular part of Sabbath observance in the synagogue and the home, and to train lay members in the skill of Torah reading and Torah chanting. Such individuals could then use their newly acquired skills to reinvigorate worship services. The hope is to pioneer a new type of Jewish spirituality through intellectual growth and emotional development.

Along with the UAHC, individual synagogues are developing new approaches to attract the many congregants who do not attend Jewish study sessions. When Congregation Beth Am in Los Altos Hills, California, hired Josh Zweiback in 1998 as adult educator, he took the first full-time position in a Reform congregation in the United States intended to "develop new frontiers of education in synagogue life," according to Richard Block, the congregation's senior rabbi. Funded by the Koret Foundation of San Francisco, Zweiback interpreted his mandate as spanning a very broad spectrum, from Torah study to "all sorts of experiences including praying and giving Tzedakah." He pointed out that "distinctions between mind and body were not made in classical times: living Torah and learning Torah went hand in hand."[36] Zweiback has tried a number of interesting ideas. On the congregation's Tikkun Olam Day, he distributed a tape about the role of social action in Judaism that included mock interviews with famous Jews throughout history, a number of Hebrew concepts relating to the subject, and the senior rabbi teaching a blessing that should be recited before performing a mitzvah.

Zweiback has adapted the traditional *chevruta* system of studying by pairing off adults interested in studying Jewish texts. He argues that the system, "road-tested over the past couple thousand years," is one of the best for adult learners because it "builds community and deep, long-lasting friendships" and "allows adults to study what they want, when they want, where they want."[37] The congregation also offers "Bagels, Lattes, and Learning," a monthly seminar that parents can attend while their children are in Sunday school. There they grapple with such contemporary issues as how parents can respond to questions their children ask about what they hear in the media.

Zweiback believes that adult education "seems to be the direction the Reform movement in the Bay Area and all of the Jewish communities are moving. We live in a time that fragments us. I think the Torah is the glue that can put the pieces together." Rabbi Leon Morris, director of the Skirball Center for Adult Jewish Learning at Temple Emanu-El and formerly director of the New York Kollel at HUC-JIR in New York, agrees. "I think that a kind of Judaism that was very organic for previous generations of American Jews is not so for us," he told me. "Contemporary Jews need to find substantive and meaningful expressions of why they should be Jewish. There is a greater urgency to find relevance in classic Jewish sources. I think that given a whole variety of circumstances, it will become increasingly difficult to transmit a strong sense of Jewish identity without a serious Jewish educational foundation." Morris said that "of all the ways that one can actualize Judaism today, we believe that it is Jewish studies which has the greatest potential for invigorating Jewish life because Jewish study is based around the sense of debate, dialectic, discussion, and disagreement. So this is what resonates with the lives of contemporary American Jews."[38]

Among new paradigms being explored are family education, where the entire family—adults and children—study and experience Judaism together, and an intensive immersion program. Peter Knobel of Beth Emet, the Free Synagogue of Evanston, Illinois, takes about fifty members of his congregation to Jerusalem for one week every other year. "They stay in the dormitory of Hebrew Union College, and I get some of the best Jewish scholars in the world to teach them. They have been required to read a serious book on Judaism by a major scholar—they all have read it and have come prepared—and for a week they study with the scholars. We do no touring; when they are not in class they are free in Jerusalem. The success of this program indicates to me that many Jews really want to learn about the faith in a serious way."[39] Unlike a special interest program for people from all over the country, Knobel's group comes from one temple in a Chicago suburb. The study trip's congregational nature accounts for its success, allowing the intense experience to include both extensive preparation and substantial follow-up.

The UAHC biennial and the other regional and national Reform conferences offer further models of serious Jewish study. Adult retreats referred to by their Hebrew designation, *kallot*, which generally run for several days and include a Shabbat experience, are particularly successful. They have expanded from their original sites on the East and West Coasts to an additional *kallah* in the Midwest and another in Canada. The courses run the gamut of Jewish studies, concentrating on spirituality, prayer, mysticism, and gender studies. One recent kallah featured "Locating God: Jewish Perceptions of Sacred Space," taught by Steven Weitzman, and "The Rhythms of Worship," taught by Jeff Klepper, a well-known cantor and songwriter, along with textual courses such as Lewis Barth's "Prayer and Worship in Biblical, Midrashic, and Talmudic Texts" and Peter Knobel's "The Siddur and Tanach, the Prayer Book and the Bible: A Conversation with God, About God, and About Us."[40] Those who have participated in the kallah experience describe it as an intimate study retreat that focuses participants on serious textual study while at the same time facilitating a meaningful spiritual encounter. For example, the Canadian kallah includes "meditation, twice-daily services, and a complete Shabbat experience with *mikveh*, singing, optional workshops and study, and Israeli dancing." A Kids' Kallah for the children of participants allows children aged four to twelve to attend a concurrent Judaica program that mirrors what their parents are doing. On Shabbat, for instance, the children are encouraged to reflect "on how Jewish learning has touched their young lives."[41]

This formula for adult education is the right type of program at the right time. In a way that their grandparents would not have understood, many people are looking for something spiritual to provide a sense of meaning in their lives. They feel adrift in a materialistic society and need reassurance that their existence has purpose in a broader context than their home environments supply. That is why the kallot—which remove the participants from their usual environment—are able to generate a sense of spiritual excitement they would not otherwise feel. Furthermore, the teachers, mostly top scholars, are exceptional in that they bring a deep emotional commitment as well as a wealth of knowledge to their teaching. The kallah is "an incredible learning and community-building experience."[42] The UAHC hopes that as more and more congregants bring the sense of inner warmth and joy discovered at kallot back to their temples, they may help their rabbis transform the worship and educational experience in their congregation. This may break the cycle of apathy that pervades many liberal congregations today.

Judaism will be able to survive only if its culture can be transmitted to the next generation in a compelling form. The children of Israel who left Egypt wandered throughout the desert for forty years, a holy nation set apart. In contrast, American Jews are thoroughly integrated into America's multicultural, multiethnic, and very pluralistic society. The Reform movement needs to develop a strategy of engaging Jews—young and old—in programs that combine spiritual meaning with community unity in a way that inspires them to look for more. When the Freies Jüdisches Lehrhaus opened in Frankfurt after World War I, Franz Rosenzweig explained that its methodology would be revolutionary. "A new learning is about to be born—rather, it has been born. It is learning in reverse order. A learning that no longer starts from the Torah and leads into life, but the other way round: from life, from a world that knows nothing of the law, or pretends to know nothing, back to the Torah." Facing the same challenges, the American Reform movement is responding with a vigor that would have pleased Rosenzweig.

Chapter 8

The Outreach Campaign

Outreach is Reform Judaism's response to the problem of intermarriage . . . We live in an open society, and intermarriage is its inevitable concomitant. It is our collective effort to convert a crisis into an opportunity, to turn the threat of a serious drain on our numeric strength into a vital source for our enlargement. . . . We have but one of two options: We can either exile our children or continue to embrace them. . . . We have resolved to take the latter course. We refuse to alienate our children... Quite the contrary, we intend to reach out to them, to embrace them. . . . Their non-Jewish partners might then conceivably be inclined to initiate the process of conversion to Judaism

—ALEXANDER M. SCHINDLER, 1995

In the Old World, intermarriage was the least of the problems Jews faced. In countries such as Poland, Lithuania, and Romania, Christian hostility toward Jews was felt as ever present. The romantic liaisons that occurred were rare, and even in the United States in the early decades of the twentieth century, were seen as curiosities more than anything else. As late as the early 1960s, most American Jewish communities had extremely low intermarriage rates.

In 1977, the warning bells went off when Harvard demographer Elihu Bergman extrapolated in an article in *Midstream* that, based on available data and likely trends, the Jewish population would decline precipitously by the year 2076. Bergman, then assistant director of the

Harvard Center for Population Studies, wrote that one hundred years in the future, the 5.7 million Jews then calculated to live in the United States would be reduced to at most 944,000, or even as few as 10,420.[1] But the sociologists whose studies Bergman had drawn on immediately came forward to refute his method as well as his conclusions.[2] The implication seemed to be that if Bergman's methodology was flawed, then there was nothing to worry about.

Indeed, many Jewish leaders in the 1980s were optimistic that the American Jewish community would not just sustain itself but thrive. Charles E. Silberman's 1985 *A Certain People*, which argued that all was well, generated a huge amount of publicity. Silberman insisted that residual anti-Semitism had collapsed, as he proudly dropped name after name of Jews who had risen to the highest levels in industry, academia, and virtually all other facets of U.S. economic and political life. He pointed to Irving S. Shapiro, chair and chief executive officer of that "bluest of blue-chip corporations," E. I. du Pont de Nemours and Company. Henry Rosovsky became dean of the Faculty of Arts and Sciences at Harvard, Edward I. Koch became mayor of New York, Henry Kissinger became Secretary of State—the list went on and on. Silberman argued not only that Jews were doing well as individuals but also that American Judaism was robust and healthy. "Most Jews are choosing to remain Jews," he claimed, although not necessarily the same kind of Jews as their grandparents or even their parents. This argument was being made by a number of academics as well, including Calvin Goldscheider of Brown University. Silberman reported both sides of the issue, but it was hard not to be swept away by his conclusions.[3]

After so much optimistic talk, the 1990 National Jewish Population Survey (NJPS) came as a rude shock: 52 percent of the Jews who had married between 1985 and 1990 had married non-Jewish spouses who had not converted. Even more distressing, only 27.8 percent of intermarried couples were raising their children as Jewish. Many Jewish leaders were dismayed. Even Silberman expressed his surprise and acknowledged that many of his optimistic prophecies had proved to be wrong.[4] Those already pessimistic now became frantic. For example, Orthodox rabbi Ephraim Z. Buchwald wrote a letter to the editor of *Moment* urging Jews to "stop the silent Holocaust."[5] Buchwald continued to speak in this vein, warning, "There are no barking dogs and no

Zyklon-B gas . . . but make no mistake: this is a spiritual Holocaust."[6] After Gary A. Tobin opened a book on conversion to Judaism with his quote, Buchwald clarified that "for the record, that statement was said about general assimilation, not intermarriage." But he went on to intro-duce a new analogy: "Ladies and gentlemen, this is the reality: Our children are drowning."[7] While Buchwald's represented an extreme response, many others felt depressed and confused. Studies showed that the children of Reform Jews were intermarrying at rates higher than were the children of Conservative or Orthodox Jews. Also, many Con-servative or Orthodox Jews who intermarry subsequently join Reform congregations. Therefore, the Reform movement had already had con-siderable experience dealing with the reality of intermarriage and its consequences for the synagogue. It is in this context that the Reform movement pioneered the development of Outreach.

Alexander Schindler and the Origins of Outreach

In December 1978 UAHC president Alexander M. Schindler gave a dra-matic speech to the UAHC Board of Trustees that called for a sustained effort to reach out to the unaffiliated and particularly the intermarried. He spoke of the increase in intermarriage since the early 1960s, and of its threat to the future of the American Jewish community. He then ad-dressed the question of how the Reform movement should respond:

> I begin with the recognition of a reality: the tide of
> intermarriage is running against us. The statistics on the
> subject confirm what our own experience teaches us:
> intermarriage is on the rise . . . we may deplore it, we may
> lament it, we may struggle against it, but these are the facts.
> The tide is running against us, and we must deal with this
> threatening reality. Dealing with it does not, however, mean
> that we must learn to accept it. It does not mean that we
> should prepare to sit *shivah* for the American Jewish
> community. On the contrary, facing and dealing with reality
> means confronting it, coming to grips with it, determining to
> reshape it.[8]

Schindler argued that intermarriage did not necessarily mean the couple was lost to the Jewish community. Rather, how such families developed over a period of a decade or longer would determine the number of Jews in the next generation. Therefore, the Reform movement could take steps to "deal realistically with the threat which intermarriage presents to our survival." In keeping with the accepted wisdom of the time, Schindler made it clear that his policy of first choice would be to encourage the non-Jewish spouse to convert to Judaism. To encourage such conversions, he recommended that the Jewish community increase its sensitivity to Jews by choice and Jews-by-choice candidates. If such individuals felt more welcome, more of them would consider becoming Jewish. Schindler bluntly stated that many in the Jewish community had not been very friendly to such individuals: "We often alienate them. We question their motivations (since only a mad man would choose to be a Jew, the convert is either neurotic or hypocritical). We think them less Jewish (ignoring that they often know more about Judaism than born Jews). Unto the end of their days, we refer to them as converts" (244). Thus the first part of the strategy involved taking steps to encourage conversion to Judaism.

But Schindler believed that this would not suffice. In 1978, 66 percent of the intermarriages consisted of a Jewish man and a non-Jewish woman, and about 25 percent of non-Jewish women who married Jewish men converted to Judaism either before or during the marriage. However, among the 33 percent of intermarriages that involved a Jewish woman and a non-Jewish man, far fewer of the spouses converted to Judaism, in terms of both percentages and numbers.

And yet, not all hope was lost. In many of the cases where no formal conversion occurred, Schindler believed that there was "Jewish drift"—the couple might drift toward an informal affiliation with the Jewish community and might develop a generally Jewish rather than Christian identity. A new study indicated that almost 50 percent of the non-Jewish husbands of Jewish women described themselves as Jews, despite not having formally committed to Judaism. Schindler hoped to encourage this trend, not only by welcoming intermarried Jews and their marriage partners, but also by inviting them to actively participate in the Jewish community, including its synagogue activities. He warned that the task would not be easy: "They may feel guilty, they may feel resentful, they are almost sure to feel some confusion and ambivalence toward active involvement in the community. They may feel inhibited out of a sense of regard for their partner's sensibilities, or out of embarrassment in the face of a community they think will be hostile to their partners" (247). This was remarkably progressive thinking for the time. Many Jews in the 1970s remained hostile to intermarriage and felt anger toward those who had intermarried. Many would see this as a tacit admission of failure, Schindler said; others would see it as destroying any possibility of intimidating Jews from "marrying out." By proposing a gentler, more nurturing approach, he was arguing both that such couples deserved compassion rather than hostility and that such a policy would be in the best interests of the Jewish community.

Finally, Schindler called for outreach efforts to include unchurched gentiles—people who may have been raised as Christians but had become alienated from Christianity, and people who had been raised with no religion and professed no religion. "I believe that the time has come for the Reform movement—and others, if they are so disposed— to launch a carefully conceived outreach program aimed at all Americans who are unchurched and who are seeking religious meaning" (248). This statement was quoted widely in national newspapers, including the *New York Times*. Schindler's advocacy of active proselytization appeared to be a completely new approach and, for that reason, generated tremendous controversy.

Those who liked Schindler's forthrightness felt his position was an overt recognition that the status of the Jews in the United States was in the process of rapid change. They felt Schindler was boldly recognizing the shift and trying to lead the Reform movement into a proactive position. Critics saw Schindler's position as a cataclysmic reversal of a religious policy in place for nearly two thousand years. Schindler spoke with confidence: "It would be easy to tiptoe here, to use obfuscatory language and be satisfied to hint at my purpose. But I will not. Unabashedly and urgently, I propose that we resume our vocation as champions of Judaism, that we move from passive acceptance to affirmative action" (249). When Schindler used the word "resume," he was referring to the generally accepted fact that Jews in the ancient world actively proselytized. Judaism could offer spiritual nourishment that Americans craved, Schindler told the UAHC board. Many had not found a sense of spiritual satisfaction in the religions of their birth and so would be receptive and appreciative if Judaism was offered to them.

On the other hand, Schindler stressed that he was not advocating a "traveling religious circus" but envisioning a dignified approach, which might include information centers and information bulletins. "Introduction to Judaism" courses could be offered and publications printed so that the Jewish people could "respond openly and positively to those God-seekers whose search leads them to our door, who voluntarily ask for our knowledge" (249).

Schindler deliberately restricted his target group to unchurched gentiles, which excluded anyone involved in any way with Christianity, to avoid giving Christian evangelical groups a pretext to justify new proselytizing initiatives among American Jews. This was a very real possibility, since many Christians believe that one must accept Jesus in order to be saved, and thus it is of paramount importance to help Jews see the light. Despite this theological justification, in recent decades most Christian denominations had avoided overt proselytizing due to the delicate nature of Jewish-Christian relations in the post-Holocaust period. Christian leaders had become acutely aware that most Jews would perceive such proselytizing as a direct attack on them and therefore restrained their missionary forces. But a new policy of Jewish proselytizing of Christians could easily upset these delicate informal arrangements, unleashing a new wave of Christian missionary efforts aimed at Jews.

Despite all the publicity, nothing much came of this proposal. Whereas Reform Jews responded with enthusiasm to the idea of outreach to intermarried couples, they remained apathetic toward the concept of active proselytization of the unchurched. Reform Jews lacked the sense of religious mission necessary to inspire them with the belief that converting others was a religious duty. And without that sense of religious mission, no sustained attempt at proselytizing was likely. Still, Schindler's recommendation to convert unchurched gentiles represented a dramatic shift in how Jews would view their religion vis-à-vis the outside world.

Subsequent Efforts to Wrestle with the Intermarriage Dilemma

In response to Schindler's speech, the UAHC and the CCAR set up the joint Commission on Jewish Outreach. Lydia Kukoff, a Jew by choice herself, became the first director, based in Los Angeles and then in New York. The commission wanted to provide support for Jews by choice and to change the mindset of the community—to help people understand that Jews by choice convert for many reasons, not just because they marry someone Jewish. Those who choose to become Jewish needed to be invited in with appropriate programs and a welcoming atmosphere. In 1983, the CCAR passed the patrilineal descent resolution, which became a key foundation for further outreach efforts. It further emphasized that American Jews who marry someone who is not Jewish may still want to raise a Jewish family.

"Times and Seasons," the pilot project, started in the mid-1980s as an eight-week discussion group to help intermarried couples define who they were and understand the issues. Arlene Chernow, who runs the Outreach program for the Pacific Southwest Region that includes Southern California, New Mexico, Arizona, El Paso, Texas, and Las Vegas, told me in an interview in April 2001: "The basic dilemma being addressed was why you can't be Jewish and Christian at the same time, and a lot of people did not understand this. The question of how can you raise Jewish children when you are not Jewish comes up in a variety of contexts. It can work very effectively under certain circumstances. In cases where the couple have an ability to communicate effectively with each other, where the synagogue is welcoming, and there are opportunities for the non-Jewish parent to learn enough about Judaism to participate with the family." For example, two non-Jewish mothers who send their children to the Temple Israel of Hollywood Nursery School decided to put together a notebook for parents like themselves. "Celebrations: A Parent's Guide to Celebrating Holidays at Temple Israel of Hollywood Nursery School" contains a brief description of each holiday, blessings, recipes, songs, and suggested family activities. As a result of the successful outreach, both of these mothers decided to enroll their children in the Temple Israel of Hollywood Day School.

The UAHC decided to hire Outreach coordinators for all the regions. Chernow's region has about eighty Reform synagogues, and she maintains contact with every congregation. The larger congregations have an outreach committee that Chernow works with on a regular basis. Many small congregations cannot afford a full-time rabbi and are unlikely to have a formal Outreach committee, although the whole congregation performs this function. Like many of the small congregations in remote locations, Congregation Beth Hamidbar of Yuma, Arizona, has extremely high levels of intermarriage: Of about forty family members, 70 to 80 percent are marriages between a born Jew and someone who is not born Jewish, Chernow said in our interview.

Yet Outreach is much more than just welcoming intermarried couples. "We've only just hit the tip of the iceberg in terms of what we can do in Outreach," Chernow said. "We want to become more active in encouraging 'Jewish grand parenting.' Adult children have intermarried and they have not yet made any decisions. So our role in that is to help the Jewish grandparents become stronger in their own Jewish identities and open doors to Jewish identity for their grandchildren." Another important Outreach focus is helping religious-school teachers and education directors become sensitive to children's comments. For example, if a child has a non-Jewish parent and talks in class about the non-Jewish grandparents, how should a teacher handle that? The Outreach directors also help congregations define the role of the non-Jew in the synagogue in terms of membership, governance, and ritual. They work with youth groups on Jewish identity and temple staff on how they can sensitively respond to questions from callers who are marginally affiliated or not affiliated at all. "You have to be an optimist to work in outreach. We see every conversation as an opportunity to open the door to Jewish learning and helping people who choose to make Jewish choices," Chernow said.

Outreach professionals have a mandate from the UAHC to do work that will help bring intermarried couples and others closer to the Reform congregation and Reform Judaism. The broad consensus in the UAHC that such work is positive and important breaks down on some specifics, including rabbinic officiation at intermarriage ceremonies. Outreach workers are careful to avoid advocacy of any position in these sensitive areas, focusing on the people and their feelings rather than trying to dictate religious policy not accepted by the movement as a whole. Rather than supporting rabbis who do officiate and implicitly attacking those who do not, they support rabbis who may make a number of different policy decisions based on their personal understanding of Reform Judaism. This neutrality makes Outreach acceptable to all rabbis and virtually all congregations. Chernow sees Outreach as contributing to the sense of excitement that many congregations feel today, she told me. "There is a wonderful vibrancy in the Reform movement today. It's not the minimalist portrait that many outsiders like to paint."

Many proponents of Outreach, including Chernow, find the continued hostility to intermarriage counterproductive. When the *Jewish Journal of Los Angeles* ran an article that implicitly recommended actively opposing intermarriage, local UAHC representatives Jerrold Goldstein and Chernow objected. Through their work in the UAHC Pacific Southwest Council, they wrote to the magazine, they had found that "it is very frequently the partner who is not born Jewish who insists on a Jewish education for themselves and their children." Goldstein and Chernow argued that strong statements against intermarriage would be ineffective: "That was tried for the last one hundred years without any success." They quoted Alexander Schindler, who believed that contemporary Reform Jewish Outreach seeks "to take intermarriage out of the house of mourning and place it in the house of study." Rather than taking a hard-line position, "we think that it is far more productive to welcome couples who wish to explore Judaism than to shut the door before they have had an opportunity to learn."[9]

Goldstein and Chernow were also concerned by the implication in the article that endogamic marriage would ensure a strong future for the Jewish community in North America. "We do not want the Jewish community to be lulled into a false sense of security by assuming that Jews marrying Jews will in itself guarantee a strong sense of Jewish identity." What they could say with certainty was that "people who chose Judaism as adults now fill temple leadership positions all over the country. Many of these people were introduced into Judaism by marrying a Jewish person." This is true, but there is another side to this question. Goldstein and Chernow seem to deliberately ignore the ethnic component of Jewish identity. If Judaism is a form of liberal religion, then the only measure of how successfully it is being transmitted is to look at who is religiously active and who is not. But if Jewishness is an ethnic characteristic passed on from generation to generation, then it matters very much who Jews marry. Los Angeles has a high percentage of first-generation immigrants, so it is no surprise that many in the local Jewish community feel their identity will be transmitted to the next generation only if their children marry partners who were born Jewish. An inherent tension exists between Reform theological assumptions and the visceral ethnic identity that many Jews continue to feel.

"I feel that Reform Jewish Outreach is such an important piece of the future of American Judaism," Chernow said in our April 2001 interview. "People don't have total control over whom they fall in love with. The place where they can make choices is how they are going to lead their lives and what lifestyle choices they are going to make. I think that Reform Judaism has tremendous potential to reach a lot of people and make their lives more meaningful regardless of how they were raised." She questioned the *Jewish Journal* article's assumption that marrying someone who was born Jewish would ensure the future of American Judaism. "I don't think that that is a correct assumption. Anyone who wants to be Jewish in this day and age has to take affirmative and positive steps with their family. Judaism just does not happen by birth or marriage."

Chernow's message will find a warm reception among many baby boomers searching for spiritual meaning and religious identity on the suburban frontier. It will be less welcome among those who retain strong ethnic ties and continue to live in urban Jewish neighborhoods. But the UAHC's Outreach policies allow Jews living in communities with high intermarriage rates to construct new forms of Jewish identity in the context of a mixed religious background household.

Responding to Internal Migration

While intermarriage attracts most of the attention, migration patterns also threaten to corrode traditional Jewish societal patterns. The 1990 NJPS found that only about one quarter of Jews in the United States were still living in the area where they were born. About one quarter had moved out of their immediate region in the previous five years. A 1996 study by Sidney Goldstein and Alice Goldstein entitled *Jews on the Move* confirmed what has long been known: Many Jews have been leaving the "Rust Belt" and settling in the South and the West.[10] Many sociologists view this internal migration to be of tremendous importance. Jews who relocate are less likely to affiliate than Jews who live in the same neighborhood that their parents and grandparents did. Those who move are more likely to intermarry than those who remain in the place where they grew up. Intermarried couples are more likely to move than Jewish-Jewish couples. The impact on "Jewish continuity" is tremendous.

Americans migrate for numerous reasons. The American tradition of immigration has fostered a "culture of migration." The individualism of American society means that people often place their personal priorities over those of their family and their community. The economic structure of the United States also encourages and often even requires mobility. Views differ on whether high levels of migration are a positive or negative phenomenon. Some believe that migration will help America innovate more. For example, Americans from diverse backgrounds and places now live and work together in places like San Diego and Denver, creating new centers of creative thought. Others see high rates of internal migration as leading to more social isolation, as people settle farther from their families and home communities.[11]

In response to these trends, the Reform movement recently launched a new project, Synagogue Match, to attract internal migrants and to help pair up new residents with Reform congregations near their new homes. "More than ten thousand Reform Jewish homes move each year, so it's really imperative that we respond and help stabilize Jewish communities," stated David Franklin, assistant director of the Commission on Synagogue Affiliation. "People are moving for a ton of reasons: new jobs, for family, for relationships. We're having people move to parts of the country that they have never moved to before, like Phoenix and Las Vegas. People are being dislocated. This is an opportunity for Jewish communities to reach out and provide a warm welcome." The program uses geographical software developed by the military, a fact that prompts Franklin to comment, "It's like turning guns into roses."[12]

At the program's web site, *www.synagoguematch.org*, newly arrived residents can type in their new address as well as any special interests. They then receive a list of three Reform congregations within twenty-five miles of where they live. At the same time, information about the new resident is sent to the three synagogues. This gives both the individual and the congregations the opportunity to introduce themselves and see if a "match" can be made.

Steven M. Cohen of the Hebrew University praises the effort, pointing out that migration has exacerbated the declining sense of community among American Jews. Despite its importance, the issue of mobility has not received the attention it requires. "It doesn't strike as deeply into the fears of American Jews for their continuity as does intermarriage. Nevertheless, mobility and dispersal are very critical problems." Rela Mintz Geffen, president of the Baltimore Hebrew University, also approves of the program. Geffen has argued that the Jewish community is continuing to rely on outdated approaches to community affiliation that no longer work. She has suggested that the Jewish community needs to create portable community memberships that would include a variety of organizational affiliations. "It's about time," she says of Synagogue Match. "This is the way to go with a continental Jewish community."[13]

Many communal leaders are deeply concerned that the high level of mobility threatens the stability of the Jewish community. When migrants are compared to those who have remained in their original communities, one model suggests that migrants are less likely to have been affiliated in their original communities; the assumption is made that they are therefore less likely than nonmigrants to affiliate in their new locations. Another model minimizes the differences between those who migrate and those who do not and suggests that influences in their new environment result in migrants' displaying new patterns of affiliation. Either way, it appears that a substantial number of migrants are using the opportunity to "recreate themselves," and many may consciously avoid any affiliation with the local Jewish community.

Some may find, on the other hand, that the experience of migrating strengthens their desire to be part of a Jewish community, and they may become intensely interested in becoming more religiously involved. The Synagogue Match project facilitates contact between existing local congregations and interested migrants. When migrants with a desire to maintain their Jewish identity search for contact with the Jewish community, "the success of such efforts will depend both on the strength of the motivation and on the degree to which the host community extends a facilitating hand."[14]

Increasing Racial Diversity in the Reform Synagogue

As the entire American Jewish community sees the results of a generation of intermarriage, conversions to Judaism, adoptions, and so forth, Reform congregations are becoming much more diverse. While many earlier Jews with obvious racial differences felt uncomfortable in synagogues that were virtually all white, many contemporary Jews with African American, Asian, or Hispanic backgrounds say they feel right at home. This may be due to the increasing numbers of nonwhite Jews, but it is also a result of the increasing acceptance of multiculturalism. Prominent black Jews, for example, include the late Sammy Davis Jr., who converted to Judaism, and Yaphet Kotto, who plays Lieutenant Giardello on the television show *Homicide*.[15] While there are no authoritative statistics, some experts believe that as much as 10 percent of the Jewish community is nonwhite.[16]

Nevertheless, being a nonwhite Jew inevitably creates identity issues not faced by white Jews. Lesli Williams of Fairmount Temple in Cleveland, Ohio, was raised as a Jew by her African American father and white mother. When her synagogue was looking for a speaker for Martin Luther King Jr. Day, they turned to her. "In connection to my race, there is always confusion about my religion. I am Jewish, I have always felt at home at Fairmount Temple," she said in her speech. Nevertheless, she expressed a bit of uneasiness about being one of the very few African Americans in the congregation. "Sometimes I find myself scanning the synagogue for other brown-skinned people. I almost always fail to find any, making me wonder what people are noticing about me."[17]

In fall 2002, Alysa Stanton became the first black woman to study to become a rabbi in the United States. A children's psychotherapist in Aurora, a suburb of Denver, she had taken courses in Hebrew and Jewish thought as an undergraduate at Colorado State University in Fort Collins. Soon she began studying with an Orthodox rabbi in Denver and at age twenty-four decided to convert to Judaism. In 1992, she began attending Temple Emanuel, the large Reform synagogue in Denver, where she felt immediately welcomed into the congregation. "I wasn't an oddity. I was just another new face." As she became more active at Emanuel, Stanton was often asked if she had ever considered becoming a rabbi. She also heard that it was becoming more common for older students to begin rabbinical school. At age thirty-eight, she applied to HUC-JIR in Los Angeles for admission to the rabbinical program. Richard Levy, the director of rabbinic studies, commented that "it is a reminder that Jews come in all colors and all ethnic groups." Stanton has said she wants "to be a rabbi who breaks barriers, inspires dreams and builds bridges."[18] As the first black women rabbinical student, she has become something of a celebrity, appearing on Black Entertainment Television and on CBS's *Early Show*.[19]

Increasing numbers of Jews are marrying Asians, some of whom convert to Judaism. Others convert without any romantic tie. Patricia Lin, a history professor at the University of California in Berkeley, wears a Magen David ring, recites the Shema every morning, and reads Torah at her local synagogue. Lin converted a few years ago in a liberal synagogue in London, where she was studying at the time. "I just knew it was the right thing. I have felt at home in the Jewish community in a way I have never felt in the Asian community." She feels that her Judaism has helped her connect to the painful events in Chinese history that her family had experienced. Her father had witnessed a Nationalist chop off the head of his neighbor in Taiwan after World War II. Yet she did not realize just how traumatized her parents had been until she attended a conference on children of Holocaust survivors. Worrying that she might not be considered "a real Jew if I was not connected to the Shoah directly," she asked her parents more about their experiences growing up in Taiwan right after the Japanese occupation. "The conference gave me a way to understand my own childhood and why I had emotional pain and outbursts. I wish that there were survivors groups for my parents because they do not talk about their experiences."

Jewish ritual life has helped Lin bond with her parents, who profess no faith and practice no religion. When her father needed open-heart surgery, he asked Lin, the only religious person in the family, to pray for his recovery. When her mother was diagnosed with cancer, Lin asked her rabbi to visit her mother in the hospital. Living in Berkeley, Lin has not had to face too many obstacles. Yet she is aware that many born Jews aren't sure what to make of her. "You don't look Jewish," some people say to her. When Lin joined a new congregation, she wondered if she should pray loudly so congregants would see that she was familiar with Judaic practices.[20] Still, many American Jews are adopting Asian babies and raising them as Jews. When such parents have asked Lin how she copes with the dual identities of being Jewish and Asian, she is reassuring. "Jews have been all around the world, and we should welcome this diversity. Asian Jewish children will still have to deal with some animosity. We have to educate. A lot of synagogues have multicultural Judaism classes. It is not just in history, but happening now."

Gail Steinberg of Petaluma, California, has found that adopting transracially requires a completely different frame of reference. She adopted her daughter, Shira, from Korea in 1962, as well as two African American children and one Caucasian child in the United States. "We think that we are a match for each other on the inside, but that doesn't mean everyone will feel that way."[21] Susan Katz, director of the adoption agency Stars of David, reports that many Jews are interested in adopting a child from overseas. Like other Americans, they are hesitant to adopt American children because of well-publicized stories of U.S. birth mothers changing their minds and trying to reclaim their children. But African American and Latino social workers' associations have taken a strong stance against transracial adoptions, leading many to adopt children from outside the United States. A substantial number go to Korea, China, and other Asian locations.

Sharon Kaufman of Washington, D.C., was a divorcee with no children when she read an article about Americans adopting children from China. "It just hit me in my kishkes, and I knew right then and there that I would be going to China." In 1997 she adopted Rebecca Joy Chufang Kaufman and brought her to be named at Washington's Reform Temple Sinai. "I was so excited to bring my daughter into the Jewish community, that when I shouted out the blessings you could have heard it in the next county." Raising her daughter as an active Reform Jew, Kaufman is also encouraging her daughter to identify as a Chinese American. Rebecca attends a Jewish day school and studies Mandarin as well.[22]

Helen Radin adopted her daughter, Jessica, in Thailand in 1976 when Jessica was five days old. Jessica Radin attended Hebrew school at

Temple Shaaray Tefila, served as president of the New York City branch of NFTY, and was sent to Israel on a Bronfman Youth Fellowship. When she visited her native Thailand, a new friend demonstrated how to bow to the Buddha. "The first thought that went though my head was, I am a bad Jew, I just bowed to an object," Jessica Radin said. She is deeply committed to the Jewish religion and does not think she could raise children who are not Jewish. At the same time, she wants to embrace her Thai ethnic identity, although "after Thailand, part of me doesn't want my child to be biracial. It feels like losing a part of me."[23]

In the shift toward multiculturalism that welcomes these adoptees, the Reform movement has also started reaching out to Latino Jews, many of whom are native Spanish speakers. The recent economic crisis in Argentina has caused an influx of Argentinean Jewish immigrants, often destitute and jobless. Reform synagogues in Miami in particular have developed programs to welcome them. "We want to help them because it's the right thing to do," Rabbi Gary Glickstein of Temple Beth Sholom in Miami Beach told me. "When the Cuban Jews came here in the early 1960s, they were not in a position to contribute much to the community because they were so overwhelmed with rebuilding their lives. But today, many Cuban Jews are playing extremely important roles in the Jewish community. The same is now true with the Argentineans. I believe that in twenty years many of the Argentineans will be leaders in this synagogue and the community generally."[24] Beth Sholom has brought in a Spanish-speaking rabbinic intern, Claudio Javier Kogan, M.D., to serve these immigrants. Kogan teaches classes and conducts life-cycle events in Spanish and writes a newsletter message in both English and Spanish.[25] Other groups of Hispanic Jews have migrated to California, New York, and a number of other states. Depending on their religious upbringing and their present predilections, some gravitate to Reform temples.

The Reform movement is going to be accommodating tens of thousands of members from multicultural backgrounds in the coming years. These Jews are going to have to work out new approaches to affirm their Jewish commitments, while also expressing their ethnic identities. The anecdotal evidence so far suggests that synagogues are making substantial efforts. But many of these individuals are torn between two or more different types of identities. Helping them enrich their commitment to Judaism while working through their ambivalence and conflicts is not going to be an easy task.

Accepting New Definitions of Jewish Identity

According to the traditional halacha, Jewish identity is determined by the mother; if a child's mother is Jewish, so is the child. If the Reform movement planned to integrate large numbers of intermarried couples in which the wife was not Jewish and had not converted, Reform synagogues would soon be raising a large pool of children who were not technically Jewish. The Orthodox would not accept such children as Jewish even if their mother converted, because Reform conversions are not conducted in accordance with the much more stringent Orthodox criteria. Even if the Reform ceremony was conducted strictly in accordance with halacha, the convert would not be accepting the beliefs and practices that Orthodox Jews felt were essential. When attempts were made in Denver and Kansas City to organize communitywide conversion programs acceptable to the Orthodox, they were criticized by most Orthodox rabbis and were eventually dissolved.

With little hope of satisfying the Orthodox, the Reform movement nevertheless needed to formalize its own conversion procedures. Under the movement's unofficial policy, children of Jewish fathers and non-Jewish mothers were routinely enrolled in Hebrew school. When they were ready for bar or bat mitzvah or confirmation, they would be regarded as undergoing a de facto conversion. Solomon Freehof had accepted this procedure in one of his responsa. But with no movement-wide official policy, each synagogue developed a different approach. As more and more children of Jewish fathers and gentile mothers enrolled in synagogue afternoon schools, the need for a standard policy became more pressing. The solution appeared simple: Allow patrilineal as well as matrilineal descent to determine the religious identity of the children. Not only would this solve the problem of how to integrate the children of Jewish fathers and non-Jewish mothers, but also it would represent one more step toward egalitarianism between the sexes.

Patrilineal descent was officially accepted at the 1983 CCAR conference, when the Reform rabbinate voted to accept the resolution entitled "The Status of Children of Mixed Marriages." According to the resolution, if one parent was Jewish, their child was "under presumption of Jewish descent."[26] While this change expanded the boundaries of who could be considered Jewish in an intermarried family, there were additional stipulations. In a dramatic departure from Jewish tradition, which regarded anyone born to a Jewish mother as Jewish, regardless of his or her beliefs or behavior, the resolution narrowed the requirements for being Jewish: Such children needed to be raised as Jews, not simply born to a Jewish parent. The requirement was in fact mostly theoretical. In practice, there were few documented cases of children with one Jewish parent who had been forced to convert because they had not been raised as Jews.

The patrilineal descent resolution was thus less a significant departure from previous Reform policy than a public declaration of inclusivity, a logical step in the open society of the United States. To move in the direction of exclusion would severely limit the pool of potential recruits, just when the Reform movement was looking for new members. The acceptance of patrilineal descent sent a clear message that the children of intermarried couples—even those who were not halachically Jewish—were welcome in the synagogue.

Developing an Educational Policy on Religious Upbringing

Most Jewish educators have long believed that it is psychologically unhealthy to raise a child in two religions at the same time, and the new inclusivity presented problems of its own. In the 1980s, more and more children attending religious schools in Reform synagogues had a Christian parent. Many of these parents were completely alienated from their Christianity, but others were not. Some took their children to church on occasion; a smaller number exposed their children to Judaism and Christianity in equal doses. This made a lot of sense to parents who felt that the best course was to teach their children about both religions, expose their children to the cultural heritages of both parents, and let them make up their own minds when they were older.

Yet synagogue leaders were deeply concerned. The presence of substantial numbers of children receiving Christian religious instruction could dilute the Jewish atmosphere of the temple religious school. Such children might even bring Christian concepts from their church schools into their temple classrooms. For example, in Milwaukee, I led a youth service on Yom Kippur afternoon at Congregation Emanu-El B'ne Jeshurun. Hoping to pose a question that most of the small children would be able to answer, I asked, "Who led the children of Israel out of Egypt?" And indeed, most of the hands went up. But when I called on one little girl, she proudly blurted, "Jesus!" We went on without incident, but it made me wonder if there were any safe questions. Such confusions are not unusual in Reform synagogues.

Obviously, the Reform movement was in no position to force intermarried couples to raise their children in one faith. What the movement could control was who would be admitted into the religious schools as students. At the UAHC biennial conference in Atlanta in 1995, a resolution was adopted to this end. "Enrollment Policies in Reform Religious Schools" declared that interfaith couples practicing two separate religions in the home and sending their children to a church as well as a synagogue-based religious school should not be allowed to enroll their children in a Reform religious school. The resolution encourages congregations to articulate a clear policy that offers enrollment in religious and day schools only to children who are not receiving formal education in any other religion.[27]

The policy of the religious school is extremely important because the school is the primary pathway through which the movement reaches out to intermarried families. Most couples do not begin their association with a temple by attending Friday night services or by enrolling in adult education courses. Rather, when their children become old enough to attend religious school, they may start to look around for a suitable congregation. Between 25 and 35 percent of intermarried families enroll their children in a Jewish religious school, usually an afternoon or Sunday school under Reform auspices. The policies of the religious school thus set the tone for these families' understanding of their entry into the synagogue.

Of parents who chose to educate their children in both a church and a synagogue, the resolution stated:

> This is a path that we as committed Reform Jews cannot
> support. First, it is contrary to our understanding of Outreach

which, while deeply respecting other religions, offers a way
into Judaism as a distinctive and precious way of life and faith.
Second, it is theologically inconsistent for a person to identify
as both Jewish and Christian (or as an adherent of any other
religion). Indeed, it is the long-standing policy of the
Commission of Reform Jewish Outreach to encourage
interfaith couples to choose a single religious identification for
their children. Third, psychologically placing the burden of
such an impossible decision on children may imperil their
healthy spiritual development. Finally, the goal of parents to
educate children in both Judaism and another religion is
incongruent with the mission of Reform religious schools.[28]

Some observers found this resolution baffling. They reasoned that
since the Reform movement was constantly advocating inclusiveness,
the sudden placement of barriers seemed incongruent. Some congregational leaders were angry as well, feeling that the resolution was an
attempt to rap them across the fingers after they had worked hard to
bring such children into their congregational schools. But Harris
Gilbert and George Markley, the chair and vice chair of the Commission on Reform Jewish Outreach at the time of the resolution, were
unequivocal: "It has long been the position of the Commission on
Reform Jewish Outreach that, in order to promote healthy spiritual
development, parents should choose a single religion for their children.
All Outreach programs are based on that premise and go on to invite
couples to choose Judaism."[29]

Apart from such reactions, the 1995 resolution had little direct
impact on congregations. Those with large numbers of intermarried
families and a history of tolerance simply ignored it. Other situations
were dealt with on a case-by-case basis. The nature of discourse in the
Reform movement has not relied on an appeal to authority. Just as the
leaders could not cite the Torah or Talmud as authoritative texts that
must be adhered to, neither could they refer to the 1995 Atlanta resolution as the basis for an unequivocal policy decision. Rather, what has
counted in the Reform movement is the ability to persuade. Resolutions, legal decisions, and platforms were only as influential as they
were convincing.

Many Non-Jews Convert to Judaism

The UAHC has introduced a series of new Outreach programs to appeal to mixed religion families, including alternative family education programs for intermarried couples, formal "Introduction to Judaism" courses, special worship services and holiday celebrations geared for mixed religion families, and interfaith couple marriage workshops. One of the most successful, "A Taste of Judaism," focuses on Jewish spirituality, ethics, and community and is advertised in local media as well as through synagogue sources to reach the maximum number of people. Dru Greenwood, the director of the UAHC and CCAR joint Commission on Reform Jewish Outreach, estimates that the program has enrolled close to twenty-five thousand people, about half of whom are Jewish. Approximately one out of seven non-Jews who take the course go on to study for conversion to Judaism. For example, "A Taste of Judaism" class at the South Street Temple in Lincoln, Nebraska, in spring 1999 drew about eighty people. When the program ended, ten of the non-Jews in the class expressed interest in conversion. According to Cantor Michael Weisser, none of the ten was married to a Jew. "I think what attracts non-Jewish people to Judaism once they get a tiny taste of it is the logic of it, the ability to argue with it." [30]

Alexander Schindler would agree. When he envisioned Outreach more than twenty years ago, he saw it not merely as a practical response to the rising intermarriage rate. Rather, he had a coherent theological justification for spreading the Judaic religious vision. "My dream was to see our Judaism unleashed as a resource for a world in need, not as the exclusive inheritance of the few, but as a renewable resource for the many; not as a religious stream too small to be seen on the map of the world, but as a deep-flowing river, hidden by the overgrown confusion of modern times, that could nourish humanity's highest aspiration." [31]

Many of the Americans who chose Judaism have become very active in Reform congregations. Considerable numbers have even become rabbis. For example, John Bush converted from Catholicism to Judaism in Lexington, Kentucky, in 1974. Bush and his wife, Joanna, decided to leave Catholicism and spent two years on an intense spiritual journey. After trying several other religions, they eventually found their way to Judaism. "I loved the ideas and concept of Judaism and I kept coming back to it. I identified with the Jewish people more than anything—that through the most terrible adversity, they've endured. But it was something I read in Talmud that really hit me: 'When a man goes before the throne of justice, the first question he is asked will not be "Did you believe in Me or follow all the rituals?" but "How did you treat your fellow man?"' This is what Judaism is all about to me. It's a religion of action." The Bushes were invited to Friday night Shabbat services, and the couple began attending regularly. They studied intensively with a rabbi for a full year and then converted to Judaism along with their daughter, Jennifer, then three years old. Their son, Ben, was born a few months later. After their conversion, they soon realized that they needed to know a lot more. In 1980, they attended an outreach conference in New York for Jews by choice. Their involvement continued to grow. Finally, at age forty-two, John Bush decided to become a rabbi. His wife recalls: "There was a sense of peace that took over John. It was all over his face."[32]

While ideological Jews by choice like the Bushes are numerous, the majority of converts to Judaism are spouses of Jewish partners. But whereas a generation or two ago most Jewish parents put a tremendous amount of pressure on the non-Jewish partner to convert before marriage, today it is much more acceptable to remain non-Jewish. The Reform movement has tried to encourage such couples to raise their children as Jews. When Marty and Wendy Smith of Denver, Colorado, married, they made no conclusive decisions about how to raise their children religiously. Marty had been raised in a traditional Jewish home, where he had participated actively in Jewish prayer and holiday observances. Yet he was ambivalent. "I had some doubts. I just didn't know if I wanted my girls to be raised as Jews." When their older daughter, Amy, was about six, she asked to go with her cousin to a program called "Stepping Stones to a Jewish Me" at a local congregation. The family participated in the two-year program designed for interfaith families who had not yet committed to a religion. The Smiths later joined Temple Micah and celebrated the bat mitzvoth of their daughters Amy and Caitlin. Caitlin said: "I'm told that when I was really little I said I wanted to be Christian—like my mom. But I've really always felt Jewish. And I've always felt special because of what I know about the Jewish holidays and traditions. To me, Judaism is a lot more than just a religion—it's a way of life. And when I meet another Jew, it's like finding a long-lost member of the family."[33]

Dru Greenwood explains, "We are all Jews by choice. It's up to us to make the choice to live and grow Jewishly, to study and learn as much as we can about our religion, to make a commitment to a congregation, and to see that our families actively participate in our synagogue community." Greenwood believes that Outreach has achieved remarkable success. "There's a saying in Hebrew, *mitvah goreret mitvah*, which means 'one mitzvah leads to another. That's what Outreach is all about. Through Outreach, Reform Jews have taken up and brought to life the mitzvah of loving the stranger and welcoming him- or her- into our Jewish tent to share the finest we have. And just look at the mitzvah that leads to! Many of the strangers we've embraced have, in turn, embraced us, which multiplies our strength and vitality a thousandfold."[34]

Rabbinic Officiation at Mixed-Marriage Ceremonies

One of the most perplexing issues that Reform rabbis faced was whether or not to officiate at intermarriage ceremonies. In spite of the Outreach programs designed to bring people closer to Judaism, the reality is that most non-Jewish spouses do not convert before or after marriage. Yet many request that a rabbi officiate, either alone or with another member of the clergy, at their wedding. The interaction with the rabbi marks the first sustained contact that the intermarried couple has with the Jewish community.

Until recently, few rabbis were willing to accommodate such couples. In the 1970s, Albert Axelrod, a Hillel rabbi at Brandeis University ordained by HUC-JIR, came under sustained attack for performing intermarriage ceremonies, even though he set conditions that had to be met before he would agree to officiate. But times have changed. A 1996 survey found that 48 percent of Reform rabbis would officiate at intermarriage ceremonies under various circumstances. Simeon Maslin, then president of the CCAR, disputed the results of the survey, estimating that the true rate was somewhere between 33 and 40 percent. Maslin pointed out that rabbis willing to take the time and energy to complete the survey were more likely to respond positively.[35]

Whatever the exact percentage, a substantial number of CCAR members are willing to officiate. Some will marry any couple that turns to them. Others have criteria so strict that few couples are willing to meet their standards. Some believe that what they are doing is for the long-term good of the Jewish people, some see their role in pastoral terms, and some officiate primarily for financial gain. Rabbi Jacques Cukierkorn explains his motivation: "In my eight years as a Rabbi, I have yet to have a couple come to ask for my permission to get married. They all come to ask for my help. I have to decide if I want to help them or not, if I want to bring Judaism to this very important event in their lives (even if one of them is not Jewish). By doing their wedding, I believe I am enhancing the probability of them raising Jewish kids. If I turn them down, then some minister will happily welcome them and probably their children as well."[36]

What has become clear over the past decade is the difficulty of requiring an interfaith couple to commit themselves to having a Jewish home and raising Jewish children. In 1990, 64 percent of Reform rabbis who would officiate at interfaith marriages required that commitment before they would agree to officiate. Only five years later, that percentage had dropped to 42 percent. As Irwin Fishbein, the director of the Rabbinic Center for Research and Counseling in Westfield, New Jersey, explains, there has been a gradual recognition that a commitment to making a Jewish home is "not something that rabbis can really require. You are dealing with the future. Very often the couple themselves do not know what they are planning to do."[37]

Another reason for the shift is that rabbis are under tremendous pressure to perform these ceremonies. Most congregants have children married to or dating non-Jews. Many are in interfaith relationships themselves. Regardless of what the religion says or what is good for the long-term future of the Jewish people, they want their rabbi to officiate at the marriage of their children. And more and more of the children are refusing to accept preconditions. This leaves the rabbi in a vulnerable situation. If he presents a series of requirements and the couple refuses, the rabbi will face the heat for turning his back on his flock in their moment of need. If he suddenly backs down, then he looks weak and indecisive. The only sensible solution is to avoid the dilemma by agreeing to officiate without preconditions.

Most rabbis hope the married couple will gravitate toward Judaism, but being realists, they understand this may not occur. According to the 1990 NJPS, only 27.8 percent of Jews were raising their children as Jewish; 30.8 percent were raising their children without any religion; and 41.4 percent were raising their children in a religion other than Judaism.[38] Fishbein sees "more and more interest today in raising children with both religions. This is contrary to traditional philosophy about what is good for families and children, but there are thousands of families out there doing this."[39] The trend threatens the future of the American Jewish community. The Reform movement is trying to formulate strategies to counteract the dissolution apparent in every city and state of the union. But it is an uphill battle.

An Impediment to Outreach—Lack of Passion

Despite Schindler's bold rhetoric, the Reform movement has not yet maximized the potential of Outreach. Most Reform Jews lack the passion necessary to recruit large numbers of new adherents successfully. Too many Reform temples are devoted to fulfilling the personal needs of individual members to the detriment of building a strong and committed religious community. As Conservative rabbi Michael Goldberg puts it: "Vibrant, lively community eludes many American Jews because even as they look for it, they carry with them the infection that kills community in contemporary American life: a culture of consumerism based on individual preference. Despite their vaunted theological differences, American Orthodox, Conservative, Reconstructionist, and Reform Jews all practice the same kind of Judaism—consumer Judaism. For the only thing their synagogues require for membership is the payment of monetary dues. Such synagogues are like religious 7-11s."[40]

The liberal theology of Reform Judaism makes it extremely difficult to set and maintain high expectations in terms of communal participation. Without an omnipotent God who compels the believer to practice a prescribed pattern of ritual behavior, the consumerism that Goldberg describes becomes the dominant ethos of the congregation.[41]

The corrosive impact of "consumer members" on religious organizations has been studied extensively. Rodney Stark has popularized ideas first developed by Dean Kelley and later, Lawrence R. Iannaccone.[42] While his work has drawn a great deal of criticism, it has been very influential. Others have written on the problems facing "low-intensity religion."[43] Stark and Roger Fink argue that "religious organizations can thrive only to the extent that they have a theology that can comfort souls and motivate sacrifice." This theory suggests that a "fundamentalist" approach to religion is more compelling than a liberal one, an idea buttressed by the experience of religious groups whose membership has declined as they have moved toward a more "refined" theology, such as the Presbyterians and Methodists. These denominations have seen the number of participants at church services and other religious activities decline as well. When theology is "shorn of mystery, miracle, and mysticism—when an active supernatural realm is replaced by abstractions concerning virtue," the authors argue, the religious denomination lacks the theological strength to motivate people to build a strong and vibrant religious community. "Theological refinement is the kind of progress that results in organizational bankruptcy."[44]

Over the long haul there is no substitute, according to this view, for a compelling God. To permanently break the cycle of apathy that leads to low attendance, which in turn creates more apathy, an American religious movement needs a theology that represents God as demanding specific behaviors at specific times. While some congregations will, of course, create innovative programming that meets the needs of a large group for a time, without such a God, they will inevitably develop a free-rider problem. Rational-choice theories of behavior seem to support this view, suggesting that the more individuals sacrifice on behalf of their religion, the more benefits they receive in return. Individuals evaluate religion the same way they evaluate all other matters of choice: They evaluate the costs as well as the benefits, including the opportunity costs that arise when one action can be undertaken only by foregoing other actions. In the end, they will consume those religious goods that maximize their net benefits.

A liberal theology leads to an emphasis on the autonomy of the individual, which is inevitably promoted at the expense of the authority of God. This theological shift escalates the problem of free riders. Why would people devote time to keeping the organization running when most other congregants are doing nothing? Rather, they can send in their check and let synagogue professionals or a small core group of devotees bear the burden. But this type of organization does not appeal to "religious seekers." It may draw in intermarried couples who have already decided to create a Jewish family, but not those looking for a healthy, dynamic religious community.

Such congregations thus create insufficient collective goods. While everyone in the organization suffers, the most active participants suffer most. Therefore it should not surprise us if people who develop a strong interest in Judaism find Reform temples emotionally unsatisfying and move on to Conservative or even Orthodox congregations. Orthodox Jewish theology is based, of course, on the belief in a compelling God who demands the observance of a large number of specific commandments. This represents a high cost, but for those willing to make the commitment, it also brings high benefit. Such individuals find themselves in a group of like-minded people willing to make a strong commitment to their God and their community. So even though they may not be conscious of it, their intimate involvement in their congregation and community is founded on the theological assumptions that are the basis for their approach to religion.

One can understand that for men, an omnipotent God may seem to offer a good deal—the traditional forms of religion almost always gave the man most of the religious power—but one might expect women to be drawn to liberal religion, which is more compatible with feminist principles. Such is not always the case, as Debra Renee Kaufman found in a group of 150 women who returned to their Jewish roots in their early adult years: Orthodoxy was more attractive than more liberal forms of Judaism, including Reform. For many of these women, "Orthodoxy provides an unambiguous belief in a transcendent God. It supplies fixed parameters in an otherwise relativistic, fragmented, and chaotic world. For the ba'alot teshuvah [returning females] I studied, rabbinical authority and Halacha take precedence over history or culture."[45]

Those attracted to a God who compels specific behaviors find that the costly demands strengthen a religious group by mitigating free-rider problems and increasing the production of collective religious commodities. Outreach for such movements thus attracts religious seekers with the highest degree of motivation. People qualify for membership by accepting the demanding nature of a compelling God, by accepting the many sacrifices that the observances required by that God will entail, and by implicitly accepting the potential social stigma attached to their religious beliefs and practices. Even in today's tolerant world, for example, being Orthodox remains difficult in many ways. Since religion involves collective action, all religious organizations are potentially subject to exploitation by free riders, but the Reform movement is much more vulnerable than Orthodoxy. The very core of liberal religion, the stress on individual autonomy, makes the free-rider problem ubiquitous among liberal synagogues and churches as well. "One need not look far to find examples of anemic congregations plagued by free rider problems . . . a visit to the nearest liberal Protestant church usually will suffice to discover 'members' who draw upon the group for weddings, funerals, and (perhaps) holiday celebrations, but who provide little or nothing in return. Even if they do make substantial financial contributions, they weaken the group's ability to create collective religious goods because their inactivity devalues the compensators and reduces the 'average' level of commitment."[46]

According to Benton Johnson and his coauthors in an article in *First Things*, published by the interreligious, nonpartisan Institute on Religion and Public Life, "The underlying problem of the mainline churches . . . is the weakening of the spiritual conviction required to generate the enthusiasm and energy needed to sustain a vigorous communal life." How might those churches deal with the spiritual inertia and membership decline of the last twenty years? "Their first step must be to address theological issues head-on."[47]

The theological avoidance that is causing severe commitment problems for the liberal Protestant denominations is an equally serious problem for synagogues in general and Reform congregations in particular. Outreach can be effective only if prospective members are brought into a vibrant religious community. There is therefore an organic connection between UAHC president Eric Yoffie's efforts to revitalize synagogue life and the Outreach campaign.

The Difficulty of Attracting and Holding Committed Members

Eric Yoffie had recently argued that the Reform movement has a decade at most to reach those on the periphery of the community or risk losing a large segment forever. The challenge that has been both its strength and its weakness since the movement's origin almost two hundred years ago remains: How can a liberal religious movement set standards?

Standards would give congregants a clear vision of what it means in concrete terms to be a Reform Jew. But this is a problem. Without a clear theology that can posit the existence of a commanding God in an unequivocal way, Reform Jews feel no compulsion to accept any system of standards as binding. Jack Westheimer explains: "Today, Reform is open to change in both directions—toward a more radical break with traditional practices and toward an unprecedented openness to traditional teachings."[48] This is a significant shift from the Classical Reform model, which established limits and prohibited traditional practices that were regarded as inappropriate or outdated, at least in the context of public worship.[49] "Whereas Reform was formerly a movement that on principal said no to some aspects of Jewish tradition, it is now a movement that is open to all Jewish possibilities, whether traditional or innovative."[50]

What guides the decision-making process in the Reform movement today is the key word "autonomy," which allows individuals to choose whatever Jewish religious expressions are meaningful to them.[51] This pluralistic approach to practice makes it extremely difficult to express a coherent theology, which was precisely why Classical Reform Judaism insisted on ceremonial conformity. Walter Jacob has argued forcefully that the richness and fullness of Jewish religious life has been lost in the Reform context, because congregants have used the ideal of autonomy as an excuse to neglect active involvement in their religion. "No one can fault this ideal but it has not worked. We need direction, standards—a system of mitzvot (observances)—and Halacha as we go beyond guidance to governance."[52] The editor of *Reform Judaism* received numerous letters objecting to Jacob's article. Many readers felt that standards were restraints on their freedom and were therefore unacceptable and even offensive. Clearly, the Reform movement has chosen the road of inclusion rather than the path of standards that would inevitably lead to exclusion.

Yet successful Outreach must carefully balance inclusiveness with a clear religious message. By offering almost everything to everyone, the Reform movement is making a concerted effort to appeal to as many

Jews and potential Jews as possible, including former Jews who are wandering off never to return—a substantial number even in the best-case scenario. But to achieve this result, the movement must rely on a theology in itself so pluralistic that it will be challenging to discern a clear and unequivocal religious message. If most Reform congregants have little idea what the movement's religious beliefs are, it will be difficult for them to pass on those beliefs to their children and grandchildren.

As the baby boomers have become the parents of the children in Reform religious schools and the bulk of the congregational membership, the movement has adopted many of their values, just as it adopted the values of earlier American generations. The movement has taken into account their growing up "in a post-60s culture that emphasizes choice, knowing and understanding oneself, the importance of personal autonomy, and fulfilling one's potential—all contributing to a highly subjective approach to religion." [53] For this generation, knowing and understanding oneself remains the most important priority of one's early years, and fulfilling one's potential the ultimate goal of life. This mentality has moved all forms of liberal religion toward an even more pluralistic model that allows for all sorts of approaches to the spiritual quest.

Without compromising the Reform commitment to autonomy and choice, it will not be possible to develop a theological statement strong enough to change dramatically the social dynamics in Reform congregations. As ethnicity continues to wane, this lack of theological clarity, along with the free-rider phenomenon, will become even more serious problems, consequences of the liberal theological perspective of American Reform Judaism.

Eric Yoffie's Renewed Call for Outreach

Eric Yoffie, while forthright in admitting that the movement has had problems, nevertheless posits a large and growing number of highly committed Reform Jews. "The Reform movement is large, sprawling, fast-growing, and diverse; for all of its problems, there are many pockets of enthusiasm, excitement, creativity, and deep commitment." [54] This enthusiasm is one of the reasons the Outreach effort has succeeded with certain groups of potential members. Thirteen-year-old Julia Bloch's impressions of her first UAHC biennial are indicative: "Five-thousand Jews were reciting prayers aloud. Some stood, some sat, some prayed in Hebrew, some in English, some chanted, some spoke, some belted, some muttered. But it was the sound of five thousand Jews praying. And there, for that moment, the room felt holy."[55] Potential Reform Jews need to see this excitement.

Yoffie argues that, more than a practical response to a sociological problem, Outreach is based on a set of theological principles that are central to its mission. In his view, "Judaism is a rejection of tribalism," which he defines as a view of Judaism that would root Jewish identity solely in race. On the other hand, Yoffie contends that it would be equally wrong to believe that Outreach is based on an extreme form of universalism. "Judaism is not a universalistic religion." The starting point for Outreach must be the same starting point as for all Jewish religious thought, "our unique destiny as a religious people, tied to God in a covenant that we trace back to Abraham and Sarah."[56]

The Jewish community has the obligation to develop the meaning that flows from the covenant between God and the Jewish people. This covenant guides the Jewish people in a world that is redeemable but not yet redeemed. Thus, Outreach begins with "an act of self-definition," rather than "an act of inclusion." Reform Jews must begin by affirming their particularism, and only then can they reach out. "The first step of Outreach—and the single most important step—is to have a clear sense of who we are and of the boundary that exists between us as Reform Jews and the society around us."[57] This is the right message at the right time. The people who will be most successful at Outreach are those who can communicate the beauty of the Jewish heritage. Those confused about what their religion stands for are ineffective ambassadors for the Reform synagogue. Yoffie's core message is that being a Reform Jew can deepen one's love of God. If this message is widely accepted, it can promote the practice and study of Torah and at the same time bring in new adherents interested in sharing the Jewish destiny as God's chosen people.

Chapter 9

The Struggle for Women's Equality

On June 3, 1972 I was ordained rabbi by Hebrew
Union College-Jewish Institute of Religion in
Cincinnati, Ohio. As I sat in the historic Plum Street
Temple, waiting to accept the ancient rite of s'micha, I
couldn't help but reflect on the implications of what was
about to happen. For thousands of years women in
Judaism had been second-class citizens. They were not
permitted to own property. They could not serve as
witnesses. They did not have the right to initiate divorce
proceedings. They were not counted in the minyan.
Even in Reform Judaism, they were not permitted to
participate fully in the life of the synagogue. With my
ordination all that was going to change; one more
barrier was about to be broken.

—SALLY J. PRIESAND, 1972

THE REFORM movement set out to offer liberal Jews a modernized form
of Jewish religious belief and ritual practice that would emphasize personal faith and ethical behavior. The movement declared that while it
would draw on the traditional rabbinic literature for wisdom and inspiration, it was not obligated by the halacha. This made it easy for
Reform to adapt to modern sensitivities and sensibilities, and it did so.
One area immediately reformed was the religious roles of men and
women. Religious education was now an obligation equally incumbent
on both sexes, and the confirmation service that marked the formal
entrance of the young Jew into the religious community would include

both males and females. Perhaps even more important, the accessible worship service conducted partly in German or English was stimulating for women with limited Hebrew language and synagogue skills. Many traditional ritual observances conducted by women in the home were eliminated or at least minimized as Classical Reform Judaism attempted to articulate a rationalistic and deritualized vision of modern Jewish life. While on the surface this appeared to place women and men on the same level, the elimination of female ritual roles actually reduced female participation in religious life. The dramatic social upheaval of the 1960s would find most Reform synagogues vaguely egalitarian in principle but male dominated in both their power structure and ritual life.

It would be hard to underestimate the influence of late-twentieth-century feminism on American Reform Judaism. Indeed, feminist values have generated much of the heat behind the "culture wars" pitting social conservatives against political liberals.[1] A number of mainline Protestant denominations have found themselves torn apart by this battle. For the liberals, religious authenticity is determined in large part by the zeitgeist of the contemporary age. Truth is viewed as a process, progressively discovered over the course of time, rather than as an external immutable authority. The progressives see nothing wrong with changing the historic role of women in light of cultural and societal changes. The conservatives, in contrast, see the traditional sex and gender roles as central to their religious values, not subject to short-term change. Unlike the Episcopalians, Methodists, or Presbyterians, the American Reform movement has no significant conservative wing. Despite the time it has taken for women to break into many traditionally male roles, there was little ideological opposition to full egalitarianism. By the 1970s, women were participating in all aspects of synagogue life, including serving as congregational rabbis.[2] Social differentiation between the sexes has virtually disappeared in the contemporary American Reform movement.

One reason social equality made such headway so quickly in the Reform movement was the absence of halachic or ideological bases for anyone to oppose it. The only barrier was the conservative nature of many Reform congregations and their leaders, often wealthy, middle-aged men who were certainly not in the forefront of the feminist movement. But they adjusted and barriers quickly fell. In the Conservative movement, on the other hand, a strong contingent vigorously opposed women's rights on halachic grounds.[3] Making the transition even easier was Reform's full acceptance of the concept of egalitarianism, at least in theory. Thus, there was no need to change Reform theology or ritual practice to accommodate a fuller role for women. Women could read prayers, serve on synagogue boards, and even become rabbis and cantors without upsetting the theoretical basis of Reform Judaism.

Family life had always been of central importance to Judaism, and the Reform movement reaffirmed this importance. But whereas in traditional Judaism the husband was the dominant figure in the family, the Reform movement stressed the equality of the spouses. Marriage continued to be seen as establishing a holy bond between a man and a woman, but this commitment was viewed as equal and mutual. The man and the woman are consecrated to each other, whereas in traditional Judaism the woman is consecrated to the man, but not vice versa.

This equality had many implications. The wedding service featured a ring exchange, whereas the traditional ceremony required the man to present a ring to the woman, but not vice versa. The *ketubah* (wedding certificate) is likewise egalitarian in nature, whereas the traditional *ketubah* is given by the man to the woman as a promissory note specifying the financial obligations he is undertaking toward his wife during and after the marriage.

The *get* (divorce document) was traditionally presented by the man to the woman. The Reform movement abolished this procedure and accepted civil divorce as sufficient. In recent years, some Reform Jews have begun using a document written in 1983 by Rabbi Simeon J. Maslin called a Seder P'reidah, a ritual of release. This was designed to introduce a positive religious dimension into what was often a highly contentious legal situation. The CCAR hoped to create a sacred space in the divorce process that could provide divine sustenance and a mechanism for spiritual healing. Maslin has emphasized that while it is a Reform divorce document, it does not serve the same halachic purpose as a *get*.[4] The Reform movement is committed to complete egalitarianism in all areas of ritual observance.

Feminism and the Reform Movement

Despite the Reform movement's never having opposed equal rights for women, the male hierarchical structure remained in place until the 1960s. The push for egalitarianism was not a high priority for the nineteenth-century Reformers, who were far more concerned with reforming the liturgy and adapting Judaism's religious beliefs to the surrounding cultural environment. Nevertheless, Reform leaders were cognizant of the desirability of full and total equality for women alongside men. For example, at the 1846 Breslau Conference of Reform Rabbis, a subcommittee that had been asked to reevaluate the role of women recommended that they be "entitled to the same religious rights and subject to the same religious duties" as men.[5]

Rabbi David Einhorn declared it a "sacred duty" of rabbis "to declare with all emphasis" the religious equality of women and men. Despite this sentiment, both European and American society maintained gender distinctions. No pressure came from the rank and file to institute dramatic changes on either the congregational or the leadership level. When changes did occur, they tended to be consistent with practices already common in the surrounding society. For example, when Rabbi Isaac Mayer Wise broke with his congregation in Albany, New York, and established a new temple, he introduced mixed seating in the new building. Despite his later claim to have pioneered this innovation, mixed seating was allowed because the church building that the reformers bought had no women's gallery and renovation would be costly. Since women sat with men in the neighboring churches, there seemed no reason to prohibit them from sitting with men in the synagogue either.

Despite his faulty memory, Wise did support moves toward greater equality for women. He comments in his 1857 *Minhag Amerika* prayer book that a minyan consists of "ten adults, male or female."[6] Rabbi Kaufmann Kohler likewise spoke of the importance the Reform movement attached to the equality of women. In the paper he presented to the rabbis at the 1885 Pittsburgh conference, he wrote, "Reform Judaism will never reach its higher goal [of spiritual and moral elevation] without having first accorded to the congregational council and in the entire religious and moral sphere of life, equal voice to woman with man."[7]

Yet until the 1960s, most Reform congregations were run by men, and their dominance was accepted without question. Fitting in was important, and congregational social mores reflected the society's. Whether immigrant or native born, American Jews adjusted to American values and wanted to see those values reflected in their congregational structure and activities. This meant that women in the typical Reform congregation were relegated to the traditional woman's role, a situation accepted by almost all parties without dissent. Sisterhoods served central functions in temple life; without them, many if not most activities would have been impossible. Whether they were baking cakes for fundraising purposes, preparing the confirmation dinner, or simply attending services, women constituted the backbone of Reform religious and social life.

But in the 1960s, the feminist movement began to challenge the traditional roles assigned to women. Through the 1970s and 1980s, its impact on the synagogue was immense. As women began to move into roles of responsibility traditionally assigned to men, there was a great deal of dissonance. Rachel Adler, an early Jewish feminist and now a lecturer at HUC-JIR in Los Angeles, in 1983 summarized the feeling of many women: "Being a Jewish woman is very much like being Alice at the Hatter's tea party. We did not participate in making the rules, nor were we there at the beginning of the party. At best, a jumble of crockery is being shoved aside to clear a place for us. At worst, we are only tantalized with the tea and bread-and-butter, while being confused, shamed and reproached for our ignorance."[8] Women in the Reform movement studied for the rabbinate, the cantorate, and other professional positions, while others became synagogue presidents rather than sisterhood presidents. What had been seen as an oddity became an accepted phenomenon, then so commonplace as to be unworthy of note.

Many of the leading feminists were Jewish, and some of them took an interest in Jewish affairs. Other women admired the feminist leaders and specifically wanted to apply their perspective in a Jewish context. The Reform movement provided an ideal setting for this synthesis because of its non-halachic nature, allowing a much greater flexibility than could have developed in Orthodox or even Conservative Judaism. Women wanted to be treated on an equal basis with men, both in the synagogue power structure and in their portrayal in the myths of the tradition.[9]

The Struggle for the Ordination of Women as Rabbis

While the issue of women's ordination is only one aspect of the struggle for gender equality in the Reform synagogue, it is important not only for its symbolic value, but also for opening the way for women to increase in their influence dramatically.[10] The ordination of Sally Priesand in 1972 was an extraordinary event, because HUC-JIR was the first major rabbinical program in the history of Judaism to ordain a woman rabbi. The issue had been debated as far back as the nineteenth century, and no persuasive religious argument prevented the ordination of women. The issue was primarily a social question; one should not underestimate the power of social convention and its inhibiting influence on women as well as men.

During the two centuries between the beginnings of the Reform movement and the Priesand ordination, periodic attempts were made to ordain women, and a few officiated as rabbis without formal ordination. On the West Coast in the late nineteenth century, newspaper accounts frequently described Ray Frank as a "lady rabbi."[11] A number of women served as unordained "rabbis" in the first half of the twentieth century as well. But these women, in isolated locations or renegade congregations, did not threaten the establishment status quo, which could be changed only if the official policy of the CCAR, HUC, or the UAHC changed.

The movement's policy on women rabbis was first put to the test in 1921, when HUC student Martha Neumark requested a High Holy Day assignment along with the male students. Female as well as male students had been admitted to HUC since its founding in 1875, but the women had studied for education degrees rather than rabbinical ones. Neumark's petition suggested that she hoped to become a rabbi. The faculty vote on whether she should be permitted to take a High Holy Day pulpit ended in a tie. Kaufmann Kohler, president of HUC, broke the tie vote in her favor subject to the approval of the designated congregation. A committee set up to study the question reported that "because of practical considerations, . . . the admission of women to the Hebrew Union College with the aim of becoming rabbis, should not be encouraged."[12] But there was a lot of support for women rabbis among the faculty, who voted unanimously to approve a resolution in favor of women's ordination. The CCAR membership was also largely in favor, voting fifty-six to eleven that females could not "justly be denied the privilege of ordination." Despite these votes, the HUC Board of Governors denied Neumark ordination, arguing that the social climate in America did not make it advisable to ordain women at that time, that very few women were interested in studying for the rabbinate, and that therefore there seemed no compelling reason to change the prevailing practice of "limiting to males the right to matriculate for the purpose of entering the rabbinate."[13]

In 1956, CCAR president Barnett Brickner formed a committee to restudy the question of women's ordination. In the thirty-five years since Martha Neumark had made her attempt to become a rabbi, an increasing number of mainline U.S. Protestant denominations had begun to admit women into Bible colleges and seminaries with the expressed purpose of allowing them to study for ordination. The committee recommended that women indeed be ordained. HUC president Nelson Glueck endorsed a proposed CCAR resolution in favor of women's ordination and enthusiastically declared that HUC would ordain any woman who passed all the curricular requirements. Nevertheless, the CCAR voted to table any action until the opponents of women's ordination could present a counter-report. No such report was ever written or presented.

By the time Sally Priesand had finished her studies at HUC-JIR, the impact of feminism had transformed the Reform movement to a degree unimaginable just a few decades earlier. Nelson Glueck supported her petition—there was little basis upon which to deny her the certificate of ordination. Unfortunately, Glueck died before he could actually ordain Priesand, and new HUC-JIR president Alfred Gottschalk conducted the ordination ceremony. After a stint as an assistant rabbi and then as a chaplain, Priesand joined Monmouth Reform Temple in Tinton Falls, New Jersey, where she continues as the rabbi today.

The Impact of Feminism on Reform Liturgy

Many modern American women found the language of the traditional prayer book restrictive and even sexist. Based on biblical models that portrayed God solely in masculine terms, the prayers assume that public worship is an obligation primarily for men. For example, the prayer that began "Praise be our God, God of our Fathers, God of Abraham, God of Isaac and God of Jacob" now seemed exclusionary. Where were the matriarchs? In 1972, a task force on equality, arguing that such language misleads worshipers about the true nature of both human beings and God, recommended altering masculine references in prayer. In the resulting effort to rewrite the prayers to reflect the growing egalitarian nature of American Jewish thinking, the names of the matriarchs were added in a series of gender-sensitive prayer books published in the early 1990s. The same prayer now reads, "Praised be our God, the God of our Fathers and our Mothers: God of Abraham, God of Isaac and God of Jacob; God of Sarah, God of Rebekah, God of Leah, and God of Rachel."[14]

Dealing with the names of God framed in the masculine form was more difficult. In English, Reform prayer books had referred to God as "He" and "Him" and called God "the Lord." These references could be changed, but the practical problem of replacing prayer books in use for only a short time was daunting. Some congregations developed a list of gender-sensitive words that could be substituted for masculine references to God. Thus, the word "God" might be used to replace "the Lord" each time that phrase appeared in the prayer book. But this could confuse congregants, who had to be exceptionally alert to make all the correct substitutions in the right places and at the right times. In the mid-1990s a series of soft-cover experimental gender-sensitive prayer books, then a hard-cover gender-sensitive version intended to be semi-permanent, gradually supplanted the original Sabbath prayer book *Gates of Prayer*. A new gender-sensitive edition is under way.

Congregations did not want to replace the new edition of the High Holy Day prayer book, *Gates of Repentance*, so soon. The solution was a gender-sensitive version that matched the original, page for page. Unfortunately, many found the mix of the two High Holy Day prayer books in the same service confusing, as their neighbors seemed to be reading from a different text than they were. But the production of new prayer books would eventually resolve such issues. Most Reform Jews adjusted to the new liturgy and accepted the gender-sensitive wording without a murmur. Many women found it empowering and exhilarating.

New Fields for Leadership

Priesand's ordination opened the door for many other women inter-ested in careers to which rabbinical ordination could provide them access. Large numbers applied to cantorial as well as rabbinical pro-grams at HUC-JIR. The Rabbi Sally J. Priesand Visiting Professorship was launched in the fall of 1999 at HUC-JIR in New York.[15] By May 2001, 373 women were ordained. At HUC-JIR in Los Angeles, the very first group of female ordainees in May of 2002 includes five women out of eight rabbinical graduates. Six women have been ordained in the Israeli program on the Jerusalem campus.[16]

The increasingly active role that women are playing in the Reform congregation has fueled concerns that an increasing number of men may walk away from active leadership involvement. This phenomenon is not new; many-nineteenth century Reform rabbis complained that their congregations on Shabbat morning were composed primarily of women, children, and the elderly. But if the new trends increase the alienation of Jewish men from the temple, the yoke of Jewish commu-nal leadership may fall more and more on female shoulders. Others worry that Jewish professional work is starting to be seen as more suit-able for women than men. There is a persistent rumor that HUC-JIR deliberately admits fewer women than men to avoid the "feminization" of the rabbinate.[17] Some older male rabbis have grumbled that the rab-binate is becoming a "woman's profession" and, like grammar-school teaching and nursing, will decline in professional status and in salary range. They cite studies suggesting that when women enter certain pro-fessions in large numbers, those fields undergo profound and—from their perspective—negative changes.

Regarding the concern in some quarters that women will never be accepted as serious candidates for the most senior positions, some sug-gest that it is not so much prejudice that prevents women from holding senior rabbi positions as their unwillingness to devote themselves single-mindedly to career goals. How many women are willing to make the sacrifices necessary to rise through the movement's hierarchy? they ask.

Yet many women rabbis complain that their career path has been blocked. In Sylvia Barack Fishman's terminology, they had to break through "Jewish ceilings."[18] Only a handful has been appointed as senior rabbis of large congregations in recent years. Paula Reimers, a rabbi in Arizona, said in 1992: "It's the same old story. Everyone is in favor of women rabbis—until it comes time to hire one. A congregation would rather take an incompetent man than a woman. Women are picked last."[19] Such complaints, frequent in the early years, seem to have diminished, if not disappeared. Although a shortage of rabbis may explain the change in part, an increasing willingness to accept women in the rabbinate is apparent. Many congregations have had positive experiences with women rabbis; many boards may have found that female rabbis are more likely to deliver the type of service their congregation needs. In the face of this pragmatic reality, any residual resistance quickly melts away. When I spoke recently as a scholar-in-residence at a Congregation Shir Hadash retreat in California, congregants told me how Rabbi Melanie W. Aron had unified the Los Gatos temple. "From the time that we were founded, there was constant conflict between our [male] rabbis and various segments of the community. And then Rabbi Aron came. Everyone liked her and the bickering just stopped."[20] Aron pointed out to me that the flip side of this issue is that so many available women educators, administrators, and cantors can create a problem for congregations seeking "gender balance."[21]

Women cantors in the Reform movement have had an easier path in the years since Barbara Ostfield Horowitz was invested in 1975 as the first female cantor. An almost continuous shortage of ordained Reform cantors has guaranteed enough pulpits for all graduates of the School of Sacred Music at HUC-JIR in New York. Furthermore, it is easier for many of the old-fashioned congregants to accept a woman cantor than a woman rabbi, perhaps because cantors are perceived as subordinate to the rabbi. The fine voices of many of the women may also have dissipated potential opposition, as congregants discovered the new cantor's leading of the service to be a pleasant experience.

An increasing number of congregations simply take the equality of men and women for granted. One of the consequences of egalitarianism is that gender roles are no longer differentiated. Rabbi Emily Feigenson was told when she first arrived at Leo Baeck Temple in Los Angeles that the congregation was a "post-feminist" one. She responded that she did not know what that phrase meant. But as she became involved in the life of the congregation, she saw that almost all of its programming was produced for men and women together. Virtually nothing was gender segregated—no classes or discussion groups designed for men or women separately, not even a sisterhood or brotherhood in the congregation. "The very idea of a temple sisterhood had seemed too 'retro' to be seriously considered."[22]

Feigenson argues that this attitude may be counterproductive, for some Jewish women's organizations can still make a unique contribution. Women of Reform Judaism (WRJ) leaders, for example, were "savvy, dedicated and high-energy women who champion a number of cutting edge causes," and "on a variety of causes that other organizations either ignore, or only make resolutions about, the WRJ acts boldly."[23] If such an important national Reform Jewish organization is gender segregated, then perhaps the time has come for the members of the Leo Baeck Temple to reconsider their "post-feminist" aversion to such a structure. The congregation has had requests for a men's group and recently received a query from the Reform movement's national brotherhood organization, the North American Federation of Temple Brotherhoods, asking if the temple might consider organizing a course for males on the pressures that men feel in allocating and designating their time, and how they might use Shabbat as a model for dedicating their Sabbath to family and rest. The pendulum may be swinging part of the way back.

Many early female Reform rabbis saw themselves as agents for change. Rabbi Janet Marder has argued that these women attempted to restructure the American rabbinate along the framework of three important values: balance, intimacy, and empowerment. Women were determined to balance their career responsibilities with their familial obligations. Perhaps because of their femininity, they were accustomed to stressing the central role of close personal relationships in the workplace. And as a consequence of their commitment to balance and intimacy, they had a vested interest in changing the power structure from a hierarchy with the senior rabbi at the top to a new model of shared responsibility.[24]

Laura Geller, the senior rabbi at Temple Emanuel in Beverly Hills since 1994, believes that she exemplifies a feminine approach to the rabbinate. "My style is one of shared leadership—I would argue that's a feminine model of leadership. Our congregation is not a hierarchy, but a series of concentric circles. One of my very clear goals is to empower lay people to mentor young people, lead services, teach, and really take responsibility for their own Jewish life." Credited with shattering the "stained-glass ceiling" by becoming the first female senior rabbi at a major metropolitan synagogue, Geller has been followed by senior rabbis Marcia Zimmerman at Temple Israel in Minneapolis and Amy Schwartzman at Temple Rodeph Sholom in Falls Church, Virginia. Geller wonders: "Are there so few of us in senior rabbi positions because we're not choosing them, or because we're not given a shot at it? The answer is a bit of both. I have come to discover, through my involvement over the years, that when women's voices are heard, a tradition changes," Geller says. "What happens when women become engaged in creating and reforming Jewish experience [is that] our experience becomes central and not marginal, and deserving of blessing and ceremony."[25]

New Modes of Religious Thought

In the last decade of the twentieth century, women thinkers made notable contributions to Reform Jewish thought in particular and Jewish religious thought in general. Basing their work in part on new research exploring gender roles in Talmudic culture, feminist scholars built new paradigms for understanding women and Judaism.[26] Various women thinkers looked at issues of religious innovation and ritual practice from new points of view that usually challenged the accepted notion that male experience could be extrapolated as universal. Some argued that Jewish theology was designed to reinforce male power and to justify the traditional gender roles.

Women theologians also proposed new paradigms for thinking about God and expressing their religious experience.[27] Many Reform women saw spirituality as involving communion with God and obeying God's teachings, in particular those that focused on morals and ethics. Ellen Umansky argues that "this understanding of spirituality, found primarily among women who either identify themselves as Reform Jews or grew up in the Reform movement, may have less to do with gender than with the teachings of Reform Judaism itself."[28] Reform women theologians found that their interest in ethics was a central theme in Reform thinking generally. But other women thinkers created theological statements that confronted not only ethics but also traditional texts and Jewish law.[29] Some of these women had experimented with Orthodoxy before deciding to become or return to Reform. Others experimented with Buddhism, meditation, New Age religion, and other alternative forms of spiritual expression.[30] Women began writing new types of prayers, including creative prayers books that reflected a distinctive female voice.[31] Others wrote creative midrashim, halachic explanations of the underlying significance of biblical texts, which took a number of different forms.[32]

One of the most important feminist theologians in recent years is Rachel Adler, who embraced Orthodoxy as a young woman, only to turn to Reform a number of years later. As a consequence, she brings to her writing knowledge of the tradition as well as the emotional investment of one who struggled to find a place for herself as a woman within that tradition and failed. The result is a theologian driven by personal passion as much as by theological interest. Borrowing from Mary Daly's *Beyond God the Father*, Adler argued that the methodology used by the Sages was incapable of truly understanding women or their experience, that Jewish law was developed by men for men and was based on masculine concepts.

The way the questions were asked in Talmudic discourse was geared to a masculine understanding of legal categories, Adler held. For example, twentieth-century Orthodox rabbis asked the halachic question of whether a Jewish man could continue to be married to his wife after the Nazis had raped her. The legal categories were constructed so that any sexual contact between a woman and a man not her husband might prohibit her from resuming a physical relationship with her spouse. The obvious extenuating circumstances were not a deciding factor in the halachic process, and the legal categories focused only on the men. There was a halachic justification for the inclusion of men and the exclusion of woman, and Talmudic discourse revolved almost exclusively around the concerns of men as expressed by men.

Perhaps because of her experience with Orthodoxy, Adler displayed a keen awareness of and sensitivity to Talmudic thinking. In contrast to a number of other Jewish feminists, she argued strongly that

Reform Judaism without halacha would be a repudiation of what is central to Jewish tradition. She became known in particular for her essay "Tum'ah and Taharah: Ends and Beginnings," published in the *Jewish Catalogue* and in the first Jewish feminist anthology, *The Jewish Woman*, during her Orthodox phase. In this essay, she justified the traditional laws of menstrual impurity by constructing a feminist theology of purity and impurity. By 1993, however, she felt the need to repudiate this piece formally, which "as a feminist Reform theologian" she could no longer "in good conscience endorse." She wrote frankly of her dilemma: Twenty years earlier as a young Orthodox woman she had written what became an influential essay, which she no longer believed in. "I have had to ask myself, what is the responsibility of a theologian when she no longer believes what she has taught to others as Torah?"[33] Theologians are not just theorists but expected to live out their religious convictions. As Adler changed her own religious beliefs and practices, she has had to adapt her theology.

In 1998, Adler published to wide acclaim *Engendering Judaism*, in which she struggles to reconcile her Reform feminist theology with a continuing interest in Jewish law. A review in the *Journal of the American Academy of Religion* reported, "Rachel Adler has written not only the most sophisticated and important book in the field of Jewish feminist thought but a study that can serve as a model for all feminist theological writings."[34] Adler focuses on the question of how rabbinic texts that appear to denigrate women can be read by a modern feminist. She asks, "What does it mean to *engender* Judaism?"[35] She explains that non-Orthodox Judaism accepts the premise that "Jews beget Judaism," meaning that the Jewish community of a given time and place can reshape the religion according to its particular needs. On that basis, Jews living in Western countries want to integrate into their Judaic theory and practice the Western ethical ideal that women are equal. Gender issues affect men as well as women, a fact that should be incorporated into any modern Jewish theology. If gender issues are regarded as synonymous with women's issues, then it must be assumed that Judaism is a completely gender-neutral entity and that women constitute an exceptional case precisely because they have a gender identity. This is obviously not so.

Adler's book was widely praised for combining traditional learning with astute criticism. Much of her work, however, is devoted to detailed discussions of arcane halachic disputes. While her ideas on how to engender Judaism are of great interest, a good portion of her writing focuses on rather technical legal issues that have tremendous importance for understanding the relationship between halacha and women's status in Judaism but that are unlikely to prove compelling reading for the typical Reform Jew. While she cites biblical texts, Talmudic sources, feminist theology, and cultural anthropology, she seldom refers to articles or books that could be labeled "Reform." One searches in vain for either European or American Reform thinkers in her footnotes. Nevertheless, Adler has had a significant impact on the Reform movement. Her advocacy of "the Jew who wasn't there"—the Jewish woman—persuaded many of the necessity for change.[36]

Many other feminist thinkers are formulating new paradigms to explain how religion can reinterpret ancient texts in a modern (or postmodern) world. Feminist thought in particular has affected how Reform Jews view sexual relationships. Men as well as women are being influenced by new theological approaches to both gender and sexual issues.

Sexual Harassment and Scandals

The new emphasis on gender issues has changed standards of private as well as public conduct. Unethical and even immoral behavior once ignored is now being confronted. Because of this new sense of accountability, a number of sex scandals have hit the Reform movement over the last decade. Rabbis in such cities as San Francisco, San Diego, Minneapolis, New York, and Birmingham have been accused of having extramarital affairs. Howard Nevison, a cantor since 1978 at Congregation Emanu-El in New York City, has been accused of molesting his nephew; Rabbi Steven Jacobs was alleged to have had an affair with Anita Green, the president of Shir Chadash/The New Reform Congregation in Los Angeles, allegedly provoking her estranged husband to order her murder; Fred Neulander, a rabbi in Cherry Hill, New Jersey, was convicted for ordering the killing of his wife.[37] Most of the rabbis accused of ethical violations that were not criminal offenses were suspended from the CCAR. They had to resign from their congregations, work for a period of time in an administrative position, and then start over elsewhere. In earlier generations such behavior was more likely to be covered up. But standards have become stricter, and punishments more severe.

The scandal that shocked many and changed the way sexual harassment issues were dealt with was the Robert Kirschner affair. A rising star in the Reform movement, Kirschner became the senior rabbi of Congregation Emanu-El while still in his thirties. From 1985 to 1991, he helped build the congregation from 1,000 to 1,500 families. In a city hard hit by the AIDS epidemic, Kirschner delivered a memorable Kol Nidre sermon about visiting a young Jew dying from AIDS. Published in *Reform Judaism* magazine, it galvanized the UAHC to respond to the AIDS crisis. Many spoke about Kirschner's becoming president of the UAHC when Alexander Schindler retired. But there were personality issues that forecast trouble. Fred Rosenbaum, the congregation's historian, writes that both synagogue employees and lay people described the rabbi as "top down, autocratic, and even abusive." Many found him lacking in warmth and collegiality. "Most remember him as being quick to anger and stinting on praise."[38] Nevertheless, he was highly regarded in most quarters.

On New Year's Day 1992, Kirschner abruptly resigned after three congregants and a temple employee accused him of sexually harassing or exploiting them. After his resignation, eight other women made formal complaints to the temple board about Kirschner's behavior toward them. At least three received financial settlements from the temple's insurance company. Kirschner himself received a generous severance package of about $230,000 that included twelve months' salary, his accrued pension, and the equity from his home, which was jointly owned with the temple. He immediately took a research fellowship at the Skirball Museum, now the Skirball Cultural Center. After the fellowship year, Kirschner was appointed program director, a position he holds to this day. Many women were outraged. When the Skirball Cultural Center opened, fliers attacking Kirschner as a sexual predator were placed around the building. When Lee Bycel, then dean of HUC-JIR in Los Angeles, tried to appoint Kirschner to the faculty in 1993, the outcry forced the idea to be quashed. Bycel argued that Kirschner "has done more repenting and more work and more dealing with this than anyone I've ever known in my life."[39] Many disagreed.

When Rosenbaum was preparing a new edition of his history of Emanu-El, Kirschner agreed to talk with him.[40] The result was a seventy-six-page chapter, "Fallen Star." Despite promising not to "make any excuses," Kirschner told Rosenbaum that he would "not accept responsibility for the allegations that were falsely and maliciously brought, that were simply untrue." Nevertheless, he accepts some culpability for the scandal. "I climbed too far, too fast, and seemed to develop a certain form of narcissism, arrogance, obliviousness to the feelings of others." Rosenbaum elaborates: "By his own admission, he had many adulterous affairs, several of them with his congregants, which he consummated in the temple." Kirschner's explanation: "When you are elevated—literally—on this pulpit with the light on your face, kind of the way I remember thinking in my youth of Jesus, you get that look from people . . . of admiration and even more. It can be very seductive; it can be toxic for someone like me. . . . I didn't have the most important attributes needed to serve in that capacity; that is self-knowledge, humility, experience." Rosenbaum suggests that the context also contributed to Kirschner's behavior. "He belonged to a generation known for its self-indulgence, and it reached the top during a decade marked by excess, in a city that celebrated sexual freedom."[41] Whatever caused Kirschner to behave as he did, many believed he was not adequately punished. The case highlighted the potential power that rabbis wield over their congregants, particularly women undergoing emotional, physical, or spiritual problems. Many felt that when women accuse a rabbi of sexual harassment or exploitation, a conspiracy of silence prevents a full airing of the charges.

When congregational meetings are held following allegations of sexual misconduct, many congregants refuse to believe that their rabbi has done anything wrong. They see him as the spiritual leader who has officiated at their marriages and their children's bar mitzvahs and deduce from this long association that he must be the victim of a smear campaign. Debra Warwick-Sabino, a clergy sexual abuse expert, explains that "when you say to someone that their rabbi is capable of this, for them to suspend their disbelief would cause such a spiritual crisis in their own lives that it's easier for them to say 'boys will be boys' than face that faith crisis."[42] Many women who have been harassed or abused by rabbis feel guilty, believing themselves somehow responsible. They also worry that their status in the community and even their marriages are at risk. Accused sexual predators are protected; alleged victims are ostracized and humiliated. Abused women are sometimes unwilling to come forward and, in some cases, suffer silently for years.

This was brought home by the resignation of HUC-JIR president Sheldon Zimmerman due to a "sexual boundary violation."[43] One of the most charismatic Reform rabbis of his generation, Zimmerman had served the Central Synagogue in New York City from 1970 to 1985 and as senior rabbi of Temple Emanu-El in Dallas from 1985 to 1995. He married Judith E. Baumgarten in 1964; the couple had four children. Zimmerman had served as CCAR president and WUPJ vice president, and was a member of the UAHC Executive Committee and Board of Trustees. With the exception of Eric Yoffie, he was the most important leader in the American Reform movement.

The emerging scandal was kept quiet while the CCAR investigated throughout the year 2000. Finally, on December 4, Burton Lehman, chair of the HUC-JIR Board of Governors, announced that Zimmerman had resigned effective immediately.[44] This followed his two-year suspension from the CCAR after a yearlong ethics investigation by the seven-member Ethics Committee had found Zimmerman guilty of violating section A2 of the CCAR ethics code. While the exact nature of the offense was not specified, CCAR executive vice president Paul Menitoff described it as a "sexual boundary violation." Under the terms of the suspension, Zimmerman was prohibited from performing any rabbinic duties for two full years. Continuing to serve as president of a rabbinical school was therefore out of the question, and Zimmerman resigned. According to Lehman: "He felt that under the circumstances, it would be unseemly for the president of the University to be suspended from practicing as a rabbi and still remain as a role model as the head of the College. I think he felt he didn't have any choice."[45]

The resignation surprised most outside of the Ethics Committee. Even Lehman was unaware of the ongoing investigation until only a few weeks before the announcement. Gary Zola, director of the American Jewish Archives, said Zimmerman's resignation "came as a big shock to the whole school. He had attended the big annual dinner in honor of the College in Cincinnati on Sunday and he was on the cam-

pus yesterday [the day of the suspension]." Zimmerman, a popular president, had taken the position five years earlier, when there had been talk
of closing one of the four campuses. His fundraising abilities ended that
speculation. Indeed, all four campuses began to hire new faculty. A
number of physical plant renovations and expansions were also undertaken. Zola said that most of the students were "devastated and hurt" by
the news. "It's a tragic loss. It's akin to grieving."[46]

The resignation opened up the issue of sexual misconduct, as
numerous articles in the Jewish press asked, "How serious is sexual misconduct?" While the Ethics Committee kept details of the investigation confidential, further information emerged when Zimmerman
applied for a position just four months later with Birthright Israel, a
new organization devoted to sending young Jews on free trips to Israel.
It appears that Zimmerman had an affair with an adult congregant
while working at the Central Synagogue in New York City a decade
and a half earlier. Interviewers asked him why the woman had waited
more than fifteen years to file an accusation against him with the
CCAR. Zimmerman explained that the woman, now a rabbi, had asked
him to write a reference for her. Zimmerman refused, and she filed the
ethics charges. Since Zimmerman has refused to discuss what happened
and the woman has chosen to remain anonymous, the details of the
incident, as well as her motivation for waiting so long to file charges,
remain unclear. The delay was unusual but not unprecedented. A court
of Episcopal Church bishops recently ruled that Charles Jones, bishop
of the Episcopal diocese of Montana since 1986, should be disciplined
for an adulterous affair nineteen years earlier when Jones was rector of a
church in Russellville, Kentucky. "God was taken away from me," the
woman wrote in her complaint.[47]

Birthright Israel officials dismissed concerns that hiring Zimmerman so soon after his suspension and resignation sent the message that
sexual misconduct was not being taken seriously. Joel Meyers, executive
vice president of the Conservative movement's Rabbinical Assembly,
expressed dismay. "It gives license to people to assume that if they do
something wrong, there is little penalty paid." Arthur Gross-Schaefer,
who teaches Jewish values and ethics at the Academy for Jewish Religion in Los Angeles, said that rabbis who had committed misdeeds
should undergo an extensive period of reflection and repentance. "If we

rush to find new positions for them, then we take away the ability for that process to come into effect." He agreed that Birthright Israel was sending the wrong message by hiring Zimmerman so quickly. "Our tradition says that the values in our actions speak more loudly than anything we say. We have to look at the values being conveyed by this type of decision." Charles Bronfman, a cofounding chairperson of the program, disagreed. Hiring Zimmerman "sends a good message about Jewish values. The sexual misconduct happened a long time ago, and Jewish values are that if one's family forgives, then the community forgives. Shelly's family forgave him a long time ago. One would find a skeleton in almost anyone's past. Does this mean they're a bad person? I'm not sure anymore."[48]

The Zimmerman case highlighted the issue of women's roles at HUC-JIR. When the *Forward* published an article on Zimmerman's resignation that cited increasing the number of women faculty as one of his achievements, Susannah Heschel of Dartmouth College wrote to correct the record: While it was technically correct that the number of females working at HUC had increased under Zimmerman, "the glass ceiling still exists for women faculty." Heschel compared HUC with her own university. HUC had 32 tenured male and 4 tenured female faculty members; in Cincinnati, 13 tenured men and only 1 tenured woman, a situation Heschel found "particularly troubling." Since 1963, she pointed out, every male faculty member that applied was granted tenure "almost automatically," but of the four women who came up for tenure under Zimmerman, two were turned down. The recent decision not to recommend the advancement of American Jewish historian Karla Goldman to the stage where she could apply for tenure was probably on Heschel's mind. In contrast, Dartmouth had 124 male full professors with tenure and 35 females. On the associate professor level, 50 are men and 45 are women. Heschel connected the inequity indirectly to the type of scandal Zimmerman had apparently been involved in. "Gender inequalities unfortunately foster an atmosphere of male dominance that carries over from the rabbinical school to the rabbinic profession. Rabbis and congregants suffer the consequences, including incidents of inappropriate sexual behavior, of which Rabbi Zimmerman has been accused." She argued that not only the few females teaching at HUC suffered, but also the entire faculty, as students could "easily fall victim to the culture of male dominance that still prevails at all of our rabbinical schools."[49]

HUC had taken steps to correct the imbalance. The Rabbi Sally Priesand Chair was created to bring in a visiting professor of Jewish women's studies. The first appointment, in the fall of 1999, brought Tikva Frymer-Krensky of the University of Chicago to the New York campus. In 2000, liturgist Marcia Falk held the visiting-professor post on the Cincinnati campus. In 2002, composer Elizabeth Swados was in residence in Los Angeles.[50] Efforts have been increased to hire new female faculty. "You really need to have ovaries to get a job at HUC today," one rabbi told me.[51] Ten of the fourteen most recent faculty appointments were women: Rachel Adler, Carol B. Balin, Nili Fox, Sharon Gillerman, Lisa D. Grant, Alyssa M. Gray, Adriane Leveen, Dvora E. Weisberg, Andrea Weiss, and Wendy Zierler.[52] Their impact will be felt not only at HUC-JIR but throughout the Reform movement.

The Increasing Influence of Women on Related Gender Issues

The Women's Rabbinic Network (WRN) proposed the original CCAR gay and lesbian marriage resolution, after passing its own resolution in March 1999 in support of rabbinic officiation at gay and lesbian weddings. That organization then decided its resolution should be ratified by the full rabbinic conference. Journalist E. J. Kessler saw this move as representing a distinctive style of feminine leadership. Kessler suggests that the passing of the same-sex marriage resolution may be remembered historically "as the instant the Reform movement's female rabbis embraced a retrograde essentialism in the name of feminism and gay liberation." According to Kessler, "the full conference—'the men'— had tried to bring a resolution, and, owing to men's warlike propensities and their insistence in arguing about such icky patriarchal quantities as Torah, tradition and precedent, they had made a mess of it." The WRN's official support of the resolution and its decision to sponsor its adoption by the CCAR linked women rabbis with support for same-sex marriage. "Those of us watching this battle knew that the gay vows struggle would clothe itself in the prestige of the regnant ideology of feminism and that any discussions of law, tradition and precedent would likely be thrown out in favor of appeals to compassion and mercy."[53] While Kessler's interpretation simplifies the many complex and interacting pressures and influences at work, it reflects the popular perceptions that women are pushing the drive for change and that the women's arguments tended to rely on empathy rather than truth.

Indeed, much of the debate used the rhetoric of justice and compassion. Rabbis were called upon to vote in favor of the resolution because the stranger, according to Torah law, is to be treated fairly and thoughtfully. CCAR president Charles Kroloff noted that it was "not just a coincidence" that it was the WRN that brought the resolution, which appealed to women's special nature and character. "In our tradition, women have a profound sense of justice, mercy and compassion. We men have a lot to learn from women. I learn from women—from my female colleagues—every day. They have a great deal to teach us men. I'm not sure that if this was brought by a men's group, they would have been able to be as flexible."[54]

In today's Reform movement, where flexibility is crucial, some hold that the women are more flexible. While it is difficult to generalize about an entire population, some see a widening "gender gap" in the movement. Certainly, polls show that Americans are divided by gender over a wide range of issues, including their preferences for presidential candidates.[55] The WRN's initiating the gay and lesbian same-sex resolution is one manifestation of the special role that women rabbis play, as a group, in the contemporary Reform movement.

That role appears to some critics to stress compassion over intellectual rigor, sensitivity over historical precedent, and egalitarianism over halachic obligation. Anecdotal evidence suggests to these critics that women rabbis have less grounding in traditional sources than men and less concern with traditional Judaic precedents, a generalization based on no quantitative or qualitative research. Many traditionally oriented younger male rabbis and Classical Reform older male rabbis, in particular, hold this impression. Women rabbis do excel as social workers, therapists, and conciliators, roles that modern Reform congregations want their rabbis to play. Women may succeed in the rabbinate beyond their wildest expectations, dominating the profession in the coming decades. As the Orthodox long understood, revolutionary change can unleash forces unanticipated at the time of the initial decision.

Despite the vulnerability of the Reform movement due to its liberal theology, it has effectively tapped into recent societal trends, harnessing the enthusiasm of previously marginalized groups. The largest and most important of these groups has been women. The increasing range of roles women play in the movement has generated tremendous energy and excitement. Women are no longer "powerless under patriarchy," to use an expression coined by Aviva Cantor, the cofounder of *Lilith* magazine.[56] Although it has created or at least exacerbated certain tensions, the overall impact of feminism on Reform Judaism has been overwhelmingly positive.

Chapter 10

The Acceptance of Gays and Lesbians

Many of us feel pity for gays and lesbians, and we agree intellectually that it is a grievous wrong to stigmatize them, to ostracize them, to hold them in moral disdain. But something more than a grasp of the mind is required; there is a need for a grasp of the heart. Something different from pity is called for; we need as a community to cross those boundaries of Otherness, those fringed boundaries where compassion gives way to identification. —ALEXANDER M. SCHINDLER, 1989

THE REFORM movement has been a relatively tolerant place for gays and lesbians for many years. Most Reform Jews are liberal, not just religiously but socially and politically as well. Tolerant, pluralistic, and open to new ideas, Reform Jews accepted woman as equal in religious terms and were among the leaders in the national struggle for civil rights. Open to changing conceptions of society and new approaches to psychology, most Reform Jews were already sympathetic when the issue of gay and lesbian rights was first discussed.

While it is certain that there were homosexuals involved in the Reform movement in earlier times, they kept their sexual identities well hidden and we have no idea who they were. There is very little written about gay and lesbian Reform Jews before the 1960s. Sexuality in general was not spoken about as openly as it is today, and homosexuality in particular was a hush-hush subject. It seems likely that certain individuals may have been rumored to have homosexual proclivities, but it was felt inappropriate to put these suspicions into writing. Certainly, no prominent Reform Jew came out of the closet before the sexual revolution.

Today, the Reform movement is committed unequivocally to supporting full social and legal equality for gays and lesbians in the United States. The UAHC has passed resolutions in favor of protecting gays and lesbians from any form of discrimination in employment, housing, and so forth. The movement has enthusiastically welcomed gays and lesbians into its congregations and has appointed a considerable number as rabbis and cantors, a trend-setting policy that to more conservative observers would appear to repudiate the biblical prohibition on homosexual activity. Yet those within the movement see this decision as a legitimate reinterpretation of an ancient textual prohibition.

The drive to accept gays and lesbians came along at a time when the bulk of the Reform movement—even those who would normally espouse rather traditional social values—was ready and willing to accept change. The acceptance of gays and lesbians as congregants could have become divisive, as happened in a number of mainline Protestant denominations. But the Reform movement integrated gays and lesbians with a minimum of conflict. Many homosexuals were attracted to special outreach congregations, while others preferred to join typical Reform temples. In both cases, most reported that they felt comfortable and accepted.

The Background of Judaism and Homosexuality

Before the early sixties, Jewish tradition on homosexuality included no alternative position. The Bible stated that homosexual behavior was a *toevah*, an abomination, and forbade same-sex sexual relations. The Torah explicitly prohibits male homosexual intercourse and lists it along with other abominations such as adultery and incest as something that could defile that holy land of Israel. The prohibition was considered so clear cut that there was relatively little discussion of it. Sifra 9:8 states: "You shall not copy the practices of the land of Egypt where you dwelt, or of the land of Canaan to which I am taking you (Leviticus 18:3). What did they do? A man would marry a man and a woman would marry a woman." The traditional view was read in the

Orthodox and Conservative synagogue every year on Yom Kippur afternoon. While the Torah does not specifically mention lesbianism, the
Talmud prohibits it, but it is a less serious violation of Jewish law than
male homosexuality.

According to HUC rabbinics professor Mark Washofsky, "To the
extent that the sources offer a rationale to these prohibitions, it lies in
the concern that homosexual relations will lead to a breakdown in the
institution of marriage, the bearing of children, and the boundaries of
'normal sexuality.' Homosexual relations, in this view, are an *indul-
gence*, a choice of carnal pleasure that is destructive of the order of
nature and of the most basic unit of social life."[1]

Contemporary rabbis interpret the traditional sources on homosexuality in one of three basic ways. The first, held to by Orthodox and traditional rabbis, reaffirms the biblical and Talmudic prohibition. Most
temper their refusal to condone homosexual behavior with a call for
compassion for the individual. Such rabbis may suggest that homosexuality is an illness more than a conscience choice. Norman Lamm, president of Yeshiva University for many years, holds this view.

> Homosexuality is no different from any other anti-social or
> anti-halakhic act, where it is legitimate to distinguish between
> the objective act itself, including its social and moral
> consequences, and the mentality and inner development of the
> person who perpetuates that act. For example, if a man
> murders in a cold and calculating fashion for reasons of profit,
> the act is criminal and the transgressor is criminal. If, however,
> a psychotic murders, the transgressor is diseased rather than
> criminal, but the objective act itself remains a criminal one. . . .
> To use halakhic terminology, the objective crime remains a
> ma'aseh averah (forbidden act) whereas the person who
> transgresses is considered innocent on the grounds of "ones"
> (force beyond one's control).[2]

Recently, Orthodox rabbi Steven Greenberg has publicly acknowledged that he is gay. Greenberg is not from an Orthodox background
and does not serve a congregation. Although he has called for Orthodox Judaism to change its attitudes toward gays and lesbians, he has
been ignored by most in the Orthodox community or dismissed as a
crank. Nevertheless, he has been able to come out of the closet as a gay

Orthodox rabbi as a direct result of the Reform movement's position on of the acceptability of gay rabbis. Greenberg has been able to work in the general community through the National Jewish Center for Learning and Leadership, where his being a gay rabbi is not a unique phenomenon. He then was able to push for a place for gay Jews and gay rabbis in the Orthodox community. He appeared in Sandi Simcha Du-Bowski's recent documentary "Trembling Before G-D," which describes the religious and social dilemmas facing gay and lesbian Orthodox Jews. While Greenberg has been a trendsetter in the Orthodox world, his accomplishment rests on the ground-breaking efforts of gay and lesbian Reform rabbis and the Reform movement.[3]

The Conservative movement's interpretation of traditional sources on homosexuality is the most difficult to characterize. Traditionalist conservatives have held views not dissimilar to those of the Orthodox. For example, Rabbi David M. Feldman writes that, "while sincere, even non-patronizing, empathy may be called for, condonation of homosexuality as an alternate way of life is not."[4] More liberal Conservative rabbis such as Bradley Artson and Elliott Dorff reinterpret the halacha in light of modern scientific understandings of homosexuality. These thinkers would not reject the halacha, but they would understand it in the context of the changing psychiatric interpretations of homosexuality.

Most Reform and Reconstructionist rabbis reject the traditional prohibitions completely. These rabbis work to meet the emotional as well as spiritual needs of the gay and lesbian Jew. The acceptance of homosexuals is taken for granted; it is understood that one no longer has to justify the legitimacy of gay and lesbian relationships, as Margaret Moers Wenig suggests when she writes that "this essay does not argue for the acceptance of openly gay and lesbian Jews as members of our community . . . [rather] this essay takes such acceptance as a starting point for that is where the American non-Orthodox community now stands—at least in principle."[5]

The Development of Gay and Lesbian Jewish Religious Groups

Although for many the Stonewall riots in the summer of 1969 mark the beginning of the modern gay rights movement, gays and lesbians formed community organizations throughout the United States as early as the 1950s. In the late 1960s, some began to consider creating religious organizations as well. In 1968, the Reverend Troy Perry, a former Pentecostal minister, founded the Metropolitan Community Church (MCC) for gays and lesbians in Los Angeles. Inspired by the MCC, gay and lesbian Jews interested in the idea of a religious community founded the Metropolitan Community Temple in 1972.[6] The congregation first met at MCC, then at the Leo Baeck Temple, and then in a dance studio run by one of the earlier congregational presidents in West Los Angeles. Later they broke ground on their current location on West Pico Boulevard. The congregation adopted a new name, Beth Chayim Chadashim (BCC), meaning New Life Congregation or Congregation of New Lives.

Eighty-one-year-old Harriet Perl has described the atmosphere: "At the time BCC started, if you were gay, it was the thing you kept secret, because coming out of the closet typically meant the loss of family, community, and employment. You don't know the kind of fear we used to have. For the first few years, I did what a great number of members did: I didn't use my last name. . . . I finally got over my own guilt about being gay, and got to the point that I wasn't afraid of what the world will do." Robin Berkovitz explains that "thirty years ago, we had to choose between identifying exclusively as Jews—and concealing our sexual orientation—or identifying only as gay or lesbian and not finding a place to nurture our Jewish selves."[7]

The new group approached the Union of American Hebrew Congregations (UAHC) for assistance and, despite some opposition, was accepted as a member. BCC was not only the first gay and lesbian congregation accepted into the UAHC, but also possibly the first accepted into *any* mainstream congregational organization. The UAHC insisted that such synagogues should not be labeled gay or lesbian—which would seem to exclude non-homosexuals—but rather should be known as having a "special outreach" to the gay and lesbian community.

Any Jew could join BCC, regardless of sexual orientation, and as the congregation developed, a number of heterosexual couples did join, among them Maggie and Dave Parkhurst. "As we got deeper into Jewish learning, we'd found ourselves increasingly out of place at most Reform temples." The Parkhursts disliked the "service station" mentality of the suburban Reform congregations they had attended, where the congregants didn't share "Dave's love of chanting Torah or [Maggie's] devotion to studying Talmud." They were looking for a congregation where people felt a personal commitment, and BCC provided that. Most of the congregants had struggled for years with their religious identity, and the Parkhursts feel they are amidst kindred spirits. Today Rabbi Lisa Edwards and cantorial soloist Fran Magid Chalin lead BCC, which has 250 membership units. Congregational leader Davi Cheng is probably the first Chinese-American lesbian Jew by choice to be a synagogue president. Stephen Sass explains BCC as a "place that acts as a conscience to us and to the rest of the world, insisting on inclusiveness and compassion. A house of new life that continues, by its very existence, to affirm the vision of our founders: that all people are created b'tzelem Elohim, in God's image."[8] The congregation is open to all, while stressing its commitment to reach out to gay and lesbian Jews in the Los Angeles area. The BCC model has been adapted by gay and lesbian Jews looking to build religious communities in major metropolitan areas throughout the United States. Many of these congregations have joined the UAHC.

When the issue of gay synagogues first arose, UAHC president Alexander Schindler turned to Rabbi Solomon Freehof of Pittsburgh's Rodef Shalom Congregation. Freehof had written hundreds of responsum and dozens of books on Reform Jewish practice, explaining the Talmudic context for a given issue based on his familiarity with the traditional rabbinic primary source material to an extent unusual for a Reform rabbi. Unfortunately, Freehof was not sympathetic to the struggle. "Homosexuality is deemed in Jewish law to be a sin," he wrote, and "to isolate [gays and lesbians] into a separate congregation and thus increase their mutual availability is certainly wrong," although they should not be completely ostracized from the Jewish community. "It would be in direct contravention to Jewish law to keep sinners out of the congregation."[9] But Freehof's view was generally ignored, and a number of Reform congregations helped gay and lesbian religious groups that were developing. By 1977 the UAHC committed itself to welcoming congregations with special outreach to the gay and lesbian population and to providing such temples with all the services offered to other affiliates. The same year, the Central Conference of American

Rabbis (CCAR) adopted a resolution that called for legislation to decriminalize homosexual acts between consenting adults and for an end to all discrimination against gays and lesbians. Further, the resolution called on Reform Jewish organizations to develop practical programs to implement this principle. In a revolutionary deviation from the traditional Jewish view on homosexuality, the Reform movement had struck a historic note in favor of gay rights.

Despite these gains, there were still no openly gay or lesbian rabbis in the United States. Rabbi Lionel Blue in the Liberal movement in Great Britain was known to be gay, but there was no similar figure in the United States. Rabbi Allen B. Bennett would be the first. An ordained rabbi who had served a congregation in Minnesota for three years and moved to California to study for a Ph.D. at the Graduate Theological Union in Berkeley, Bennett told me: "My coming out was not directly connected to anything happening in the Reform movement. Rather, it was a result of the anti-homosexual teacher initiative."[10] He was referring to the Briggs Initiative, put on the ballot in 1978, which proposed barring gays and lesbians from employment in California's public schools. Opponents mobilized against the proposal and in the end defeated it 58 to 42 percent. The campaign against the proposition had called Bennett and told him they were trying to organize gay and lesbian clergy willing to declare themselves and publicly oppose the initiative. But when they found out that there was no openly gay rabbi anywhere in the country, they changed their minds; they felt such a sensational announcement would overshadow the anti-Briggs focus of the story. Meanwhile, a local paper ran a series of stories on gay life in the city, which featured Allen, identified only by a pseudonym, as one of the local gay personalities. Later with his permission the paper revealed his name. Other newspapers and magazines picked up the story of the first gay rabbi, including *Time* magazine.

Bennett's coming out helped the Reform leadership put a face to the issue. He met Alexander Schindler in New York shortly afterward, and Bennett remembers thinking, as Schindler welcomed him to his office in a creased shirt and without a tie, "So this is the king of the Jews?" But Schindler immediately impressed him with his quick and nimble mind. He asked, "How many gay Jews do you think there are in the United States?" Bennett said he didn't really know but that the

number of gays and lesbians in the general population was usually esti-
mated at 10 percent. "So that would be about 600,000 gay Jews then?"
Schindler asked. "Now that's interesting!" Schindler explained that he
was looking for population groups that might be interested in Reform
congregations. "How many gay and lesbian Jews are already members of
synagogues?" Bennett told him maybe two thousand. "Now that's interesting!" A large number of gay and lesbian Jews were not only potentially recruitable but also predominately in the age bracket where they
would be able to provide support and leadership.

Bennett was at a conference in San Francisco when Joseph Glaser,
the executive vice president of the CCAR approached him. "I want to
talk to you," he told Bennett sternly. "What you have done [by coming
out of the closet] has caused a great deal of difficulty for the movement
and will probably cause a great deal of difficulty for you as well. Why
would you do something like this?" Bennett replied simply, "Because it's
the truth. Why would you want me to lie as a rabbi?" Glaser's tone soft-
ened, and he asked Bennett to explain what it had been like to be a
homosexual in the rabbinate. "I told him not only what it was like for
me, but more importantly, what it was like for all those people who
were still afraid to come out." The meeting began a process of reevalua-
tion for Glaser, and over the next few years he shifted from an out-
spoken opponent to a strong advocate for respectful treatment of gay
and lesbian rabbis. Bennett believes that the Reform movement's support of gay and lesbian rights was "very much a top-down decision." He
credits Schindler with being instrumental in setting the new policy.

Bennett became the first rabbi at Sha'ar Zahav, a gay and lesbian
outreach congregation in San Francisco founded in 1977, where he
originally went to worship with no intention of "coming out" as a rabbi.
Bernard Pechter, one of the founders of the congregation, started chat-
ting with him and asked him what he was doing. Bennett at first said
that he was a graduate student, but eventually "I swallowed hard and
told him the truth—that I was a rabbi." Pechter gave him a big hug and
said, "We have been waiting for you." Bennett served the congregation
for a couple of years and was followed by Rabbis Yoel Kahn, Jane Litman, Martha Bergadine, and, since 2000, Camille Angel. Kahn served
the congregation for nearly twelve years, becoming a model for gay
Jewish leadership throughout much of the worst of the AIDS epidemic.

With his partner, Dan, and his son, Adam, Kahn remains active at Sha' ar Zahav. The congregation now has more than five hundred units, about 20 percent of whom are heterosexual (mixed-gender couples).

Current Rabbi Camille Angel explains that the congregation is particularly proud of its many children. "When the congregation began in 1977, there was no thought of there being a religious school. Now there are 149 children in our congregation. Sha' ar Zahav was the very first gay and lesbian outreach congregation to create and sustain a religious school. Not only are we teaching Jewish values, but we are bringing the experience of lesbian, gay, bisexual, and transgendered people to bear on Jewish values." She argues that "the experience of coming out, the experience of being on the margins, if not altogether invisible, helps us to identify with the stranger and the oppressed. For so many LGBT Jews, we feel that we have come out of Mitzrayim [Egypt]."[11]

Alexander Schindler had hoped that gay and lesbian Jews would one day be able to help build not only Reform congregations, but also other Jewish institutions. This is now a reality. Many of the Sha' ar Zahav congregants serve on the boards of Jewish organizations throughout the Bay Area, including the Jewish federation, the Brandeis Hillel Day School, and the *Jewish Bulletin*. One of the four founders of the congregation, Daniel Chesir, is the president of the UAHC Northwest Region.

The CCAR and the Issue of Homosexual Rights

The issue of homosexuality cuts to the heart of how the Reform movement deals with the conflicting demands of tradition and modernity. Here is a case where the tradition could not be clearer—homosexuality was prohibited in the strongest terms. Yet liberal American Jews felt they had to find a way to reconcile this condemnation with their contemporary values. How the Reform rabbinate handled this sensitive question is worth a close look.

The CCAR first dealt with the issue of homosexuality in the mid-1970s and soon after was supporting human rights as well as civil liberties for gays and lesbians. Most Reform rabbis took liberal positions across the board and so were quick to embrace what many saw as another liberal social cause. One issue that concerned still closeted gay and lesbian rabbis was the impact on their career trajectory should they declare themselves publicly. HUC-JIR did not officially admit openly gay students, and the CCAR did not guarantee to support gay rabbis looking for congregational employment. In 1986, Margaret Moers Wenig and Margaret Holub proposed a CCAR resolution that recommended a nondiscriminatory admissions policy for HUC-JIR and a nondiscriminatory placement policy for the Rabbinical Placement Commission (RPC). The motion was not voted on but referred to the newly created Ad Hoc Committee on Homosexuality and the Rabbinate chaired by Selig Salkowitz.

The seventeen-member committee—eight congregational rabbis and representatives of HUC-JIR, UAHC, and the RPC—met regularly for study and deliberation for more than four years. They talked often with leaders of other Jewish denominations as well as with the Progressive movement in Israel. Consulting with Reform leaders in Israel was particularly important because any American resolution favoring gay rights would be used as a political weapon by the Orthodox in Israel, who opposed religious pluralism in the Jewish State. Israeli Reform rabbis told the Americans that any such resolution would make their already difficult position even more so, but this information had little impact.

In the belief that gays and lesbians were entitled to equal religious as well as civil rights, many Reform rabbis felt it was important to push ahead. Whereas the Orthodox saw homosexuals as violating an explicit commandment of the Torah, most Reformers saw them as people who needed and wanted the same spiritual sustenance available to heterosexuals. Alexander Schindler, well known for confronting controversial issues head-on, gave a public address in November 1989 adding his voice to those already supporting gay rights. "If those who have studied these matters are correct, one half million of our fellow Jews, no less than one hundred thousand Reform Jews, are gay. They are our fellow congregants, our friends and committee members and, yes, our leaders both professional and lay."

In June of that year at a CCAR meeting in Seattle, there was a debate on a widely publicized report issued by the CCAR's Ad Hoc Committee on Homosexuality and the Rabbinate. As a part of the educational process, the committee invited four Reform rabbis to prepare and submit papers on the topic of "Homosexuality, the Rabbinate, and Liberal Judaism."[12] Despite the appearance of an active debate, it was clear that the movement as a whole would support greater rights for gays and lesbians. It was less clear exactly what the CCAR would decide concerning some of the technical questions.

In 1990 the committee issued a report noting that the Bible uses the harshest terms to condemn male homosexual behavior, referring to it repeatedly as a *toevah*, an abomination. The Talmud and Codes reinforce the position that any male or female homosexual activity was strictly prohibited. Nevertheless, the committee rejected this position as untenable and stated that "all Jews are religiously equal, regardless of their sexual orientation." While the committee recognized that, in the Jewish tradition, heterosexual monogamous procreative marriage is the ideal, "there are other human relationships which possess ethical and spiritual value, and . . . there are some people for whom heterosexual, monogamous, procreative marriage is not a viable option or possibility."[13] Thus the committee took the position that a homosexual relationship could possess spiritual value for those who could not form a heterosexual union.

One of the most pressing questions was how HUC-JIR should deal with gay and lesbian applicants to the rabbinical program, for although the two are separate organizations, it was expected that all rabbinic graduates of HUC-JIR would become Reform rabbis and join the CCAR. Gary Zola, HUC-JIR's national dean of admissions, showed the committee a written policy statement issued by HUC-JIR president Alfred Gottschalk on February 8, 1990. Gottschalk wrote, "The College will consider any qualified candidate in terms of an applicant's overall suitability for the rabbinate, his/her qualifications to serve the Jewish community effectively, and to find personal fulfillment within the rabbinate." The HUC-JIR Dean's Council felt that sexual orientation should not be a consideration in a candidate's decision to apply for admission; "I underline, however, that this does not commit us to the acceptance or rejection of any single student. Each applicant is judged as an individual on the basis of his total profile."[14] Nevertheless, until the early 1970s, there was an unspoken assumption that a homosexual candidate would not be admitted. Homosexuality was seen as a serious sexual deviance or even a mental illness; it was assumed that congregations would be scandalized if they found out their rabbi was gay.[15]

While this attitude had all but disappeared by the early 1990s, concern remained that gay and lesbian rabbis would have trouble finding positions or keeping their jobs once they revealed their homosexuality. In 1990, the CCAR Ad Hoc Committee on Homosexuality in the Rabbinate issued a warning: "Publicly acknowledging one's homosexuality is a personal decision that can have grave professional consequences. Therefore, in the light of the limited ability of the Placement Commission or the Central Conference of American Rabbis to guarantee the tenure of the gay or lesbian rabbis who 'come out of the closet,' the Committee does not want to encourage colleagues to put their careers at risk."[16] Despite this word of caution, there was no question that homosexuals were becoming more acceptable to the rank and file in Reform congregations throughout the country.

The possibility that gay men or lesbians could become rabbis and not have to hide their sexual identity was a heady thought. Donald Goor recently said that today "the greatest joy for me is it's not an issue at all." But when Goor officially came out to the largest Reform congregation in the San Fernando Valley in 1995, his speech made headlines in the local papers and even the *New York Times*. Goor had graduated from the Hebrew Union College in 1987, three years before the CCAR passed a resolution approving the ordination of gays and lesbians. He began serving as the associate rabbi at Temple Judea in Tarzana, a suburb in Southern California. When the senior rabbi was preparing to retire in the mid-1990s, Goor was the obvious candidate to take his position. But once the temple launched the obligatory national search, Goor felt he should tell the search committee that he was gay. While he had never concealed his sexuality from the congregation, he had never spoken about it either. His revelation sparked a media feeding frenzy, and he was besieged with requests for interviews. The issue was a hot one, and Goor's coming out put a face on a widespread trend that many were beginning to recognize. "People who are straight do not have to come out. It is a very personal disclosure that shouldn't have to be," Goor said. He was hurt by only one commentator, Jewish radio personality Dennis Prager, who attacked the rabbi as amoral and unfit to be a spiritual leader. Otherwise "the media was very positive." In the congregation, the younger members said that they had no objections but worried that the older generation would be more conservative. The older members told Goor that they had no objections but thought his homosexuality might be an issue for the young couples just beginning to start families. The senior rabbi did not object to Goor's gayness but felt it should not become national news. In the end, Goor was appointed as senior rabbi and remains in that position to this day.[17]

Not all Reform rabbis supported gay rights. For example, Philmore Berger of Temple Avodah of Oceanside, Long Island, said, "It's my duty as a rabbi to love all human beings, but it's not my duty as a rabbi to approve of the behavior of all human beings." Berger cited the passage in Leviticus 18:22, which calls homosexual behavior a *toevah*. "So far as I know," he commented sarcastically, "no Jewish biblical scholar has reinterpreted the meaning of that verse." This comment cuts to the heart of the problem. The Reform movement, as well as many other American liberal religious denominations, faced a crisis in trying to reconcile a liberal political agenda with religious traditions. Many felt they could not ignore the unequivocal statements made in the Bible and Talmud. HUC-JIR professor Leonard Kravitz, for instance, stressed that the Jewish tradition had an unequivocal position on homosexuality: "Unlike so many other issues such as birth control, for instance—on which different voices in our tradition say 'yes,' 'no,' 'maybe'— here is an issue on which the tradition speaks with one voice, and it says, 'no.' There are no analogues or precedents anywhere in our tradition for homosexual rabbis, as there are, for example, for women rabbis or for the patrilineal descent issue. The Reform movement has begun to pay greater attention to the voice of tradition. We are taking kashrut and Shabbat more seriously; we don't just disregard what the Torah says."[18]

But social pressure was pushing the Reform movement in diametrically opposed directions. As Kravitz notes, many Reform congregations were becoming more traditional. But that return to tradition meant the performing of more rituals and the reintroduction of previously jettisoned observances; it did not mean the Reform movement was embracing a commitment to the halachic system. Indeed, Reform was moving with a great deal of enthusiasm to embrace a number of liberal social positions and issues, including that of gay rights. Jack Wertheimer called this process "change in both directions."[19]

Many Orthodox leaders were predictably horrified by the CCAR's increasingly tolerant position on homosexuality. Hillel Goldberg, an Orthodox rabbi who edits a Jewish newspaper in Denver, wrote: "For the CCAR to affirm the propriety of homosexual rabbis is to stand in diametrical opposition to the authority and the content of Judaism's unanimous teaching. . . . It is one thing to adapt and modify Judaism . . . it is quite something else to be 'radical,' to 'get at the root' . . . In what sense, then, can the CCAR claim to represent Judaism?"[20] Rabbi Moshe David Tendler, professor of Talmud and chairperson of the Biology Department at Yeshiva University, quoted Jonah of Gerondi's thirteenth-century moral treatise, *Gates of Repentance*, on shame as essential to the repentance process. "Would one not be ashamed to sin in the presence of others? Should one not be ashamed after one has sinned in the presence of God? Today . . . we have lost our sense of shame for our own sins, and with it our indignation at those of others. We have become non-judgmental." Tendler claims that a major mode of the transmission of AIDS "is an activity referred to in Torah as 'an abomination, punishable by death'. It is theologically abhorrent; it menaces our lives and those of our children. Yet we refer to homosexuality with the euphemism, 'an alternative lifestyle.' " This, Tendler argues, "is not the way of Torah." Rather, one should rebuke one's fellow Jew in order to develop a moral society. The failure to express rejection means that one is condoning such behavior.[21] Tendler's strident views reflect a widely held opinion in traditional circles. How can rabbis condone something so explicitly condemned by the Torah?

Gay Marriage and Reform Rabbis

If many Orthodox rabbis were shocked by Reform rabbis willing to tolerate homosexuals in general, they were baffled by those willing to officiate at gay and lesbian commitment ceremonies. Yet Reform rabbis were still unsure about what type of ceremony might be appropriate for homosexual couples. The technical question centered on whether such a ceremony could be regarded as *kiddushin*, the halachic term for a Jewish religious sanctification of a marriage. According to the Talmudic literature, kiddushin requires the fulfillment of a number of specific conditions, and it was impossible to interpret the traditional sources as allowing kiddushin for a same-sex couple.

But many gay activists who wanted their commitment ceremonies sanctified were not willing to settle for a weak decision that would encourage rabbis to officiate at same-sex unions while urging them to avoid referring to it as kiddushin. They expected to marry in the way and with the degree of religious sanctification for which a heterosexual couple would be eligible. The motivation to have gay and lesbian commitments blessed, sanctified, celebrated, and acknowledged came less from a political agenda than from a religious and spiritual desire. Of paramount importance was meeting the personal spiritual needs of gay Jews and their families. Denise Eger explains that "for many of us, the final notion of inclusion and acceptance within our movement was acknowledging and ritually celebrating our family structure as a mishpachah [Jewish family]." She argues that "if gay and lesbian relationships cannot be sanctified and celebrated and ultimately honored as sacred, then there isn't full inclusion. If I am only an individual, not seen in the context of my family relationship, then I actually remain hidden within the Jewish community and synagogue structure."[22]

The CCAR annual convention in March 1996 passed a resolution supporting the rights of homosexual couples to a civil marriage, "On Gay and Lesbian Marriage."[23] Much attention focused on the state of Hawaii, which was about to vote on a law that would allow gay and lesbian civil marriage. For gay activists, the law would be a watershed in their struggle for civil recognition of such marriages, particularly as most states had agreements recognizing civil marriages performed in other states. At the UAHC biennial conference in Dallas in October 1997, the General Assembly passed "Civil Marriage for Gay and Lesbian Jewish Couples," a resolution that supported secular efforts to promote legislation that would give gays and lesbians the opportunity to marry civilly. The resolution also encouraged UAHC congregations to "honor" monogamous gay and lesbian domestic relationships.[24]

In June 1998, the CCAR's Ad Hoc Committee on Human Sexuality, chaired by Selig Salkowitz, presented an extensive interim report to the CCAR convention that covered all facets of Reform Jewish sexual values. Concerning the issue of rabbinic officiation at gay and lesbian weddings, the report concluded that "Kiddushah [holiness] may be present in committed, same gender relationships between two Jews, and that these relationships can serve as the foundation of stable Jewish families, thus adding strength to the Jewish community. In this spirit, we believe that the relationship of a Jewish, same-gender couple is worthy of affirmation through appropriate Jewish ritual, and that each rabbi should decide about officiation according to his/her own informed rabbinic conscience. We call upon the CCAR to support all colleagues in their choices in this matter."[25]

That is not to say that everyone was wholeheartedly in favor.[26] For example, Dow Marmur argued that rabbis are "not allowed to give away that which is not theirs to give."[27] Sanctification is restricted only to male-female unions through the process of kiddushin and no rabbi can change that fact. Other Reform rabbis such as Jeffrey Salkin and Cliff Librach have also expressed opposition to specific aspects of rabbinic officiation at same-sex union ceremonies. But even such relatively conservative rabbis would be regarded as liberal in almost any other American religious denomination.

The CCAR continued to progress on this issue. Based on a resolution passed in March 1999 by the Women's Rabbinic Network (WRN), a new "Resolution on Same-Gender Officiation" (Resolution #12) was circulated.[28] The WRN, which had supported officiation ceremonies that would sanctify the relationship between two Jews of the same gender, urged the CCAR to endorse this view. Although Resolution #12 reaffirmed many of the arguments in the CCAR's Ad Hoc Committee on Human Sexuality 1998 report, it generated a great deal of controversy. At the 2000 CCAR conference in Greensboro, North Carolina, the group voted to accept a resolution urging rabbis to look favorably on same-sex commitment ceremonies.

All major U.S. papers headlined the news: "Reform Rabbis Back Blessings of Gay Unions" (the *New York Times*); "Gay Unions Affirmed by Reform Rabbis" (the *Los Angeles Times*). Lisa Edwards, a lesbian rabbi serving Beth Chayim Chadashim, opened her monthly statement in her synagogue's newsletter by asking, "Did you think you would ever live to see such headlines?" The April 10, 2000, issue of *Newsweek* printed a quote in its "Perspectives" section by Valerie Lieber of the Gay and Lesbian Rabbinic Network praising the Reform rabbis who declared gay unions "worthy of affirmation": "We have gone beyond a time of tolerance and acceptance to a time of embracing the souls of gay and lesbian Jews."[29] Many Christian liberals praised the boldness of the CCAR, while most Christian fundamentalists looked on in disgust.

Some Jews agreed with the Christian fundamentalists. The ultra-Orthodox Agudath Israel of America took out a quarter-page ad on the April 14, 2000, *New York Times* op-ed page, responding to the CCAR's assertion that "the relationship of a Jewish, same-gender couple is worthy of affirmation through appropriate Jewish ritual."[30] The ad charged that Reform rabbis have "gravely misled not only other Jews, but the entire world, by fostering the notion that Judaism tolerates homosexual acts." Agudath Israel believes that the Torah is the eternal word of God and that Judaism should reflect that reality. What particularly upset the organization was that this resolution would seem to suggest that the CCAR was willing to endorse any social trend that gained acceptance in America. Therefore, they put in large print at the top of the page, "Judaism Is Not a Mirror of Society's Shifting Mores." The text of the advertisement states: "Let it be said loudly and clearly: the Torah, the very basis of the Jewish faith, explicitly considers such acts and relationships deeply sinful, condemns them without qualification, and leaves no room for their formal recognition."

Agudath Israel representative Avi Shafran explained to a reporter that the advertisement was not placed with the intention of provoking a fight with the Reform movement. Rather, it was aimed at doing one thing: "making sure the general public, both Jewish and non-Jewish, realizes this is not a Jewish move of a Jewish movement and doesn't reflect Judaism as it has been historically defined."[31] While Shafran was probably sincere in his comment that the ad did not seek to antagonize Reform Jews, repudiating the CCAR's position was bound to be interpreted as a direct challenge of a most unfriendly nature. For the ultra-Orthodox, the acceptance of homosexuals and homosexuality was one more indication of how far the Reform movement had strayed from authentic Jewish values. For the Reform movement, the hostile Orthodox response was a predictable consequence of the perceived hostility of the Orthodox toward the movement as a whole.

Paul Menitoff, executive vice president of the CCAR, responded to the Orthodox attack stoically: "My sense was before the resolution passed, and now that it's over, that while other groups may disagree and disagree strongly with our stance, that ultimately our friends will remain our friends, and our detractors will remain our detractors." Menitoff preferred to think about the many more liberal-minded people who were enthusiastic about the resolution. "What's been heartening is the tremendous positive response from certainly lots of individuals in the Jewish community, both straight and gay and lesbian. This has meant on a deep level a great deal to not only gay and lesbian Jews, but to non-Jews." Many non-Jewish clergy had privately "expressed their admiration for what we've done and indicated that they hope their respective groups would be able to follow suit in the not-too-distant future."[32] This was a reference to the three Protestant denominations that had scheduled votes on the same issue for their conferences that very summer. None would pass any of the proposed resolutions, leaving the Reform Jewish movement the only one to take a strong stand in favor of gay and lesbian rights.

Although most Reform rabbis favored the resolution, a small but influential group opposed rabbinic officiation at same-sex ceremonies. Rather than stress their opposition to a resolution that was bound to pass, they emphasized that its original draft did not adequately provide for a full range of pluralistic responses. These rabbis argued that the movement's respect for pluralism meant that the final resolution should recognize that the CCAR had taken a number of different positions over the previous two decades, that the Reform movement had a wide range of views on the topic, and that no one view was seen as decisive. Among these documents was the 1995 Responsa that argued that gay relationships "cannot be called Kedushin." As a consequence of their pressure, the resolution avoids the use of the word "marriage" and also shies away from the word "wedding." The final draft also removed a statement arguing that kedushah, holiness, "may be present in committed same-gender relationships between two Jews." Supporters of gay marriage, wanting to avoid an open confrontation at the conference, rewrote the resolution shortly before the final vote to say not only that "we support the decision of those who choose to officiate at rituals of union for same-gender couples" but also that "we support the decision of those who do not."[33] Not all gays and lesbians were satisfied with the wording of the final resolution. Some felt it had been watered down by compromises before the conference, removing any reference to the holiness of gay marriage on a par with heterosexual marriage. For some this was a critical deletion. If the goal was to affirm that homosexuals could "marry" in the same way and with the same degree of sanctification as heterosexuals could, then the final resolution fell far short.

Despite the last-minute compromising, supporters of the marriage resolution were pleased with the vote for same-sex commitment ceremonies. Shira Stern of West River, New Jersey, for example, believed that "the essential nature of the resolution remains," because the final resolution "affirms the sacred relationship between two Jews who are gay and lesbian and says that we are going to create materials to reflect that affirmation." The CCAR has now decided to prepare and distribute liturgy, Ketubot, and other materials and resources to rabbis who plan to officiate at gay and lesbian wedding ceremonies. Yoel Kahn, who was "very proud to be a Reform Jew and to be a Reform rabbi because of today's vote," hopes the resolution will help the movement reach out to gay and lesbian Jews who feel "invisible or marginalized. This is our statement that we finally and completely have a place for you."[34]

Reform rabbis on the whole supported the resolution in its final version. In line with today's therapeutic culture, the focal point for most rabbis was how the resolution could help people feel affirmed and accepted. As Howard Voss-Altman put it: "These are our friends, our relatives, our sons and daughters who are in need of Jewish life. Their lives are no different from ours—they work, they worship, they give *tzedakah*, cook dinner together, and they love each other. Perhaps someday they will walk down the street together holding hands. Perhaps someday they will walk into *Kabbalat Shabbat* together, proudly and openly. Someday."[35] The feeling is that gays and lesbians are just like heterosexuals, and what prevents them from being accepted in society is the prejudice of many of those heterosexuals.

Effects on Interfaith Marriage Issues

Despite the fact that the proponents of the resolution denied any connection between the two issues, many rabbis who did not officiate at intermarriage ceremonies disagreed, fearing that the acceptance of gay and lesbian commitment ceremonies would bring unbearable pressure on them to capitulate on the intermarriage issue.

They frequently cited Jerome Davidson as an example of their concern. Davidson, senior rabbi at Temple Beth-El of Great Neck, Long
Island, had hired Karen Bender, a lesbian, as assistant rabbi in 1994.
When Bender announced plans to have a commitment ceremony in
Encino, California, Davidson readily agreed to bless the couple in the
synagogue about two weeks before the marriage. Davidson differentiated between the case of a gay or lesbian couple who were both Jewish
and committed to the covenant and a heterosexual union involving a
Jew and a gentile, where there was obviously no commitment to the
covenant between God and the Jewish people. While this rationale
had sound logic behind it, some of Davidson's congregants were furious.
Many had accepted his refusal to officiate at their children's intermarriage ceremonies because they respected his belief that to do so would
violate his fidelity to the tradition. But once they heard he had blessed
two lesbians on the *bimah*, they found his refusal to accommodate their
family needs more difficult to accept. In response to the furor, Davidson
announced that he would take time to reevaluate his officiation policies. He created an ad hoc committee of rabbis to study new perspectives on the possibility of intermarriage officiation, and as a result, he
later decided that he would perform interfaith marriages under certain
circumstances.

Davidson announced his change of heart on Rosh Hashannah
1997. He told the assembled congregation he had decided "to do more
to support such couples . . . some of us want to find ways to bless and
perform their marriages. This is a big step, but I believe today that it is
necessary and right, and ultimately will strengthen our faith." Davidson
explained that in his view, "The situation has changed from the way it
was years ago when [mixed couples sought rabbis to perform their marriages largely for] cosmetic reasons. Now couples want to do it to seal
the commitment [to Judaism] they both already made. And in cases
where the commitment is supported by real action, we should do something." Unlike most rabbis who perform interfaith marriages, Davidson
said he would insist on "some very clear and demanding requirements"
that would include a commitment that Judaism would be the exclusive
religion in the home, family participation in Jewish activities, synagogue affiliation as a family, the serious study of Judaism on an ongoing
basis, and regular meetings with a rabbi. Davidson, who lives in a heav-

ily Jewish area with a high Orthodox representation, said, "I want us to open the widest doors we can to such couples, unlike the Orthodox who want to close them."[36]

Rabbis opposed to officiation at interfaith ceremonies pushed hard to moderate at least the language of the gay and lesbian officiation resolution. But one supporter of the resolution told me, "Most of the rabbis opposing rabbinic officiation at gay and lesbian wedding ceremonies are old-fashioned and narrow minded." Others believed the opponents were outright "homophobic." Whatever their motivations, they succeeded in changing the language of the resolution to emphasize the diversity of opinion on this issue in the Reform movement, and the differences that currently exist among Reform rabbis.

Reconciling the Marriage Resolution with the Torah

Some in the Reform movement have taken the faith's historic religious documents and reduced their message to simplistic liberal truisms. Love, justice, and compassion are the core values of the Torah; everything else is based on historical settings that have changed, or interpretations valid only in a different context, and so forth. What remains is the core message of the Torah as understood by the Reform movement: tolerance and inclusivity. Reminding congregants that they should be studying the Torah and the Codes to bring their behavior into conformity with Judaism's dictates would seem narrow, rigid, and unbending. Yet Judaism is based on the concept of divine revelation and the giving of divine commandments. It is the Jew's obligation—at least in the traditional conception of the religion—to fulfill God's will by performing certain ritual acts and abstaining from other forms of behavior and activity.

Many supporters of the marriage resolution and similar positions see themselves as warriors for liberal causes fighting against the forces of darkness, among them Voss-Altman, who explains, "We have taken a stand—a stand that most people, and many Jews, not only disagree with, but actually revile." The implication in his words is that people who disagree with his stand on the issue "revile" gays and lesbians, not because they have a well-thought-out set of religious values, but because they are homophobic and probably filled with all sorts of other

irrational prejudices. He continues to stress the leadership responsibilities of the Reform rabbinate and ties the support of gay and lesbian
marriage to the dictates of the Torah and the prophets. "It is never easy
to lead. It is never easy to take a position that is contrary to most
people's values and insist that it is right. But we have always been a
counter-cultural people. We have always stood outside the mainstream,
clinging to the revolutionary idea that justice and compassion must be
extended to everyone—the poor, the disabled, and the homosexual.
There is still much to do. But in the spirit of Torah and our prophetic
tradition, we are in pursuit of justice."[37] This is a common rhetorical
device among Reform rabbis, but it is a big intuitive leap to say that
fighting for gay and lesbian marriage rites/rights is in the spirit of the
Torah and the prophetic tradition. It is hard to imagine a single prophet
finding the idea even remotely acceptable.

Some rabbis indeed recognize the potentially problematic consequences of this reductionism. Daniel Rabishaw, the associate rabbi at
Congregation Beth Israel in Houston, asked the obvious question,
"How can rabbis justify something that seems to contradict the Torah
so blatantly?"—and then answered it. "The answer, at least in my mind,
can be found in the autonomy that all Jews—especially Reform Jews—
feel when confronted with important issues that cross into the religious
arena. We all have to make informed decisions about how we engage
the Torah and the lessons it contains. Our faith community holds in a
high regard the right of the individual to be confronted with an issue,
to study the relevant texts and then, with information in hand, render
a decision which is, at least in the mind of that individual, grounded in
Judaism."[38] Rabishaw stresses study as a critical prerequisite for informed
choice in the Reform decision-making process. The individual has the
right to study, gather information, and then render a decision. Not a
posek, a halachic expert. Not a Talmudic scholar. Not a Jewish historian. But every Jew. And that decision will be "grounded in Judaism . . .
at least in the mind of that individual."[39] One feels that Rabishaw himself senses the intellectual feebleness of this approach. But it is certainly
democratic, pluralistic, tolerant, and, most important, inclusive.

The Reform movement has come to regard acceptance of gays and
lesbians as a central value. When the Boy Scouts of America expelled
gay scout leader James Dale and the expulsion was challenged in court,

CCAR executive vice president Rabbi Paul Menitoff resigned his BSA membership. "As a fifty-eight-year-old heterosexual male, I decided that I could no longer be associated with an organization that engages in discrimination against homosexuals. It is an unacceptable affront to the principles upon which both Reform Judaism and our great country stand. Moreover, I believe the Boy Scouts' stance nurtures a climate of bigotry in the United States." Menitoff's call to boycott the Boy Scouts carried weight because he had earned the rank of Eagle Scout and received the Ner Tamid Award, the highest religious award bestowed upon a Jewish scout. He published his letter of resignation in the CCAR *Newsletter*, and the media picked up the story. Menitoff argued that the Reform movement must take an unequivocal stance on the "exclusionary policy" of the Boy Scouts. He explained that "we are each created in the image of God. It is no badge of honor to be heterosexual and it is no sin to be homosexual, just as it is no honor to be White and no sin to be Black. It is simply who we are."[40]

The Current Scene

As a result of the movement's openness, some alternative congregations thrive. Congregation Kol Ami broke off in 1992 from Beth Chayim Chadashim, the first gay, lesbian, and bisexual outreach congregation, with thirty-eight founding members who rented space from the West Hollywood Presbyterian Church. Rabbi Denise Eger said that being guests in a Christian congregation's building was unsettling. "I spent a lot of time carrying the Torah around."[41] Having a permanent home became an important priority. Only a decade old, Congregation Kol Ami has developed into a warm and vital synagogue that has recently dedicated its new building, marking the culmination of an arduous effort to build a permanent home.

Kol Ami wanted to distinguish its synagogue from the suburban congregational architecture of the post–World War II period that many congregants associated with superficiality and heterosexual centrism. They wanted their temple building to reflect their values, which stress simplicity as well as beauty. For example, instead of the usual bronze commemorative plaques, the Yahrzeit boards are simple wooden shelves with understated nickel-plated and engraved markers. Next to each board is a small basket of polished stones that family and friends can place in their loved one's space. This recreates the traditional experience in the cemetery, providing an emotional connection for many who can not visit the gravesites of their loved ones.

Los Angeles architect Joshua Schweitzer included in the building's design some features of his popular designs for the Border Grill restaurants. He wanted the space to be sunny and open so that gays and lesbians who had often felt excluded would feel welcomed. The congregation also wanted to show that it was serious about Judaic text. Schweitzer explains, "The rabbi and I talked about how text can become part of the building, the idea that the building can actually speak to you." On the sage-green and brown building, stenciled metal letters spell out the Hebrew words Shalom (peace) and Zedek (justice); the sun shining through the stenciled cutouts creates interesting shadows on the wall of the temple. Wrapped around the sanctuary above colored windows are Hebrew words based on the ten aspects of God in the Jewish mystical tradition: love, holiness, commandment, joy, compassion, justice, eternity, blessing, understanding, and faith. Eger states, "These are ideas and concepts that are critical to who we are." The congregation now has 330 member units, including not only gays and lesbians but also heterosexual family members, intermarried, and interracial couples.[42]

If the women's issue has been largely settled in favor of complete equal rights, the issue of gay and lesbian participation is well on its way to being similarly resolved. Unlike some of the more liberal Protestant denominations that have had ongoing confrontations over the question of gay and lesbian ordination and homosexual marriage, the Reform movement settled the issue in favor of these practices with a minimum of open conflict. Further, the pluralistic nature of the Reform movement has allowed different opinions on this, like other controversial issues, to coexist in relative harmony.

The hope is that gays and lesbians can bring renewed energy to the Reform movement in much the way that women have over the past twenty or thirty years. If gays and lesbians indeed commit themselves to making Reform Judaism even more vibrant, then the Reform revolution will certainly succeed.

Chapter 11

The Battle over
the Future of
Reform Judaism

I foresee great changes. I foresee our being open to
bringing God more creatively and forcefully into our
lives; I foresee more and more sustained Torah learning
. . . I foresee our people filling their lives with more
opportunities to actualize the kedushah which lies just
below the surface of their daily activities.
— RICHARD N. LEVY, 1998

WHEN THE 110th annual Central Conference of American Rabbis (CCAR) convention in Pittsburgh passed a new set of principles in May 1999, the vote represented the culmination of eighteen months of debate over a Reform platform, the latest clash between two very different approaches to Reform Judaism. The Classical Reformers have vigorously objected to the many changes the neo-Reformers have instituted. The neo-Reformers have looked with disdain on the Classical style of worship as sterile and lifeless. The debate over the platform reflects how the interaction between the two groups is working and where the struggle for the soul of the Reform movement may lead in the coming years. Then–CCAR president Rabbi Richard N. Levy justified the need for a new statement of religious principles on the grounds that the movement since the 1976 San Francisco statement had made a number of momentous decisions, including the patrilineal descent resolution of 1983, the development of an outreach program to intermarried families and others, and the establishment of a significant number of congregations with special outreach to gays and lesbians.

The proposal of a new statement of principles raised the hope that Reform Judaism could stir the passions buried in the hearts of what appeared to be a largely apathetic congregational body. Many hoped that the enthusiasm so apparent at the Union of American Hebrew Congregations (UAHC) biennials would spread throughout the movement and that Reform Jews would begin to experiment with Judaic ritual in a great spiritual awakening. Instead, the proposed platform became the arena for an ugly fight over who controlled the movement. The debate focused on the overriding religious meaning of the innovations over the past two decades and on the idea that Reform Jews should try out a wide variety of traditional rituals. Only a series of political compromises enabled the CCAR to pass the final draft. By the time of the vote, most of the substance of the original document had been removed, and all hope that the platform could serve as a rallying point for a Reform renaissance had been lost. The debate over the platform and the resulting controversy have forced many Reform Jews to ask themselves what their synagogues stand for.

The Need for Consensus Building

The debate over the 1999 platform highlighted the dynamics of consensus building within the Reform rabbinate. With autonomy a central feature of the entire movement, "Reform Judaism changes through consensus building—and that takes a long time," the UAHC's Dan Freelander told me. "Power is not centralized, but rather leadership is exercised through inspiration, planning, and programming. That is why the resolutions of the UAHC or CCAR don't mean much unless accompanied by program implementation, significant ongoing public relations, and formal endorsement by brother and sister organizations."[1] Declarations, resolutions, and institutional decisions are most effective when they are passed at the end of a long and inclusive process of consensus building. Otherwise, the position is usually ignored.

This sets the Reform movement apart from denominations that accept the religious concept that the Sages possess wisdom and insight that others lack. The Orthodox *posek*, or halachic expert, has tremendous authority, for the Orthodox believe that specialized expertise in Jewish law is needed to make halachic decisions. Because halacha is viewed as divinely given and then passed down from generation to generation, it would be unthinkable for the Orthodox to ignore a halachic ruling by a prestigious *posek*. In the Conservative movement, the Talmud faculty at the Jewish Theological Seminary had a degree of this type of religious authority, particularly when Talmud professor Saul Lieberman was alive. Reform Judaism rejects this model of leadership and refuses to acknowledge the binding nature of Jewish law.

Despite this position, many Reform Jews have pushed to restore traditional language and concepts. Particularly important has been the rehabilitation of the word "mitzvah." When *Gates of Prayer* was published in 1975, it was the first time an official publication of the Reform movement used the word: "Be mindful of all My mitzvot and do them." This restoration of the concept gave W. Gunther Plaut and the Committee on Reform Jewish Practice a rationale for preparing a guidebook on practice, published as *Gates of Mitzvah* in 1979. The small volume used such phrasing as "It is a mitzvah to . . ."— language suggesting that the writers were urging Reform Jews to consider performing more rather than less mitzvah, and as rituals rather than as mere ceremonies.[2] In addition to the descriptions of various mitzvahs, the book contained four brief essays on the meaning of mitzvah. Shim Maslin, who solicited the essays, explains: "I felt that it was necessary to get four prominent Reform rabbis to write about their very different concepts of mitzvah in order to forestall any major objections to the use of the word. The use of the word mitzvah in American Reform Judaism today might seem quite natural, but its rehabilitation was a real struggle just a quarter of a century ago."[3] Not just another book put together by an individual or a small committee, the *Gates of Mitzvah* underwent a full process of critique and formal vote by the entire CCAR membership before publication.

The Reform belief in religious autonomy means that individuals should evaluate a given mitzvah and decide whether and in what way it might be spiritually meaningful for them. This precludes an authoritarian power structure, since the individuals on the congregational level make the final decision on religious policy. This approach had a profound impact on the institutional culture of the American Reform movement, beginning in the mid–nineteenth century.

Despite this autonomy, the Reform movement has taken vigorous positions on issues and has supported position papers. In some cases, these positions were not regarded as held by consensus, and the CCAR has reversed policies in place for years, sometimes even decades. The most effective and long-lasting resolutions have been those voted on by the CCAR or UAHC after an extensive process of dialogue, negotiation, and reformulation. For example, the patrilineal descent resolution was first raised by then–UAHC president Alexander Schindler long before it was brought to a vote and passed in 1983. Schindler engaged in an educational effort to convince both leaders and rank-and-file members in his organization that it was in their interest to accept the children of Jewish fathers and gentile mothers as Jewish, that this was a logical and legitimate religious policy to adopt.

Likewise, the CCAR resolution supporting rabbinic officiation at gay and lesbian commitment ceremonies was not sprung on the rabbis out of the blue. Both the UAHC and CCAR had been discussing aspects of the issue for years. Committees had studied the issue, and extensive discussions had been held in various contexts. A great deal of related work had also been done on parallel subjects, such as the Reform movement's position on civil rights, the adoption of an nondiscrimination policy for Reform congregations and the movement, membership policies as they related to a number of categories of "nontraditional" members, and the appropriate response to pending laws in Hawaii and later Vermont allowing for a civil equivalency to marriage for gays and lesbians. Because consensus was reached on most of these other issues, the leadership was willing to push ahead with an explicit rabbinic policy on the officiation issue. A potentially divisive difference of opinion between the liberal majority and a small group of traditionalists was negotiated privately in the months before the vote on the resolution at the 2000 Charlotte, North Carolina, conference.

And yet Reform's apparent tranquility should not deceive us. The movement is feeling the same pressure as other similarly placed religious movements to split into factions. One group supports a politically correct social agenda, while another wants to preserve "traditional" standards. The question that arises is, Just what is "traditional"? For a Reform Jew, the traditional approach to Judaism is the high-church Classical Reform model. For the eastern European Jew who has entered the Reform movement in the last generation or two, "traditional" refers to something more akin to *Fiddler on the Roof*. The debate over the

1999 Pittsburgh Platform is a fascinating case study of how different camps in the Reform movement see their past from different perspectives. The struggle over the religious direction of the movement will determine the future of Reform Judaism in the United States.

The Context

Rabbi Richard N. Levy understood the problem as early as 1969:

> The American Reform synagogue is in trouble. It has generally defaulted on all three of its traditional functions—as a house of prayer (*Bet Tefilah*); as a house of study (*Bet Midrash*); and as a house of meeting (*Bet Knesset*). There are few Reform synagogues where prayer is a regular and significant event for the majority of members; even fewer where there is serious study of Jewish literature and ideas, either alone or in conjunction with secular study; and as Reform congregations grow in size, "meeting," in any sense beyond occasional social affairs where few members know each other, has become equally rare.[4]

Thirty years later, his concern was even greater. The platform that Levy would propose to the CCAR would become, if it passed, the fourth major statement of beliefs by the American Reform rabbinate in its history, after Pittsburgh in 1885, Columbus in 1937, and San Francisco in 1976.

During 1998 and the first half of 1999, Levy would redraft his document six times, as the proposed set of principles went through an extensive and relatively transparent process of debate and evaluation. Even the movement's official publications published at least some dissenting views. Leadership played a key role in initiating the process, but it would be effective only to the extent that it could enthuse the congregational members. No rabbinic or lay leaders would even attempt to draw solely on authoritarian models of religious leadership, holy texts, or legal precedents to justify their policy positions. They understood the need to win over not only the neo-Reform majority, but also the 20 to 25 percent of the movement still committed to Classical Reform. The debate process was facilitated by the quarterly magazine *Reform*

Judaism, which all members of the movement receive automatically as part of their membership in their UAHC-affiliated synagogue. The Internet discussion groups sponsored by the UAHC, CCAR, and HUC-JIR also greatly facilitated open debate. This would prove important not only for the passing of a platform but even more for the pushing of a revolution.

While much of the debate over the new platform centered on the so-called move toward tradition (however defined) that the Reform movement is in the process of embracing, much of its subtext concerned the recent sociological studies on American Jewry. The premise of Reform Judaism had been that it was possible to become Americanized and yet be able to pass on a perhaps attenuated form of Jewish identity to succeeding generations. But the 1990 National Jewish Population Survey had called this assumption into question. Even worse, it was not at all clear how many Reform Jews still cared. A number of recent journalistic reports suggest that the obsession with Jewish continuity and survival worries lay and professional leaders almost exclusively, and that most Reform Jews and most American Jews generally are just living their lives. Their attitude is, what happens, happens. As the intermarriage rate dramatically increased, the consensus in the Jewish community shifted from rejection of intermarriage to grudging acquiescence and then to acceptance. The Reform movement reacted to the change in social context by proactively advocating and implementing new approaches to issues facing Jews and Judaism today.

A Move Toward Tradition?

To placate the approximately one-quarter of the movement's members who were Classical Reformers, most of the references to specific ritual acts were removed from Levy's original proposal draft. The suggestion that Reform Jews might consider eating kosher food, taking ritual baths in a *mikveh*, and even wearing tefillin (phylacteries) was shocking to many. Some considered such proposals an attack on their entire approach to religious life. *Reform Judaism* magazine, the official organ of the movement, published the third draft of Levy's "Ten Principles for Reform Judaism"—the number ten presumably was intended to remind readers of the original ten principles given to Moses by God, the Ten

Commandments. Many reacted emotionally, positively or negatively, to the accompanying cover photo of Rabbi Levy wearing a tallith and a yarmulke.

While many applauded the tone and the substance of the proposed platform, others were distressed and saddened by what they felt was an abrogation of the historical positions of the Reform movement. Letters and e-mails attacked Levy personally, suggesting he would feel a great deal more comfortable in the Conservative or even the Orthodox movement. Others stressed that Levy's long career at the Hillel Foundation, a Jewish university campus organization, prevented him from understanding the mentality of the congregational Reform Jew. For those who associated tradition with "medievalism," Levy's proposals struck a raw nerve and precipitated a major debate over the direction the Reform movement should take. Some of the criticism was very harsh. "Abandonment, hurt, outrage, violation, betrayal. These are just a few of the first words that came to mind after I read Rabbi Richard Levy's proposal," wrote a reader from Mequon, Wisconsin. "I don't recognize and can't even participate in it . . . there is so much Hebrew in the service, I not only don't understand it, but I can't even follow where I am suppose to be in the prayer book." Paul Uhlmann Jr. from Kansas City, Missouri, stated frankly that "we do not need a Rabbi Levy to burn bridges in our country, isolating ourselves into little 'Williamsburgs'. As a friend of mine wrote, we 'cannot be lemmings following him over the Orthodox cliff'." Another reader commented sarcastically: "It was quite a surprise to read the contents of Rabbi Levy's article. . . . I did have to check the cover to make sure it said Winter 1998 and not Winter 1698."[5]

Levy was surprised by the ferocity of the responses, and the CCAR leadership discussed abandoning the effort, but Levy wanted to push on. Working closely with other CCAR and UAHC officials, he produced a fourth draft, much more moderate in tone than the original. This new document, discussed at the December 1998 UAHC board meeting, still contained a number of issues that caused difficulties for certain members of the board, mainly the urging to read and speak Hebrew, and the encouragement to make aliyah—move to Israel. But Judge David Davidson summed up the board's ultimate response: "The issue generated a lot of apprehension, some heat, and even some dismay, but after hearing Rabbi Richard Levy's very personal and very open presentation yesterday, the apprehension is largely dissipated and most of the heat is gone."[6]

Although the CCAR had announced that no vote would be taken on the proposal at the Pittsburgh conference, a new announcement went out to declare that the platform would indeed be brought to a vote. The leaders of the CCAR now united behind Levy in support of the new platform. They urged its passage as a way to show those who were watching that the Reform movement was moving forward and that the platform could serve as a stimulus for discussion and further study. Many found this a rather weak argument for passing a platform, but the final document had been so severely modified that it was difficult to find anything in it that would seriously offend anybody. Consensus prevailed over ideological agendas.

On May 26, 1999, the CCAR met at the historic Rodef Shalom Congregation in Pittsburgh. This congregation had hosted the 1885 Pittsburgh Platform that symbolized, for many, the rejection of Jewish tradition, and, for all, the hallmark of Classical Reform Judaism. At 11:30 A.M., the rabbis voted to adopt a new platform by a vote of 324 to 68, with nine abstentions, A Statement of Principles for Reform Judaism.

In the end, a platform was passed by the CCAR only because of Richard Levy's willingness to rewrite it six times, even though this rewriting substantially watered down the original thrust of the document. In fact, the final draft contained virtually none of the distinguishing features of the original.

What the Return to Tradition Means

The controversy over the platform has reinforced the impression that Reform is moving in two directions at the same time. Since the 1960s, the positions taken by the Reform movement have been shaped by two very different impulses that seem contradictory. On one hand, the Reform movement has reintroduced many traditional rituals and practices that had been rejected by Classical Reform, including the wearing of yarmulkes and prayer shawls for men and now women and, perhaps most noticeably, the increase in the Hebrew in the Friday night services of many Reform temples. At the same time, the Reform movement has adapted to changing social realities by sanctioning a significant change in the traditional definition of who and what is a Jew—the patrilineal descent resolution of 1983, which accepted the children of Jewish fathers and gentile mothers as Jewish if they were raised as Jews, even without a conversion. They went even further when they decided to ordain first women and then gays and lesbians as rabbis and cantors. These innovative responses to changing social trends reveal how sensitive the leadership of the movement is to the needs of the typical congregant. They show a willingness to meet the needs of atypical Jewish congregants who are very much a part of a rapidly changing society.

These contradictory trends were already present when the debate began over the proposed platform. E. J. Kessler of the *Forward* wrote in September 1998 that the draft of "Ten Principles for Reform Judaism" promoted "rituals and observances . . . that many associate with Orthodoxy."[7] Kessler noted that the proposed platform had been written for the most part by younger male rabbis who have become more observant of the mitzvoth, who were finding holiness in traditional practices, and who wished to move from the rational ways of their German-Jewish ancestors to embrace a new spirituality. While Kessler points out that "some exponents of Classical Reform Judaism" opposed the document for its advocacy of certain ritual observances, she noted that other critics attacked the document for not being assertive enough about the importance of outreach to intermarried families and gays and lesbians. Thus from the beginning of the debate, there was pressure from both left and right. Sometimes the same groups or individuals seemed to apply contradictory pressure. Heightened ritual observance and liberal social positions were not seen as contradictory.

More central voices too criticized the original draft of the new platform. Alexander Schindler argued that the language was not inclusive enough and needed strengthening. He accepted the trend toward traditionalism as authentic and legitimate and pointed out that the language "continues trends manifest in Reform Judaism for over the last century, and is therefore simply a continuation of pre-existing trends."[8] He also believed that the document failed to emphasize adequately the Reform movement's commitment to inclusivity. After the platform passed, Schindler emphatically argued that it was of virtually no theological or even sociological significance. He told me in a telephone interview in

October 1999: "It's nothing. It's nothing from nothing. It's not good, not bad, it's not really an advance over the Centennial issue [statement] . . . it is much ado about nothing. It really is. I mean it doesn't go beyond anything that [Eugene] Borowitz said in the Centennial Statement, not one iota. So I don't know what all the hullabaloo was all about."

Others believe that the movement's embracing of contradictory trends cannot continue forever, and that the platform may serve to galvanize opposition to either neo-traditionalism or to the politically correct liberal social agenda. But it is certain that the religious trends affecting the Reform movement cannot be seen in isolation from broader sociological patterns influencing the entire American Jewish community and indeed all Americans.

Reactions from the Press—and the Spin from the Rabbinic Leadership

Most of the general press initially reported that the platform was a "radical" move toward traditionalism. The *New York Times*, in a front-page article the day after the vote, wrote that the "Statement of Principles" would "encourage the observance of traditional rituals . . . that were set aside at the movement's founding." Like most of the other general U.S. news media, the article noted only in passing that earlier drafts of the platform had specifically mentioned many of the traditional rituals that Reform Jews might consider readopting. One reason early news accounts presented such an unbalanced view was probably that many reporters had heard for months about the earlier drafts that were so traditional in their approach. Ten days after the vote, *Time* magazine titled an article on the platform "Back to the Yarmulke," although there is no mention of the yarmulke in the document, which the *Time* writer certainly knew. The article conveyed the impression that the Reform rabbis had published the platform primarily to urge the reembracing of traditional practices. An Associated Press wire report stated that the CCAR had "approved a return to traditional values such as the wearing of yarmulkes, keeping kosher and praying in Hebrew." While this was true to some degree, the emphasis on a "return to tradition" created an impression that could be misleading, even inaccurate.

Later newspaper accounts were more likely to get the story right. Three weeks after the conference, the *Las Vegas Sun* reported that the platform was far more a compromised document than an unambiguous move to the right, and that it reflected pushes and pulls in different directions.[9]

Writers for many of the regional and national Jewish newspapers were likely to stress the final draft as watered-down compared to the original proposal. Some Jewish newspapers reported that the platform had been edited in such a way and to such a degree that the Classical Reformers were the actual victors, the opposite of the national media's reading. For example, the *New York Jewish Week* wrote: "The new Platform is seen as a victory for the Classical wing of the movement, which rejected attempts by Reform leaders to inject more tradition and observance into daily practice." Others stressed that the final draft was less a religious statement than an attempt to begin healing wounds opened by Levy's advocacy of the original three drafts. Reporters had heard a great deal about the Levy cover photo that had created so much controversy, and so this made sense. Rabbi Lance Sussman noted some months after the conference that he saw schisms developing within the movement immediately following the publication of the controversial winter issue of *Reform Judaism*, and that the elected platform was in part "an attempt to keep the unraveling process from going out of control." According to this interpretation, the final drafts removed the controversial references to the performance of specific rituals in order to begin restoring consensus and equilibrium.[10]

If the goal was damage control, then the closer the 1999 platform was to the 1976 statement the better. Certainly many rabbis found the two remarkably similar, among them Rabbi Sanford Akselrad of Congregation Ner Tamid in Las Vegas: "There is nothing in it about traditional ritual that wasn't in the previous Statement of Principles, written in 1976." Akselrad, who voted in favor of the final platform, noted that many news reports had been misleading, because the final draft of the platform made no specific mention of mitzvoth. He explained that the focus on traditionalism had occurred because the debate on defining the Reform movement had been going on for a long time.[11] But this debate had not been resolved in the platform, which was as neutral as it could possibly be.

CCAR executive vice president Rabbi Paul Menitoff, who remains a strong advocate of the platform, shared his view of the media's reaction to the platform's passage with me.

> I think by and large the media—as in many ways our own people—focused in on the dramatic or radical part of . . . the principles and that's the one under the Torah section that said we're committed to the ongoing study of the whole array of mitzvot, and to the fulfillment of those that address us as individuals and a community. Some of these mitzvot have long been observed by Reform Jews. Other ones, both ancient and modern, demand renewed attention . . . as a result of the unique context of our own times. And that paragraph talks about traditionalism. It's a radical departure from a lot of what we were talking about before. And really in a very forceful way says that we as Reform Jews are open to the full range of our tradition, our sources, our sacred texts, and that we don't see any of that, of our roots, as being inferior to other segments of the Jewish people.[12]

Menitoff suggested that it was natural for journalists to focus on the most visible expression of change, because the press transmits information in concrete terms. Reporters had seen a fight going on over the nature and direction of the Reform movement, which they wanted to report. They needed a way to illustrate the actual, rather abstract, process and why this was such an important story. It was therefore understandable that reporters—particularly those writing for the general media—would stress concrete manifestations of the supposed trend toward "traditionalism." Menitoff saw their take on the platform as accurate. There had indeed been a resurgence of "tradition" throughout the Reform movement. While the final platform might not be the best indication of this trend, the movement was indisputably changing its attitude toward ritual practice. Menitoff noted that out of almost 4,500 people who attended the last UAHC conference, almost 60 percent were wearing kippot (head coverings).

At the same time, Menitoff stressed the need for accommodation toward the Classical Reformers within Reform Judaism, whose less ritualistic approach should continue to be seen as just as valid as the more traditional approach. The spiritual and intellectual search for religious meaning for all Reform Jews should continue unabated in a pluralistic atmosphere, he said.

But Classical Reformers were nevertheless voicing a great deal of concern. Many remained fearful that they were losing their own synagogues. If the Levy cover photo had generated a great deal of controversy, the national reports on the final platform further agitated many Classical Reformers, and their residual resentment would carry over to the new millennium.

The Rabbinic Evaluation of the 1999 Pittsburgh Platform

The overwhelming response of most pulpit rabbis to the platform was to equivocate. Many leaned toward a traditionalist approach but did not want to risk agitating congregants already upset by the perceived direction of the platform. After returning to their congregations, most rabbis who had attended the CCAR conference thus spoke in broad generalities: The new platform would provide opportunities for study, for discussion, and for dialogue. Many wrote articles for their synagogue newsletters praising the openness of the process but avoiding a blunt analysis of the platform itself. Part of this was due to the nature of the document. The vagueness of the final draft made it difficult to generate either great enthusiasm or fervent hostility. Some rabbis were not sure themselves what the platform meant, although they certainly understood that it was not the unconditional embrace of tradition much of the press suggested it was. But what was it? Therefore, the safest political tack was to draw attention to the platform as an opportunity to study more about Judaism and deepen one's insights. Who could object to that?

The final version of the 1999 Pittsburgh Platform was neutral enough even for many Classical Reformers. Rabbi Jeffrey Stiffman of Congregation Shaare Emeth in St. Louis, quoted in the *Forward* as very critical of the early drafts, wrote to express his satisfaction with the final result. "The Platform has much less of an emphasis on ritual and more on social action than the earlier drafts. It is more balanced."[13] But Richard Levy continued to argue that the platform did move Reform toward greater ritual practice. He told reporters that its passage indicated that many Reform Jews were moving toward traditionalism in an effort to bring holiness into their lives through a search for spiritual meaning. This was certainly his original intent, and his views are evident in some of the earlier drafts, for example, "We know that what may seem outdated in one age may be redemptive in another." But it is not at all clear that his position survives in the final document.[14]

Many rabbis stressed that the platform represented only one view of many. In his July 1999 message in Temple Sholom's newsletter, Rabbi Aaron Petuchowski suggested that it provides only a fleeting picture of where the Reform rabbinate sees the movement at this time. "It is a snapshot. Just as a snapshot cannot convey the depth and breath of its subject, nor does this statement intend to capture it all." Petuchowski emphasized the pluralistic nature of both belief and practice in Reform Judaism and noted the importance of autonomy to Reform Jews, while exploring the wide range of practice and belief available to them. He cited the Reform movement's change in attitude toward a Jewish state as an example of "the swinging pendulum of Reform ideology."[15]

A number of rabbis chose to discuss the platform in terms of the increasing amount of ritual in and out of the synagogue. Rabbi Steven Fuchs of Congregation Beth Israel in West Hartford, Connecticut, told of how he traveled to Columbia, Maryland, over the Memorial Day weekend to perform a wedding at the congregation where he had served from 1973 to 1976. He was surprised at the number of congregants there who "feared that Reform Judaism now requires adherents to keep kosher, wear yarmulkes and use more Hebrew in services." Fuchs told them, "Honestly, I do not think the Reform Judaism that the 'Principles' describe is different in any way from the Reform Judaism I have taught since I first became your rabbi twenty-six years ago." Fuchs stresses that Reform congregants were alarmed by the new "Statement of Principles" because of the way it was presented in the media. He explained that it has become common for many rabbis, cantors, and congregants to wear kippot and tallitot during services. Further, many Reform Jews observe at least some of the traditional dietary restrictions, and the overwhelming majority of Reform synagogue kitchens, while not kosher according to Orthodox standards, do not serve pork or shellfish. Therefore, the new statement was no cause for alarm. Individual congregations could continue to observe whatever degree of ritual they felt comfortable with.[16]

Many rabbis believed that to emphasize only the move toward tradition does not present a balanced perspective of the new document. Rabbi David Castiglione of Temple Beth El of Bloomfield Hills, Michigan, said that the platform "accepts and encourages ritual participation. It doesn't mandate ritual observance. But it's also quite a difference from the previous [Pittsburgh] Platform. Early Reform distanced itself from the exercise of ritual and concentrated on the intellectual pursuit of biblical scholarship and involvement in social justice."[17] He too stressed that there was nothing to be frightened of.

And yet, many were embracing long-forgotten traditions. Shortly after the platform was passed, Rabbi Harry K. Danziger of Memphis, Tennessee, announced in the temple newsletter that he would start wearing a yarmulke at services. He wanted to make it clear, however, that this decision was not a direct result of the platform: "Timing requires a disclaimer: What I share here has nothing to do with the much-publicized 'Declaration of Principles of Reform Judaism.' What is here was my intention long before that document was born. The place of the *kippah* or yarmulke has changed enormously in Reform Jewish life. For years, few American Reform Jews wore head coverings. It was virtually a symbol of being Reform to wear one no longer!"[18]

Danziger noted that a number of rabbinic interns have worn yarmulkes on the *bimah* during services in his congregation and that the rabbis and cantor have worn yarmulkes at weddings and other ceremonial occasions when requested. He said that although he had not worn a kippah during regular services for some years, he now finds religious meaning in wearing it, and so would begin to do so. If we take him at his word, Danziger is reinforcing the impression that many Reform leaders are embracing some degree of ritual observance. But this trend did not begin with the 1999 Pittsburgh Platform.

A Gap Between Rabbis and Congregants

The debate over the platform reinforced the impression that what most concerned the rabbis did not worry the congregants, and what concerned the congregants did not interest the rabbis. Speaking to about 130 Reform rabbis in a teleconference call on August 17, 1999, Eric Yoffie addressed a question submitted in advance by Rabbi Herb Brockman of Congregation Mishkan Israel of Hamden, Connecticut: Was there a noticeable "disconnect" between the leadership of the movement on one hand and many of the people in the congregations on the other? Brockman suggested that most congregants see the principles as representing the values and behavior of the movement's leaders, but holding little prescriptive value for how congregants live their lives.

Yoffie explained how he believed the dynamic worked. To understand the strong reaction from so many congregants, it is necessary to go back to the third draft, which focused on theological issues. Yoffie remarked that as president of the UAHC, he had traveled to a great many congregations throughout the country and had heard and observed how people felt about the third draft of the platform. A recurring theme that came out of these observations centered on the questions of abandoning rationalism and subordinating modernity to tradition. While the rabbis reacted on a theological level to the third draft, the laity generally focused on the draft's references to Jewish practices, such as using the *mikveh*, wearing tefillin, observing kashrut, and learning and reading the Hebrew language.

Yoffie agreed that there was a wide gap between the Reform rabbinate and lay people but not necessarily just over the "return to tradition" issue. Rather, the rabbis have focused on the theory of Reform Judaism; the lay people are concerned primarily with practical issues. It was not the advocacy of tradition that worried the congregants but what Yoffie terms the "re-ritualization of Reform Judaism." The issue is not a matter of the acceptance of halachic standards; the movement had already embraced patrilineality, gays and lesbians, and creative approaches to worship. Reform Judaism has been going through a process of "re-ritualization," and while the majority of the Reform movement has adapted to the changes, up to 33 percent of congregants today remain uncomfortable with the process. The conflict already brewing among congregants was accelerated when the new platform proposal came to light. A generational difference in ritual observance could be seen at the most recent UAHC biennial, in which twenty older officers were to be installed before 4,500 participants. Not one of the officers wore a kippah, but over half the assembly wore kippah, and many wore *tallitot* as well.

For decades, male worshipers in American Reform temples had prayed bareheaded. This practice was of course completely contrary to the traditional Jewish custom of covering one's head and was based on the American expectation that one should remove one's hat during solemn occasions and particularly during worship. But in recent decades, many Reform Jews no longer find religious meaning in this standard of decorum. Indeed, it appears that this type of formality has been rejected by American society as a whole. Rather, many are looking for a spiritual experience that is more emotional, and they feel that a ritual that draws on traditional forms can fulfill their needs.

Others see the kippah as a symbol of the traditional Judaism that they reject. They resent the reappearance of this religious symbol and remain determined to fight it as one more indication of the encroachment of Orthodoxy on Reform. The Reform movement has not taken a formal position on this or other ritual choices. According to Reform religious doctrine, one may legitimately express one's personal religious autonomy through a wide variety of rituals. Similarly, the tallith is a ritual item that Reform Jews can choose to wear or not. According to the tradition, the tallith was worn by worshippers during the morning service because the observance of *tzitzit* (the fringes hanging from the four corners of the tallith) is possible only during the daytime. But the rabbi in the Classical Reform synagogue had always worn a robe with an *atarah*, a thinner version of a tallith. Therefore, worshippers were accustomed to seeing a ritual item similar to the tallith and tended not to react as strongly to its reappearance.

Some see this pluralism as conflictual, while others see it as a sign of healthy, vigorous debate. The discourse of disagreement in the movement is based on the universal acceptance of the concept of religious autonomy. But this discourse has changed profoundly over the course of the past few years. Consciously or unconsciously influenced by postmodernism, many Reform Jews are seeking out spiritual meaning rather than basing their decisions on reasoned explanations of religious development. Others remain committed to the old ways.

While a certain percentage of congregants have been unhappy for the past ten years, they have been accepting and tolerant of the differences. So why did the one-third of Reform Jews who were uncomfortable with the process of "re-ritualization" seem to go along with the changes until now? Yoffie cites at least three reasons. The first is that Reform rabbis who grew up as Reform Jews are introducing the ritual practices. Second, the rabbis have not imposed ritual or tradition on their congregations in the past. Third, many Classical Reform–oriented congregants understood the "return to tradition" to be the result of widespread social change being willingly accepted and even embraced by the younger generation; Yoffie said they see it as a "grass roots phenomenon," changing the lives of their children and grandchildren, and on some level they are delighted to see the young people embracing rituals they left behind years ago.

That still leaves the question of why the third draft of the platform provoked such a storm of hostility. Yoffie suggests that many Classical Reformers perceived the photo of Rabbi Levy that accompanied the draft published in Reform Judaism as representing an extremely traditional image; "It would have been a totally different debate in the absence of the picture." Furthermore, many people saw the platform's passage as setting a standard for the movement, and they were not part of the consensus. They viewed it as "a credal affirmation, as an oath of allegiance, as a litmus test."[19]

Surely that is a reasonable inference for Classical Reform Jews to make. If the movement was so concerned about them, why did the CCAR propose any new platform? Or why not make sure that everyone understood the nature of the proposed platform—whatever that was— and that people felt comfortable with the process before pushing ahead?

Yoffie's central message is that the Reform movement continues to proceed in different directions simultaneously, the "return to tradition" and the boundary stretching to make the movement as inclusive as possible. And what is the message? The movement is changing, and the "re-ritualization" of Reform Judaism is a dynamic that accurately reflects the belief structure of many. It meets the needs of longtime congregants as well as the new generation of Reform Jews. The movement remains inclusive and pluralistic, embracing all in a healthy diversity.

Nevertheless, many rabbis remain troubled by what they see as an attempt to "spin" the platform to avoid facing the leadership's mistakes.

Rabbi Mark Shook of Temple Israel in Creve Coeur, Missouri, was upset by what he saw as the CCAR's manipulative portrayal of the debate. "Following the convention there was more 'spinning taking place than a dreydl in Kislev,'" Shook wrote, arguing that the platform passed at the conference was a shadow of the original.

> The "spin doctors" have arrived in the Reform movement. Faced with the reality of a movement unwilling to be coerced into becoming "Conservative Lite," the leadership of the Central Conference of American Rabbis (CCAR) was forced to present a heavily watered down statement of principles for a vote at its annual convention in Pittsburgh. The principles voted on and passed by an overwhelming majority of the convention attendees bore little resemblance to the "Ten Principles for Reform Judaism" presented last winter to the Reform community in the pages of Reform Judaism magazine. What remained was an updated version of the Centenary Perspective—Version 3.1 instead of 3.0. Women, homosexuals, and intermarrieds were all accounted for in the new version. Interfaith activity was encouraged. Despite all efforts to portray the document as a move back to 'tradition,' whatever that is, nothing of the sort took place.[20]

The final Pittsburgh Platform is thus simply a slightly updated version of the 1976 Centenary Perspective and is therefore superfluous.

Many rabbis expressed concern about the distortions in the press, noting that very little had been written about the heavy opposition by Reform laity to the earlier versions of the platform. Because the media emphasis had been on the "return to tradition," many Reform Jews were outraged over what they considered to be a betrayal by the Reform rabbinate. Even though there was much debate about returning to tradition, Shook observed, the principles "studiously avoided explicit mention of the traditions in question." Shook noted that because the platform is in no way creative or reflective of original theology, the final version is acceptable to everyone. "Nothing in the final adopted version of the principles contradicts Reform Judaism's central principle. The individual Jew is still the final authority on that level of practice that is religiously meaningful. The dreydl spins both ways."[21] In short, nothing significant had happened.

CCAR president Rabbi Charles A. Kroloff ignored such criticism. In his view the platform will prove valuable for the congregants; 90 percent of those he met with before the vote, he noted, believed that it would be a good idea to clarify the meaning and practice of Reform Judaism, and that it would help them clarify their understanding of Reform Judaism. Speaking at the August 17, 1999, teleconference, Kroloff praised the platform as an "extraordinary document," a "tremendous source for study and for personal growth." He wrote me on October 31: "It is a superb educational tool . . . it describes for all the world to see where Reform is and/or is heading. . . . It helps Reform Jews arrive at self-definition. They don't have to accept any or all points, but it provides something clear to bump up against, to test ideas, to try out new and not so new ways of looking at things. Self-definition is [an] important exercise for liberal Jews who sometimes feel like we are all things to all people." Kroloff did not acknowledge any problem with the platform or with the process of its writing and adoption. He did stress during the teleconference that nothing is obligatory, that the points are basically voluntary guidelines within the very broad sense of the Reform movement.

What Is Still Missing

The Reform movement has come forward in recent decades with a series of bold new policies that have been welcomed by some as groundbreaking and criticized by others as deviating from thousands of years of Jewish tradition, destroying any possibility for Jewish unity in the future. These new policies were not ideologically driven, but rather were practical responses to the crisis of Jewish "continuity" that has been growing since the 1960s. These innovations, rear-guard actions, attempted to control the damage that might be done to the integrity of the Jewish community. As practical strategies, they have partly succeeded. But it has become apparent that these measures are not going to be enough. Having accepted mixed married couples, gays and lesbians, and in some congregations even practicing Christians, inclusivity has reached its full potential. It may be necessary to find a new direction to keep the numbers up. But is the sole objective maintaining numerical strength? Having 700, 900, or 1,300 family units may sound impressive. But when many of these congregations are drawing only sixty, seventy, or eighty people on a Friday night and may not even have a Saturday morning service in the absence of a bar mitzvah, there is a problem.

The push toward tradition that generated so much publicity was a valiant attempt to formulate a religious vision that could captivate religious seekers. As Leon Morris observes, the movement lacks passion:

> Some will argue that a Reform document which mentions kashrut, tallit, tefillin and mikveh would alienate the masses of American Jewry with whom we rabbis are apparently out of touch. But what about all the serious Jews who leave our movement because they were never able to find the kind of religious community Reform claimed to be but never lived up to? I personally know many people who went to our summer camps and participated actively in our youth movement who reached a point where they felt that they outgrew the Reform movement. For those who do not become rabbis and cantors, there isn't enough the movement offers them. . . . Jews who desire a framework for an impassioned engaging liberal Judaism feel frustrated and go elsewhere.[22]

Concurrent with the drive for inclusiveness, there is a need for greater intensity. This was one reason so many supported the early drafts of a new platform that would send a clear message that Reform Judaism stood for passion and commitment.

Chapter 12

Where Do We Go from Here?

"Cheshire-Puss," Alice began rather timidly. . . .
"Would you tell me please, which way I ought to go
from here?"
"That depends a great deal on where you want to
go," said the cat.
"I don't much care where," said Alice.
"Then it doesn't matter which way you go," said the
cat.

—LEWIS CARROLL

CONFLICTING—one might almost say contradictory—strands run through contemporary Reform Judaism. The movement is rushing to embrace more of what used to be regarded as traditional Judaism, while eagerly accepting social innovations that even today strike many as on the left fringe. It has begun to use the word "mitzvah," which means commandment, while insisting on its commitment to personal autonomy. It seems eager to reaffirm and even reinforce its historical links with the Jewish people around the world and in particular with the State of Israel but takes measures that seem to diminish or even destroy the possibility for reconciliation and unity.

These contradictory strands emanate out of a uniquely American environment. American Jews want to hold on to their sense of familial loyalty, but they want to do it on their own terms. They want to be pragmatic and to bring their religious views into sync with the way they live their lives. They refuse to be "rejectionists," preferring to adapt to changing social conditions rather than break off from society to build an insulated Jewish life. They are thus "adaptationists," accepting consensus opinions on virtually every topic of importance. If society as a whole adopts new standards of behavior, most American Jews will go along. Reform Judaism allows them to embrace quickly changing American trends and at the same time retain a link to the past. But it is more than a link to the past. The beauty of Reform Judaism is that it allows the group to evolve consciously in response to events. Whereas in traditional Judaism, religious evolution had to be a slow and unconscious process, in Reform change can be debated and accepted. This conforms nicely with the American view of how things should be done.

In the United States, Jews are a minority in a pluralistic and multicultural environment. They carry within them the memory of their parents, and perhaps their grandparents, and the Jewish tradition their loved ones possessed and tried to pass along. This historical memory, which gives a degree of meaning to their lives, is significant only to the extent that it confirms and reinforces whatever seems of current importance. I would argue that the Reform movement has endured because it is able to walk a tightrope between the historical memory that ethnic Jews carry with them, and the contemporary spiritual relevance that so many baby boomers seek in the American religious marketplace.

Like members of other ethnic groups, American Jews have seen themselves as part of an extended family, of a group with a common past, a family into which they are born and with whom they intend to remain associated. This "historical familism" means that Jews have a responsibility for each other that transcends physical well-being. Much of this feeling survives even amidst the extensive intermarriage, low affiliation rates, and all the other manifestations of radical assimilation in twenty-first-century America. As a consequence, the synagogue attracts many Jews and has the opportunity, first, to connect with such "Jewish seekers," then to cement a bond that can develop into an enduring connection and commitment. But such a long-term relationship has to be based on values that the individual holds dear, and those values are twenty-first-century American ones. Gone is traditional Judaism's notion of the Jewish people's having a unique covenant with God that requires the observance of myriad commandments under all circumstances and at all times. Today, most American Jews are willing to observe a degree of religious ceremony, but only if it holds personal significance or practical utility for them. They follow what some have called personalism, "the tendency to transform and evaluate the tradition in terms of its utility or significance to the individual."[1]

Personalism coupled with voluntarism—the voluntary nature of what used to be regarded as obligatory commandments—defines the Reform movement structure. Reform Judaism stands firm in defense of the right of each individual to complete autonomy. Reform Jews may choose observances that they find meaningful, try out new ceremonies, or observe them on special occasions. Such Jews are not moving toward a halachic level of observance, but they may be fully practicing Reform Jews. Personal religious choice has a sanctity of its own. This approach fits the needs of American Jews both to feel a bond with their familial ancestry and to act in a way that reflects their American commitment to individualism.

Sociologists report that the coming decades may see a large increase in the number of "census Jews," people who do not deny or even reject their Jewish background but do not incorporate identifiably Jewish beliefs or practices into their lives. They also predict an increasing number of part-Jews, individuals who descend from Jewish and non-Jewish ancestors. While these trends may bode ill for the size of the American Jewish community, they open up new opportunities for the Reform movement, which is most flexible and thus best able to accommodate itself to the evolving self-definitions of American "Jews." More and more people are saying that a Jew is someone who identifies himself or herself as one. Whether or not this makes sense from a religious point of view, more and more people out there do not fit traditional definitions. The Jewish denomination able and willing to accommodate itself to this trend will be in a position to recruit substantial numbers of such individuals. One can already see the tremendous pressure on many Conservative synagogues to ignore their own movement's standards in favor of a far more flexible approach that is welcoming and inclusive.

On the other hand, the Reform movement has taken firm, decisive steps to correct its gradual slide toward low-intensity, churchlike dynamics that threaten to sap its strength and drive off many of its most enthusiastic supporters. Eric Yoffie has played a key role in this process, as have many pulpit rabbis and lay leaders. The new Reform movement has begun to embrace a wide spectrum of ceremonies and rituals that a decade or two ago would have been regarded as outside the pale. As long as this process remains moderate, it will reinvigorate the core membership while encouraging many of those on the periphery to become more involved.

No one can predict the course of the Reform movement. Without knowing how society will evolve, no one can determine the direction of a religious denomination that has tied its future so closely to that of societal trends.

Much will depend on demographics. If the American Jewish population declines, then it will be difficult to maintain the numbers necessary for a vital movement. If the trend toward post-denominationalism continues, American Jews may drop denominational affiliations in favor of Jewish religious activities unconnected with any of the major Jewish religious movements.

Financial stability will also be crucial. A younger generation is inheriting tremendous wealth, but it is uncertain if they will support Jewish causes to the same degree as their parents. The UAHC is supported by its consistent congregations, but will temples grow resentful of paying about $100 per member unit? If the economy slows down, the Union's investments may produce less income and budgetary short falls will result.

Much will also depend on what happens religiously in the State of Israel. The Reform movement has been fighting a vigorous, but so far unsuccessful, battle for full recognition in the Jewish State, possibly one of the few places in the world where Jews are still discriminated against on the basis of religion. If the Reform movement is unable to break through and achieve some measure of official recognition there, the image of the movement will suffer throughout much of the world outside the United States. Jews in, for example, Australia and France will shy away from association with a religious movement that lacks legitimacy in the one place where such legitimacy carries tremendous weight for Jews throughout the world.

Despite these threats to the position of the movement, the coming years promise to be full of excitement. The contribution of women will continue to be great, as more and more take on the responsibilities of leadership. Now that the gay and lesbian issue has largely been settled, it will be interesting to see whether that group has a noticeable impact on the movement. With the platform controversy behind it, the movement awaits the publication of a new prayer book, which I predict will find ready acceptance; many congregations are still using the *Gates of Prayer* from the mid-1970s, and those who have bought copies of the "grey book" of 1994 understand that it is only a stopgap. In any case, those who find certain sections of the new siddur less than ideal can use the accompanying CD-Rom to create their own version—a perfect example of how the ideology of the Reform movement blends seamlessly with the individualism of twenty-first-century American society.

When Alexander Schindler gave his UAHC State of the Union message in Houston in November 1983, he spoke about the problem that religious autonomy posed for the Reform movement. Schindler stressed that Reform Judaism had achieved a remarkable degree of external success, emerging as the predominant synagogue movement on the North American scene. Yet "an honest self-appraisal compels us to confess that the quality of our synagogue affiliation is lacking, that in too many instances, it is only marginal, mere form without substance." Why? Perhaps because "as liberal Jews, we assert our autonomy; we insist on the right to choose. But all too often we choose nothing at all."[2]

This problem is the sore underbelly of the Reform movement, the Achilles' heel of liberal religion. If the Reform movement is to prosper and grow, both numerically and religiously, it is going to have to develop a coherent, effective strategy for reconciling autonomy and authority. The Reform leadership, accused of having made too few demands on its constituency beyond the financial, is working overtime to address this concern and to reverse the widely held perception that Reform Judaism is only a religion of convenience and that the Reform movement is a denomination where questions are not asked and demands are not met. Schindler's warning in 1983 remains true in the new century: "Our numeric burgeoning can excite our hopes and ambitions, but our efforts will sink into nothingness unless we perceive and embrace Judaism as a serious religious enterprise."[3]

Afterword

A modern American religious movement, particularly if it is progressive in orientation, is certain to be a messy affair. The United States is a diverse country with a stubbornly individualistic population and a multiplicity of belief systems. When Americans come together to form a religious movement, they refuse to leave their proud individualism behind, especially if their religious group is a liberal one that lacks a precisely defined and authoritative theology. Thus, large American religious movements of the liberal sort are always contentious and pluralistic and caught in a constant struggle between autonomy and authority.

American Reform Judaism fits this description, and Professor Dana Kaplan has done a superb job of describing it to us. Although he does not use the word, the movement that he portrays is messy indeed. While the nature of his task forces him to impose a measure of order on his topic, the untidiness of the subject continually breaks through. What we are left with is a many-sided Reform Judaism that is vibrant, rebellious, argumentative, frequently inconsistent, and always in search of the ethical and the holy.

This book, as the title suggests, makes no attempt to offer a comprehensive history of American Reform Judaism. It focuses instead on the issues, the values, and the controversies that enable the reader to see through the conflicting trends and to grasp, as best one can, the true identity of American Reform. What can we say about the religion that emerges from Professor Kaplan's book?

We see a religion/movement that has demonstrated a cyclical pattern of growth and creativity on the one hand and retraction and stagnation on the other. Kaplan astutely describes the intellectual strengths of Classical Reform Judaism, the decline of Reform in the in the earlier part of the twentieth century, the post–World War II surge, the doubts and uncertainties of the sixties and the seventies, and the revival and confidence of the last three decades.

We see a religious tradition that is distinctively American. Reform Jews, like all Jews before them, affirm their unique destiny as part of the Jewish people and the covenant that ties them to God and extends back to Abraham and Sarah. But America as a home to Jews is unique in Jewish experience, and Kaplan notes that America has imposed its culture on Reform just as Reform Jews have enthusiastically embraced American ideals.

As I have argued elsewhere, the distinctive values of American Reform Judaism are the following: a commitment to the history and the traditions of the Jewish people combined with a commitment to change and adapt those traditions to the needs of the day; a commitment to the absolute equality of women in all areas of Jewish life; a commitment that when the boundaries of the Reform community are drawn, they will be drawn with the intention of being inclusive rather than exclusive; a commitment to social justice as a central value and organizing principle of Reform; and a commitment to enhance the role of lay people and to create a true partnership between rabbinate and volunteer leaders.

Kaplan touches upon all of these points. His chapters on women in Reform Judaism and on outreach and inclusiveness are particularly compelling. He wisely focuses on worship practice as the best example of how change actually happens in the Reform movement. We see how individual rabbis and congregations took the initiative in creating new approaches to worship, and how this grassroots phenomenon was then encouraged and promoted by national leaders. Kaplan also makes clear how complex the process of change actually is. According to conventional wisdom, change in Reform Judaism is to be equated with "becoming more traditional." But he shows that, in fact, an embrace of once-discarded rituals and other "traditional" practices coexists with a theological radicalism that has redefined the status of homosexuals in Judaism and changed the definition of who is a Jew.

Professor Kaplan mentions in passing the role of lay leaders in Reform Judaism, but it seems to me that this is an important point that does not receive adequate attention. In the Conservative and Orthodox movements, religious decisions remain primarily in rabbinical hands, while the synagogue movements are relatively weak and exert only modest influence. The synagogue arm of Reform Judaism, however, is large, high profile, and activist; the result is that lay leadership is empowered and far more involved in movement affairs than is true elsewhere. Yet interestingly enough, an empowered lay leadership has not meant constant battles between rabbis and volunteers. In fact, the opposite is true. An impressive degree of cooperation between rabbis and lay people and among the major institutions of the movement—the rabbinical body, the congregational body, and the rabbinical seminary—has developed and is the envy of the other major movements. This cooperation has created a seeming anomaly: the religious movement most committed to individual and congregational autonomy is also the religious movement that has created the strongest, most centralized national organizational structure and a national leadership that is usually able to transcend narrow institutional differences and work together to advance the values of Reform Judaism.

This volume does not hesitate to lay out the pressing problems faced by Reform Judaism in America. Professor Kaplan discusses in a straightforward manner the need for more home observance and religious passion by Reform Jews; the shortage of Reform rabbis and other Reform clergy and professionals; the complicated relations between Reform Jews and Israel, caused in some measure by the discrimination in Israel against Reform Judaism; sexual improprieties by a few leading Reform rabbis; and the simple fact that there may be limits to how much pluralism any religious movement can tolerate. These are all legitimate concerns.

He also gives considerable emphasis to the problems caused by the absence of a coherent Reform theology, using the debate over the 1999 CCAR Pittsburgh Platform as an example of the dangers of theological anarchy. While I do not agree completely with his conclusion, I found Kaplan's chapter on this platform to be fascinating.

In many ways, the story told is a humorous one. Professor Kaplan shows how the press completely misrepresented what the platform was really about and sensationalized much of the story. We also see how the various factions involved in the discussions tended to view the debate in apocalyptic terms, although these factions somehow arrived at completely opposite conclusions. Thus, some rabbis saw the final product as a betrayal of Reform's liberal principles, while others saw the watering down of the early drafts as an unfortunate and pusillanimous distancing from Reform's newfound traditionalism.

Professor Kaplan's recounting of this story is wonderful, but he mistakenly concludes that Reform's apparent theological chaos could mean that "the movement is unraveling." I suggest that there is no reason to reach such a conclusion. Indeed, in the three years since the platform was adopted, it has receded into the background, and apart from an occasional article here or there, it is rarely mentioned.

I myself had reservations about the decision to adopt a new platform, but I never felt that the process was truly dangerous or that it would lead to a split in the movement. Who can deny that Kaplan is correct when he says that theological clarity is desirable, and that it is easier to pass along one's beliefs when one knows what they are? But American Jews are resolutely pragmatic and resistant to theological speculation, and always have been. Theological struggle is to be encouraged, but the absence of theological consistency has rarely been a major problem in America for Jews of any stripe. I continue to believe, as I always have, that the major task for Reform Jews is to build on the religious revival now occurring in our ranks, to encourage Jewish study and the observance of both the ethical and the ritual *mitzvoth*, and to strengthen our ties with the Jewish people in the Land of Israel and throughout the world. In short, we need to immerse ourselves in Jewish *doing*, guided always by our liberal principles, and if we do so, appropriate theological formulation will be developed afterwards.

But whatever one thinks about Jewish theology, there is no better way to learn about Reform Judaism today, or—if one is so inclined—to begin the process of renewing oneself religiously, than by reading this wonderful book.

Eric H. Yoffie
President, Union of American Hebrew Congregations

Notes

Introduction

1. This expression is used by Deborah Dash Moore in *At Home in America: Second Generation New York Jews* (New York: Columbia University Press, 1981).
2. Eric H. Yoffie, "Realizing God's Promise: Reform Judaism in the 21st Century," address, Sixty-fifth UAHC Biennial Convention, Orlando, Fla., 1999, 2–3; see *http://uahc.org/orlando/speakers/ysermon.shtml*.
3. Roger Finke and Rodney Stark, *The Churching of America, 1776–1990: Winners and Losers in Our Religious Economy* (New Brunswick, N.J.: Rutgers University Press, 1992), 40.

Chapter 1 A Historical Overview

1. Richard Hirsh, "Two Trains Passing: Reconstructionism and Reform in Twentieth-Century American Judaism," in Dana Evan Kaplan, ed., *Platforms and Prayerbooks: Theological and Liturgical Perspectives on Reform Judaism* (Lanham, Md: Rowman and Littlefield, 2002), 183–206. My thanks to Serena Leigh for all of her help in the editing of that manuscript, and Erin McKindley for her assistance during the production phase.
2. Hasia Diner and others have demonstrated that many of the "German" Jews were actually Polish, Bohemian, Moravian, Slovakian, French or even eastern European. See Hasia R. Diner, *A Time for Gathering: The Second Migration, 1820–1880* (Baltimore: Johns Hopkins University Press, 1992), 49. On Jewish conversion to Christianity, see Todd M. Endelman, ed., *Jewish Apostasy in the Modern World* (New York: Holmes and Meier, 1987).
3. Max Weiner, *Abraham Geiger and Liberal Judaism: The Challenge of the Nineteenth Century*, translated from the German by Ernst J. Schlochauer (Cincinnati: Hebrew Union College Press, 1981); and Susannah Heschel, *Abraham Geiger and the Jewish Jesus* (Chicago: University of Chicago Press, 1998).
4. Michael A. Meyer, "Alienated Intellectuals in the Camp of Religious Reform: The Frankfort Reform Freunde, 1842–1845," *AJS Review* 6 (1981): 61–86.
5. For an overview of the social history and sociology of the American Jewish community from its origins until the early 1980s, see Chaim I. Waxman, *America's Jews in Transition* (Philadelphia: Temple University Press, 1983).
6. Gary P. Zola, "The First Reform Prayer Book in America: The Liturgy of the Reformed Society of Israelites," in Kaplan, *Platforms and Prayerbooks*, 99–117. The prayer book was edited by Isaac Harby, David Nunes Carvalho, and Abra-

ham Moïse. Robert Liberles, "Conflict over Reforms: The Case of Congregation Beth Elohim, Charleston, South Carolina," in Jack Wertheimer, ed., *The American Synagogue—A Sanctuary Transformed* (Hanover, N.H.: Brandeis University Press, 1989), 274–296.

7. Gary Phillip Zola, *Isaac Harby of Charleston, 1788–1828: Jewish Reformer and Intellectual* (Tuscaloosa: University of Alabama Press, 1994).

8. Avraham Barkai, *Branching Out: German-Jewish Immigration to the United States, 1820–1914* (New York: Holmes and Meier, 1994).

9. Leon Jick, *The Americanization of the Synagogue, 1820–1870* (Hanover, N.H.: Brandeis University Press, 1992).

10. James G. Heller, *Isaac M. Wise: His Life, Work, and Thought* (New York: UAHC Press, 1965); and Sefton D. Temkin, *Isaac Mayer Wise: Shaping American Judaism* (Oxford: Littman Library of Jewish Civilization, 1992).

11. Wise and Lilienthal both founded congregations in Cincinnati, where they continued to work together closely. On Lilienthal's congregation, see Jonathan D. Sarna and Karla Goldman, "From Synagogue-Community to Citadel of Reform: The History of K. K. Bene Israel," in *American Congregations*, vol. 1, ed. James P. Wind and James W. Lewis (Chicago: University of Chicago Press, 1994), 159–220; also see Karla Goldman, "In Search of an American Judaism: Rivalry and Reform in the Growth of Two Cincinnati Synagogues," in Jeffrey S. Gurock and Marc Lee Raphael, eds., *An Inventory of Promises: Essays on American Jewish History in Honor of Moses Rischin* (Brooklyn, N.Y.: Carlson, 1995), 137–150, with notes on 355–359.

12. On liturgical developments in American Reform, see Eric L. Friedland, *"Were Our Mouths Filled with Song": Studies in Liberal Jewish Liturgy* (Cincinnati: Hebrew Union College Press, 1997).

13. Isaac Mayer Wise, ed., *Minhag Amerika: Tefillot Beney Yeshurun/Daily Prayers* (Cincinnati: Bloch, 1857). For a description of this prayer book, see Friedland, *Were Our Mouths Filled with Song*, 50–54.

14. Lance J. Sussman, introduction to Kerry M. Olitzky, Lance J. Sussman and Malcolm H. Stern, eds., *Reform Judaism in America: A Biographical Dictionary and Sourcebook* (Westport, Conn.: Greenwood Press, 1993), xv.

15. Michael A. Meyer, "Thank You, Moritz Loth: A 125-Year UAHC Retrospective," *Reform Judaism*, fall 1998, 30–39.

16. Author interview with Elliot L. Stevens, CCAR, New York, March 2001.

17. See, for example, Aryeh Rubinstein, "Isaac Mayer Wise: A New Appraisal," *Jewish Social Studies* 39 (winter/spring 1977): 53–74. Rubinstein concludes that "Wise's conservative pronouncements were only lip-service, while his rationalist, Deist-like statements represented his true opinions. . . . what makes Wise so complex is that his opportunism impelled him to cover his tracks" (74).

18. Benny Kraut, *From Reform Judaism to Ethical Culture: The Religious Evolution of Felix Adler* (Cincinnati: Hebrew Union College Press, 1979).

19. "Authentic Report of the Proceedings of Rabbinical Conference Held in Pittsburgh, November 16, 17, 18, 1885," in Walter Jacob, ed., *The Changing World of Reform Judaism: The Pittsburgh Platform in Retrospect* (Pittsburgh: Rodef Shalom Congregation, 1985), 91–123.

20. Max Wiener, "The Conception of Mission in Traditional and Modern Judaism," *YIVO Annual of Jewish Social Science* 9 (1947/1948): 2–3.

21. Emil Hirsch, *My Religion* (New York: Macmillan, 1925).

22. Yaakov Ariel, "Miss Daisy's Planet: The Strange World of Reform Judaism in the United States, 1870–1930," in Kaplan, *Platforms and Prayerbooks*, 50.

23. Dana Evan Kaplan, "W. E. Todd's Attempt to Convert to Judaism and Study for the Reform Rabbinate in 1896," *American Jewish History* 83, 4 (1995): 429–444.

24. Edward N. Calisch Collection, file SC–1558, Jacob R. Marcus Center of the American Jewish Archives, HUC-JIR, Cincinnati, Ohio.

25. Henry L. Feingold, *A Time for Searching: Entering the Mainstream, 1920–1945* (Baltimore: Johns Hopkins University Press, 1992).

26. Edward S. Shapiro, *A Time for Healing: American Jews Since World War II* (Baltimore: Johns Hopkins Press, 1992).

27. Maurice N. Eisendrath, *Can Faith Survive? The Thoughts and Afterthoughts of an American Rabbi* (New York: McGraw-Hill, 1964).

28. Samuel E. Karff, ed., *At One Hundred Years: Hebrew Union College–Jewish Institute of Religion* (Cincinnati: Hebrew Union College Press, 1976).

29. Author interview with Catherine Kahn, New Orleans, April 2000.

30. During the 1980s and 1990s, numerous local Jewish Federations conducted sociological studies within certain geographical boundaries of those identifying themselves as Jews. See Ira M. Sheskin, ed., *How Jewish Communities Differ: Variations in the Findings of Local Jewish Population Studies* (New York: Mandell L. Berman Institute/North American Jewish Data Bank, 2001), 72–73. My thanks to Jonathan Gibs for helping with this source.

31. There are many possible explanations for why the percentage of Reform Jews varies. How the specific survey was conducted may certainly be one factor. But generally speaking, the older established Jewish communities with relatively small Orthodox contingents in the Midwest and South have relatively high percentages of Reform Jews. At the other end of the spectrum, the larger urban communities with many first-generation immigrants have lower percentages. The percentage of Reform Jews reported in various communal studies is as follows. In Florida: Broward County, 24%; Martin–St. Lucie Counties, 51%; Orlando, 30%; Sarasota, 47%; St. Petersburg, 39%; South Broward County, 28%; South Palm Beach, 28%; West Palm Beach, 34%. In the rest of the South: Atlanta, 34%; Charlotte, 40%; Dallas, 48%; Richmond, 29%; Tidewater, Va., 33%. In New Jersey: Atlantic County, 29%; Essex-Morris Counties, 42%; Monmouth, 26%. In Pennsylvania: Harrisburg, 22%; Philadelphia, 28%; York, 48%. In the rest of the Northeast: Baltimore, 29%; Boston, 41%; Buffalo, 33%; Hartford, 40%; Rhode Island, 32%; Rochester, 41%; Washington, D.C., 38%; Wilmington, Del., 29%; Worcester, Mass., 49%. In the West: Denver, 37%; Los Angeles, 40%; Palm Springs, 42%; Phoenix, 49%; San Francisco Bay Area, 42%; Seattle, 33%. In the Midwest: Columbus, 41%; Detroit, 34%; Toronto (Can.), 24%.

32. "Report of the Committee on Patrilineal Descent on the Status of Children Mixed Marriages," CCAR report and resolution, 1983; available at CCAR, New York.

Chapter 2 An Introduction to Reform Jewish Belief

1. For a basic text on the beliefs and practices of Judaism written from a Reform perspective, see, for example, Morris N. Kertzer, *What Is a Jew?* revised by Lawrence A. Hoffman (New York: Collier Books, 1993). For a detailed description of Reform practice and its justifications, see Mark Washofsky, *Jewish Living: A Guide to Contemporary Reform Practice* (New York: UAHC Press, 2001).

2. Neil Gillman, "Four Basic Religious Issues That Divide Us," *Moment*, May 1988, 42–45.

3. Maurice Eisendrath, *Can Faith Survive? The Thoughts and Afterthoughts of an American Rabbi* (New York: McGraw-Hill, 1964), 243–244.

4. Kertzer, *What Is a Jew?* 31, 32.

5. Kaufman [sic] Kohler, *Hebrew Union College and Other Addresses* (Cincinnati: Ark, 1916), 164.

6. *Charleston Carrier*, March 20 1841, quoted in W. Gunther Plaut, *The Growth of Reform Judaism: American and European Sources until 1948* (New York: World Union for Progressive Judaism, 1965), 9.

7. Max Lilienthal, "Here Is Our Zion," quoted in Plaut, *The Growth of Reform Judaism*, 145.

8. On the historical school, see Moshe Davis, *The Emergence of Conservative Judaism: The Historical School in 19th Century America* (Philadelphia: Jewish Publication Society of America, 1963).

9. Moritz Lazarus, *The Ethics of Judaism*, vol. 2 (Philadelphia: Jewish Publication Society, 1900–1901), 123.

10. Marshall Sklare and Joseph Greenblum, *Jewish Identity on the Suburban Frontier*, 2d ed. (Chicago: University of Chicago Press, 1979), 57.

11. Bernhard Felsenthal, *Kol Kore Bamidbar Über jüdische Reform* (Chicago: Chicago Sinai Congregation, 1859), 30, quoted in Plaut, *The Growth of Reform Judaism*, 265–266. See Deut. 14:21; also Lev. 11:44, 20–25.

12. Ibid.

13. *www.ccarnet.org*.

14. Joseph Krauskopf, "Fifty Years of Judaism in America," in *American Jews' Annual* (Cincinnati: Bloch, 1888), 73.

15. Solomon B. Freehof, "Reform Judaism and the Halacha," *CCAR Yearbook* 56 (1946): 279.

16. W. Gunther Plaut, *A Shabbat Manual* (New York: CCAR Press, 1972).

17. Eugene B. Borowitz, *Liberal Judaism* (New York: Union of American Hebrew Congregations, 1984), 410.

Chapter 3   The Evolution of American Reform Theology

1. Brennan R. Hill, Paul Knitter, and William Madges, *Faith, Religion and Theology: A Contemporary Introduction* (Mystic, Conn.: Twenty-third Publications, 1991), 251.

2. I have argued that there is a connection between the perception of religious crisis and the writing of each of the Reform platforms. See Dana E. Kaplan, "Reform Jewish Theology and the Sociology of Liberal Religion in America: The Platforms as Response to the Perception of Socioreligious Crisis," *Modern Judaism*, February 2000, 60–77.

3. The 1885 platform was written before the founding of the Central Conference of American Rabbis (CCAR) in 1889. In the first *Yearbook*, the CCAR reprinted earlier statements and platforms, including the Pittsburgh Platform, but no vote was ever taken on it.

4. Alexander Kohut, *The Ethics of the Fathers* (New York: American Hebrew, 1885), quoted in Michael A. Meyer, *Response to Modernity: A History of the Reform Movement in Judaism* (New York: Oxford University Press, 1988), 267.

5. On the Pittsburgh Platform, see Walter Jacob, ed., *The Changing World of Reform Judaism: The Pittsburgh Platform in Retrospect* (Pittsburgh: Rodef Sha-

lom, 1985). Also see the review on this collection by Jonathan D. Sarna, "New Light on the Pittsburgh Platform of 1885," *American Jewish History* 76 (1986–1987): 358–368.

6. Kohler wrote a number of books, including his masterpiece, *Jewish Theology, Systematically and Historically Considered* (New York: Macmillan, 1918). Many of his essays have been collected in *Hebrew Union College and Other Addresses* (Cincinnati: Ark, 1916); *Studies, Addresses, and Personal Papers* (New York: Bloch, 1931); and Samuel S. Cohon, ed., *A Living Faith* (Cincinnati: Hebrew Union College Press, 1948).

7. David Kaufman, *Shul with a Pool: The "Synagogue-Center" in American Jewish History* (Hanover, N.H.: Brandeis University Press, 1999), 13.

8. Morris Selz, *The American Jewish Archives*, manuscript collection 56, 2/4.

9. Jacob Neusner, "When Reform Judaism Was Judaism," in Dana Evan Kaplan, ed., *Contemporary Debates on American Reform Judaism: Conflicting Visions* (New York: Routledge, 2001), 69.

10. Meyer, *Response to Modernity*, 297. This book is the classic account of the Reform movement.

11. Beth S. Wenger, *New York Jews and the Great Depression: Uncertain Promise* (New Haven: Yale University Press, 1996), 166.

12. On HUC, see Samuel E. Karff, ed., *Hebrew Union College–Jewish Institute of Religion at One Hundred Years* (Cincinnati: Hebrew Union College Press, 1976).

13. Louis Binstock, "Dogma and Judaism," *CCAR Yearbook* 35 (1935): 266.

14. Some of Cohon's writings include Samuel S. Cohon, *What We Jews Believe* (Cincinnati: Hebrew Union College Press, 1931); *Judaism: A Way of Life* (Cincinnati: Hebrew Union College Press, 1948). For an overview of his views of the Reform movement, see his "Reform Judaism in America," *Judaism* 3 (1954): 333–353. On his perspective on the theology of the Reform movement of the time and how he felt it should change, see his analysis of the Union Prayer Book: "The Theology of the UPB," *CCAR Yearbook* 38 (1928): 246–294. For an overview of Cohon's thought, see Michael A. Meyer, "Samuel S. Cohon: Reformer of Reform Judaism," *Judaism* 15 (1966): 319–328.

15. Samuel Cohon, "Report on the Guiding Principles of Reform Judaism," *CCAR Yearbook* 36 (1936): 104.

16. Meyer, *Response to Modernity*, 369.

17. Eugene B. Borowitz, *Reform Judaism Today*, vol. 1, *Reform in the Process of Change* (New York: Behrman House, 1983), xii.

18. Ibid.

19. "Reform Judaism: A Centenary Perspective (1976)," printed in its entirety in Meyer, *Response to Modernity*, 391–394. The perspective can also be found on the CCAR web site, www.ccarnet.org.

20. Sherwin T. Wine, *Judaism Beyond God: A Radical New Way to Be Jewish* (Farmington Hills, Mich.: Society for Humanistic Judaism, 1985).

21. Lawrence Bush, "Focus On: The God Debate. Can We Accept a Congregation That Does Not Worship God?" *Reform Judaism*, winter 1994, 25.

22. Later, Donald Day, president of the World Union for Progressive Judaism, would successfully refute such objections by pointing out that article 3, section 1 of the constitution included the phrase "upon approval by the Board of Trustees," which justified the UAHC's right to exclude a congregation. Day also pointed out that the preamble's words "under protection of benign Providence" would prevent Beth Adam from affirming the constitution in good conscience.

23. This same gap in perception would resurface in the UAHC vote on religious school restrictions on children being raised in more than one religion. Small congregations in remote locations are likely to express a much greater degree of tolerance.

24. W. Gunther Plaut, "Learning as a Road to Faith," in Michael Brown and Bernard Lightman, eds., _Creating the Jewish Future_ (Walnut Creek, Calif.: Alta-Mira, 1999), 60.

25. Robert Bellah, Richard Madsen, William Sullivan, Ann Swidler, and Steven Tipton, _Habits of the Heart: Individualism and Commitment in American Life_ (Berkeley: University of California Press, 1996).

26. Herbert Weiner, _9 1/2 Mystics: The Kabbala Today_ (New York: Collier, 1992); first published in 1969.

27. David A. Cooper, _God Is a Verb: Kabbalah and the Practice of Mystical Judaism_ (New York: Riverhead Books, 1997).

28. For example, see Nilton Bonder, _The Kabbalah of Envy: Transforming Hatred, Anger, and Other Negative Emotions_, trans. Julia Michaels (Boston: Shambhala, 1997).

29. Heather Robinson, "Meet the Rock 'n' Roll Rabbi," _Reform Judaism_, fall 2002, 79.

30. William Janz, "As Woman's Best Friend, a Dalmatian Gets His Due, _Milwaukee Journal Sentinel_, July 13, 1997. I would like to thank Kelly Jackson for her help in locating material relating to this episode.

31. David Cohen, "Ceremony of Thanks for Dog Was No Joke for Grateful Family," letter to the editor, _Wisconsin Jewish Chronicle_, August 8, 1997, 11.

32. David Cohen, correspondence with the author, September 3, 2002.

33. Peter Pitzele, _Our Father's Wells: A Personal Encounter with the Myths of Genesis_ (San Francisco: HarperSanFrancisco, 1995); Carol Ochs, _Our Lives as Torah: Finding God in Our Own Stories_ (San Francisco: Jossey–Bass, 2001).

34. "Renewing Spiritual Life and Leadership," promotional literature, Jossey–Bass, 2001.

35. Eugene B. Borowitz, _Liberal Judaism_ (New York: Union of American Hebrew Congregations, 1984), 129–131.

Chapter 4 The Reform Revolution of the 1990s

1. Eric H. Yoffie, "Realizing God's Promise: Reform Judaism in the 21st Century," address, Sixty-fifth UAHC Biennial Convention, Orlando, Fla., 1999, 2–3; see _http://uahc.org/orlando/speakers/ysermon.shtml_.

2. Ibid.

3. Ibid.

4. Charles S. Liebman and Steven M. Cohen, _Two Worlds of Judaism: The Israeli and American Experiences_ (New Haven: Yale University Press, 1990), 124. The information is from an unpublished 1988 study, Steven M. Cohen and Paul Ritterband, "The Utilization of Jewish Communal Services in Queens and Long Island," United Jewish Appeal/Federation of Jewish Philanthropies, New York.

5. Roger Finke and Rodney Stark, _The Churching of America, 1776–1990: Winners and Losers in Our Religious Economy_ (New Brunswick, N.J.: Rutgers University Press, 1992), 254. This theme will be explored in more depth in chapter 8.

6. Howard Lovy, "Can Shul Be Cool?" _www.beliefnet.com_, October 22, 2000.

7. Commission on Religious Living, "UAHC Worship Initiatives," _www.uahc.org_.

8. Eric H. Yoffie, "Thoughts on the Ten Principles: Closing Remarks to the Board of Trustees," speech delivered in Memphis, Tenn., December 5, 1998; see *UAHC Report*, "Remarks from the President," 6.

9. Julia Goldman, "Reform Judaism Confronts 'Crisis' over Rabbi Shortage," *Forward*, *www.forward.com/issues/2001/01.02.09/news2.html*.

10. Gary Zola, correspondence with the author, November 2001.

11. Ellenson has written more than two hundred articles and three books: *Tradition in Transition: Orthodoxy, Halakhah, and the Boundaries of Modern Jewish Identity* (Lanham, Md.: University Press of America, 1989), *Rabbi Esriel Hildesheimer and the Creation of a Modern Jewish Orthodoxy* (Tuscaloosa: University of Alabama Press, 1991), and *Between Tradition and Culture: The Dialectics of Modern Jewish Religion and Identity* (Lanham, Md.: University Press of America, 1994).

12. Netty C. Gross, "The Dynamic Reformer," *Jerusalem Report*, December 3, 2001, *http://www.jrep.com/Jewishworld/Article-10.html*.

13. Lewis M. Barth, "Two Very Important Programmatic Developments," memo, February 25, 1999, author's files; "Hebrew Union College–Jewish Institute of Religion's Board of Governors Approves Ordination at Los Angeles School," HUC–JIR press release, February 19, 1999.

14. Andy Altman–Ohr, "Area Rabbis Praise Pluralistic Seminary Planned for Los Angeles," *Jewish Bulletin of Northern California*, September 24, 1999, 12A; also see "Los Angeles Getting New Seminary," *Forward*, July 2, 1999, 3.

15. "HUC at 125," *New York Jewish Week*, April 13, 2001, 3.

16. Sheldon Zimmerman, letter to colleagues, April 26, 1999.

17. Goldman, "Reform Judaism Confronts 'Crisis.'"

18. Charles A. Kroloff, correspondence with the author, April 2001.

19. Liebman and Cohen, *Two Worlds of Judaism*, 124–126.

20. Ibid, 126.

21. Sheldon Zimmerman, "Transforming the Reform Jew," in Dana Evan Kaplan, ed., *Contemporary Debates in American Reform Judaism: Conflicting Visions* (New York: Routledge, 2001), 249–250.

Chapter 5 The Worship Revolution in the Synagogue

1. For example, Arnold Jacob Wolf wrote: "Like most of his allies, including myself, he grew up in Reform Judaism, but with no need to find reasons to reject an Orthodoxy he had never known. But, donning Tallit and T'fillin for a cover story in *Reform Judaism* magazine, he unleashed a hailstorm of dissent and unfair recrimination." "Reforming Reform Judaism," *Judaism* 48, 3 (summer 1999): 368.

2. Richard N. Levy, "Ten Principles of Reform Judaism," *Reform Judaism*, winter 1998, 14–16.

3. David A. Whiman, "Reform Judaism's Little Black Book," *Congregation Beth Israel Bulletin* (Houston), September 1, 2000, 1.

4. Chaim Stern, ed., *Gates of Prayer* (New York: CCAR Press, 1975).

5. Caesar Seligman, Ismar Elbogen, and Hermann Vogelstein, eds., *Einheitsgebetbuch* (Frankfort am Main: M. Lehrberger, 1929). On the *Einheitsgebetbuch*, see Jacob J. Petuchowski, "The Development and Design of a German-Jewish Prayerbook," in Moses Rischin and Raphael Asher, eds., *The Jewish Legacy and the German Conscience* (Berkeley, Calif.: Judah L. Magnes Museum, 1991), 171–187.

6. David Einhorn, *Olath Tamid: Gebetbuch fur Israelitische Reform Gemeinden*

(New York: Thalmessigner and Cahn, 1858). For an analysis of this prayer book, see Eric L. Friedland, "David Einhorn and Olath Tamid," in *Were Our Mouths Filled with Song": Studies in Liberal Jewish Liturgy* (Cincinnati: Hebrew Union College Press, 1997), 17–49.

7. Isaac Mayer Wise, *Minhag Amerika: Tefillot Beney Yeshurun/Daily Prayers* (Cincinnati: Bloch, 1857). A revised edition was issued as *Minhag Amerika/The Daily Prayers for American Israelites* (Cincinnati: Bloch, 1872).

8. Kaufmann Kohler, "The Origin and Functions of Ceremonies in Judaism," *CCAR Yearbook* 17 (1907), 226. The text is reprinted in Michael A. Meyer and W. Gunther Plaut, eds., *The Reform Judaism Reader: North American Documents* (New York: UAHC Press, 2001), 104.

9. David Polish, ed., *Maaglei Tzedek-Rabbi's Manual* (New York: CCAR Press, 1988), 229, 30. The text is reprinted in Meyer and Plaut, eds., *The Reform Judaism Reader,* 105–106.

10. Author interview with Alan Bitterman, Albany, Georgia, May 2002.

11. Jack Stern, "Observations of a Rabbi Who Never Became a Bar Mitzvah," *Reform Judaism,* winter 1997, 15, 16.

12. Lawrence A. Hoffman, "The Liturgical Question," in *Gates of Understanding* (New York: CCAR Press, 1977), 3.

13. Herbert Bronstein, *A Passover Haggadah* (New York: CCAR Press, 1974).

14. A. Stanley Dreyfus, remarks on the dedication of *Gates of Prayer,* from Lawrence A. Hoffman, "The Liturgical Question," in *Gates of Understanding* (New York: Central Conference of American Rabbis, 1977), 8, note 1.

15. Stern, *Gates of Prayer,* xi–xii.

16. David Ellenson, "Reform Judaism in Present-day America: The Evidence of the *Gates of Prayer,*" in Abraham J. Karp, Louis Jacobs, Chaim Zalman Dimitrovsky, eds., *Threescore and Ten: Essays in Honor of Rabbi Seymour J. Cohen on the Occasion of His Seventieth Birthday* (Hoboken, N.J.: KTAV, 1991), 379. I would like to thank David Ellenson for presenting me with a copy of this essay.

17. Michael P. Sternfield, introduction to *The Union Prayerbook,* Sinai edition (Chicago: Chicago Sinai Congregation, 2000), v.

18. Peter S. Knobel, "The Challenge of a Single Prayer Book for the Reform Movement," in Dana Evan Kaplan, ed., *Platforms and Prayerbooks: Theological and Liturgical Perspectives on Reform Judaism* (Lanham, Md.: Rowman and Littlefield, 2002), 161.

19. Elyse Frishman, "An Update on the New Siddur, *CCAR Newsletter,* September 2002, 2.

20. Michael Sternfield, correspondence with the author, July 10, 2002.

21. Interview with Amanda Chau in Albany, Georgia, September 11, 2002.

22. Author telephone interview with Rabbi Joel Levine of West Palm Beach, Florida, September 2002.

23. Peter S. Knobel, *Gates of Repentance for Young People* (New York: CCAR Press, 2002), iii.

24. Eric H. Yoffie, "Iv'du B'Simchah: Worship with Joy" in UAHC *Worship Initiatives,* booklet, author's files.

25. *Let Us Learn in Order to Do: A Study Program for Worship/Ritual Committees* and *Entering the Dialogue: A Procedure for Self–Study of Congregational Worship.* This UAHC workbook was adapted from the CCAR study, *Lay Involvement in the Development of Liturgy.*

26. Yoffie, "Iv'du B'Simchah."

27. Summit is quoted in Michael Endelman, "Turning to the Spiritual Sounds of

Synagogue Life: A Book Examines the Relationship Between Ritual Music and American Jewish Identity," *Forward*, April 13, 2001; *www.forward.com/issues/2001/01.04.13*. See also Jeffrey A. Summit, *The Lord's Song in a Strange Land: Music and Identity in Contemporary Jewish Worship* (New York: Oxford University Press, 2000).

28. Endelman, "Turning to the Spiritual Sounds."
29. E. J. Kessler, "Rabbis Bucking for Friday Nights at the 'Synaplex': Trend Sees Practice of Holding Several Smaller Minyans Within a Synagogue," *Forward*, June 5, 1998, 2.
30. Ibid., 1.
31. On religion in the 1960s, see Robert S. Ellwood, *The Sixties Spiritual Awakening: American Religion Moving from Modern to Postmodern* (New Brunswick, N.J.: Rutgers University Press, 1994).
32. Kessler, "Rabbis Bucking for Friday Nights," 2.
33. Elliott Abrams and David G. Dalin, eds., *Secularism, Spirituality, and the Future of American Jewry* (Washington, D.C.: Ethics and Public Policy Center, 1999), 57–58.
34. Kessler, "Rabbis Bucking for Friday Nights," 2.
35. Lawrence Hoffman, "Why Congregations Need to Change," *Reform Judaism*, summer 2000, 78; for more on Synagogue 2000, see *www.s2k.org/index.html*.
36. The quoted material throughout the description Westchester's project is from Richard Jacobs, "Forsaking the Status Quo in Scarsdale: How We Transformed Westchester Reform Temple," *Reform Judaism*, summer 2000, 51–59.
37. Samuel G. Freeman, *Jew vs. Jew: The Struggle for the Soul of American Jewry* (New York: Simon and Schuster, 2000), 338.
38. Jacobs, "Forsaking the Status Quo," 59.
39. Benton Johnson, "On Church and Sects," *American Sociological Review* 28 (1963): 539–549.
40. Roger Finke and Rodney Stark, *The Churching of America, 1776–1990: Winners and Losers in Our Religious Economy* (New Brunswick, N.J.: Rutgers University Press, 1992), 40.
41. H. Richard Niebuhr, *The Social Sources of Denominationalism* (New York: Holt, 1929).
42. Roger Finke and Rodney Stark, *Acts of Faith: Explaining the Human Side of Religion* (Berkeley: University of California Press, 2000), 273.
43. The 1990 National Jewish Population Survey found that 74 percent of the eighteen- to twenty-nine-year-olds "always or usually" light Hanukkah, compared to only 53 percent of those over age fifty; 78 percent of the younger group "very often" attend a Seder, compared to 65 percent of those over fifty; 61 percent of the younger group fasts on Yom Kippur, versus 44 percent of those over fifty; and 39 percent of those in the younger group buy kosher, versus 24 percent of those over fifty. The percentages decline over the entire spectrum of cohort groups.
44. Sylvia Barack Fishman, *Jewish Life and American Culture* (Albany: State University of New York Press, 2000).
45. Author interview with Kathy Butt, Milwaukee, April 1998.
46. Evan Moffic, correspondence with the author, July 5, 2002.
47. Religious Action Center of Reform Judaism, promotional literature, author's files.
48. "Saperstein, Marking a Milestone, Disputes a Rightward Drift," *Forward*, April 23, 1999, 1, 21.

49. Leonard Fein, *Where Are We? The Inner Life of America's Jews* (New York: Harper and Row, 1989).
50. Leonard Fein, "These Statistics Don't Lie," *Forward*, April 20, 2001, 13.
51. Ibid.
52. Dan Polish, "Capital Punishment on Trial: Does Judaism Condone Capital Punishment?" *Reform Judaism*, summer 2002, *www.uahc.org/rjmag/02summer/focus.shtml*. Also see the WRJ website, *www.RJ.org/WRJ*.
53. Ibid.
54. Evely Laser Shlensky, "Jewish Faith and Social Justice (1994)," in Michael A. Meyer and W. Gunther Plaut, eds., *The Reform Judaism Reader: North American Documents* (New York: UHC Press, 2001), 156. Originally published as "Wholeness and Holiness: Social Justice as a Vital Component of Religious Living, *New Menorah*, summer 1994, 5,11.
55. Terry Bookman, *God 101: Jewish Ideals, Beliefs, and Practices for Renewing Your Faith* (New York: Perigee, 2000), 132.
56. Joe Eskenazi, "800 Jews, Catholics Join Rodef Sholom 'Mitzvah Day'," *Jewish Bulletin of Northern California*, November 10, 2000, 33A.
57. See *www.S2K.org*
58. George Gallup, Jr., and Jim Castelli, *The People's Religion: American Faith in the 1990s* (New York: Macmillan, 1989), 15, 116.
59. David Kaufman, *Shul with a Pool: The "Synagogue–Center" in American Jewish History* (Hanover, N.H.: Brandeis University Press, 1999), 285.

Chapter 6 The Struggle for Recognition in the State of Israel

1. Daniel J. Elazar and Rela Mintz Geffen, *The Conservative Movement in Judaism: Dilemmas and Opportunities* (Albany: State University of New York Press, 2000), 131.
2. Bernard Lazerwitz, J. Alan Winter, Arnold Dashefsky, and Ephraim Tabory, *Jewish Choices: American Jewish Denominationalism* (Albany: State University of New York Press, 1998).
3. Ephraim Tabory, "The Legitimacy of Reform Judaism: The Impact of Israel on the United States," in Dana Evan Kaplan, ed., *Contemporary Debates in American Reform Judaism: Conflicting Visions* (New York: Routledge, 2001), 221.
4. Matthew Gutman, "New Campaign for Jerusalem Pol: Religious Pluralism," *Forward*, May 31, 2002, *www.forward.com/issues/2002/02.05.31/news10.html*.
5. Charles S. Liebman and Steven M. Cohen, *Two Worlds of Judaism: The Israeli and American Experiences* (New Haven: Yale University Press, 1990), 9. They are following up on an observation made by the late Israeli scholar Uriel Tal.
6. Wendy Elliman, "Reform Judaism Creates Its Own Israeli Identity," *Jewish Post of New York*, October 1998, *www.jewishpost.com/jp0410/jpn0410b.html*.
7. Ammiel Hirsch, "The Making of a New Zionist Platform", *Reform Judaism*, Winter 1997, 65.
8. Ibid.
9. *WUPJnews*, October 7, 1999, *www.WUPJ.org*.
10. Ibid., April 19, 2000, *www.WUPJ.org*.
11. Ibid., September 25, 2000, *www.WUPJ.org*
12. Elliman, "Reform Judaism."
13. Ibid.
14. Ibid.

15. Gary Rosenblatt, "American Jewish–Israel Bond Continues to Fray Despite Intifada," *Kansas City Jewish Chronicle*, June 1, 2001, 27A.

16. For an overview of this phenomenon up to the late 1980s, see Chaim I. Waxman, *American Aliya: Portrait of an Innovative Migration Movement* (Detroit: Wayne State University Press, 1989).

17. Steven T. Rosenthal, *Irreconcilable Differences? The Waning of the American Jewish Love Affair with Israel* (Hanover, N.H.: Brandeis University Press, 2001), 31.

18. Ibid., xv.

19. Joe Eskenazi, "S.F. Rabbi Now Doubts Palestinians Ever Wanted Peace," *Jewish Bulletin News of Northern California*, March 15, 2002, http://www.jewishsf.com/bk020315/sfp10a.shtml.

20. Spencer Michels, "Split Sentiments," *Online NewsHour*, April 15, 2002, http://www.pbs.org/newshour/bb/middle_east/jan–june02/split_4–15.html.

21. Nathan Jones, "U.S. Reform Judaism Leader Denounces Netanyahu Policies," *Washington Report*, March 1997, www.washington-report.org/backissues/0397/9703045.html

22. Ibid.

23. Paul Menitoff, letter to George W. Bush, "Bush Must Intervene Forcefully in the Middle East Conflict," August 7, 2002, http://www.ccarnet.org/menitoff.html

24. Alexandra J. Wall, "'Refusenik' Speaker at Emanu–El Event Stirs Backlash," *Jewish Bulletin*, June14, 2002, 20A.

25. Stephen Pearce, correspondence with the author, July 7, 2002.

26. Elliman, "Reform Judaism."

Chapter 7 New Challenges in Reform Jewish Education

1. Emanuel Gamoran, "The Role of Jewish Education in Developing a Creative Jewish Center in America," *Jewish Education*, fall 1952, 15–16.

2. Michael A. Meyer, "Reflection of the 'Educated Jew' from the Perspective of Reform Judaism," *CCAR Journal*, spring 1999, 8, 9.

3. Ibid., 20.

4. Jonathan S. Woocher, *Sacred Survival: The Civil Religion of American Jews* (Bloomington: Indiana University Press, 1986), 67–68.

5. Jonathan S. Woocher, "Spirituality and the Civil Religion," in Elliot Abrams and David G. Dalin, eds., *Secularism, Spirituality and the Future of American Jewry* (Washington, D.C.: Ethics and Public Policy Center, 1999), 19–25.

6. Sara Bershtel and Allen Graubard, *Saving Remnants: Feeling Jewish in America* (New York: Free Press, 1992), 43.

7. This phrase is from Wade Clark Roof, *A Generation of Seekers: The Spirituality Journeys of the Baby Boom Generation* (San Francisco: HarperSanFrancisco, 1993).

8. For an analysis of the NJPS data connected to young people, see Ariela Keyser, Barry A. Kosmin, and Jeffrey Scheckner, *The Next Generation: Jewish Children and Adolescents* (Albany: State University of New York Press, 2000).

9. Michael Lerner, *Jewish Renewal: A Path to Healing and Transformation* (New York: Grosset/Putnam, 1994), 1.

10. D. R. Miller, "The Study of Social Relationships: Situation and Identity and Sound Interaction," in S. Kerch, ed., *Psychology: A Study of Science* (New York: McGraw-Hill, 1963).

11. Lee Hockstader, "'Selling' Jewishness: Program Flies Youths to Israel," *Washington Post*, January 17, 2000.

12. Janet Marder, "The Trouble with . . . Jewish Education," *Reform Judaism*, summer 1993, 19.
13. Ibid.
14. "Breaking Out of the Educational Box," *Congregation Beth Israel Bulletin* (Houston), December 15, 1998, 1.
15. Marder, "The Trouble with . . . Jewish Education," 19.
16. Michael Hechter, *Principles of Group Solidarity* (Berkeley: University of California Press, 1987), 27.
17. Jan Katzew, "How Can We Make Hebrew Schools Work Again: With Right Priorities, Learning in the Home Becomes the Primary Focus," *Forward*, January 19, 2001, 17.
18. Ibid.
19. Elissa Gootman, "Hebrew Schools May Land a New Role," *Forward*, November 6, 1998, 14.
20. Emily Grotta, "Leader of Reform Judaism Calls for Overhaul of Religious Education," press release, December 8, 2001, *http://www.uahc.org/pr/2001/011208. html*.
21. "New York Day School Finds Itself in Mother of all Brouhahas," *Forward*, May 18, 2001, *www.forward.com/issues/2001/01.05.18/news3.html*.
22. A. Smith, I. Cohen, and T. Hanover, "Memo on the Temple Youth Group Leader Assembly," UAHC, New York, July 1997, author's files.
23. Eric H. Yoffie, speech to the UAHC board, Memphis, Tenn., December 1998, author's files.
24. North American Federation of Temple Youth, *http://shamash.org/reform/nfty/index.html*.
25. "Renaissance Drive Turns to Youth Groups," *Forward*, December 11, 1998, 18.
26. Lee T. Bycel, "Thinking Ahead to Summer," *Anshe Chesed Fairmount Temple (Cleveland, Ohio) Bulletin*, January 7, 2000, 2.
27. Jane Ulman, "Jewish Overnight Camp Is Powerful Antidote to Alienation," *Jewish Bulletin of Northern California*, August 21, 1998, 17.
28. Bycel, "Thinking Ahead to Summer," 2.
29. Olin-Sang-Ruby Union Institute, promotional literature.
30. Pauline Dubkin Yearwood, "Camp Spirit: Olin-Sang-Ruby Union Institute Celebrates a Half-Century of Bringing Judaism Out of Doors and into the Hearts of Reform Jewish Kids," *Chicago Jewish News*, July 21–27, 2000, 11.
31. Yearwood, "Camp Spirit."
32. Hank Bordowitz, "Singing unto God," *Reform Judaism*, summer 2002, 65.
33. "Torah Study," resolution adopted by the General Assembly, Union of American Hebrew Congregations, Dallas, Texas, October 29–November 2, 1997.
34. Debra Nussbaum Cohen, "Jewish Education: Never Too Late," *Chicago Jewish News*, November 13–19, 1998, 13.
35. Ibid.
36. Joshua Schuster, "A First for Reform Synagogues—Beth Am Hires Rabbi for Adult Ed," *Jewish Bulletin of Northern California*, November 20, 1998, 30.
37. Ibid.
38. Author interview with Leon Morris, New York, April 16, 2001.
39. Abrams and Dalin, *Secularism*, 55.
40. *Kallah 2000* (New York: UAHC Department of Adult Jewish Growth, 2000), 13.
41. Ibid.

42. *Live Together, Learn Together: A Congregational Kallah Retreat Manual* (New York: UAHC, 2000), 1.

Chapter 8   **The Outreach Campaign**

1. Elihu Bergman, "The American Jewish Population Erosion," *Midstream*, October 1977, 9–19.
2. Samuel S. Lieberman and Morton Weinfeld, "Demographic Trends and Jewish Survival," *Midstream*, November 1978, 9–19.
3. Charles E. Silberman, *A Certain People: American Jews and Their Lives Today* (New York: Summit Books, 1985), 83.
4. Jonathan D. Sarna, "The Secret of Jewish Continuity," *Commentary*, October 1994, 55.
5. Ephraim Z. Buchwald, "Stop the Silent Holocaust," letter to the editor, *Moment*, December 1992, 4.
6. Quoted in Craig Horowitz, "Declining Birth Rates. Rampant Intermarriage. The 'Seinfeld Effect.' Are American Jews Assimilating Themselves out of Existence?" *New York*, July 14, 1997, 31–37.
7. Ephraim Buchwald, "Conversion and the American Jewish Agenda," *Judaism*, summer 1999, 274.
8. Alexander M. Schindler, "The Case for a Missionary Judaism," in Steve Israel and Seth Forman, eds., *Great Jewish Speeches Throughout History* (Northvale, N.J.: Jason Aronson, 1994), 244. Succeeding quotations from this speech are cited by page number in the text.
9. Jerrold Goldstein and Arlene Sarah Chernow, "Intermarriage," letters column, *Jewish Journal of Greater Los Angeles*, March 16, 2001, 4.
10. Sidney Goldstein and Alice Goldstein, *Jews on the Move* (Albany: State University of New York, 1996).
11. Patricia Gober, "Americans on the Move," Population Bulletin 4, November 1993, 2–40.
12. Ami Eden, "Reform 'Plays Matchmaker,'" *Forward*, April 13, 2001, 1.
13. Ibid.
14. Goldstein and Goldstein, *Jews on the Move*, 5–6.
15. Enid Weiss, "Life Full of Contradictions for Black Jewish T.V. Actor," *Jewish Bulletin of Northern California*, April 2, 1999, 42.
16. Elicia Brown, "From Bangkok to BJ—and Back," *New York Jewish Week*, July 14, 2000, 46.
17. "Young Congregant Speaks from the Heart," *Anshe Chesed Fairmount Temple (Cleveland, Ohio)*, January, 2001, 3.
18. Colleen Slevin, "Convert Takes Another Leap of Faith—Enters Rabbinate," *Jewish Bulletin*, April 5, 2002, 52.
19. Rachel Brand, "Rocky Road to the Rabbinate," *Jewish Journal of Greater Los Angeles*, www.jewishjournal.com/home/preview.php?id=8508.
20. Joshua Schuster, "Asian Jewish Woman Faces Confused Looks," *Chicago Jewish News*, August 27–September 2, 1999, 18–19.
21. Ibid.
22. Ibid.
23. Joshua Brandt, "How Jews Blend Three Cultures with Asian Adoptions," *Jewish Bulletin of Northern California*, August 25, 2000, 1.
24. Author interview with Gary Glickstein, Miami, June 2002.

25. Claudio Javier Kogan. "Elu V'Elu," *Hakol (Miami, Fla.)*, July 2002, 2, 10.
26. "The Status of Children of Mixed Marriages," resolution adopted by CCAR, March 15, 1983. See www.ccarnet.org.
27. "Enrollment Policies in Reform Religious Schools," resolution adopted by the General Assembly, Union of American Hebrew Congregations, Atlanta, November 30–December 3, 1995. The complete text of this resolution can be found at *www.uahc.org.*
28. "The Resolution: Enrollment Policies in Reform Religious Schools," *Reform Judaism*, spring 1996, 59.
29. Harris Gilbert and George Markley, "Choosing Exclusion? Why Outreach Proposed This Resolution," *Reform Judaism*, spring 1996, 58.
30. Gustav Neibuhr, "For Jews, a Little Push for Converts, and a Lot of Angst," *New York Times*, June 13, 1999, 3.
31. Alexander M. Schindler, "Not by Birth Alone: The Case for a Missionary Judaism," in Dana Evan Kaplan, ed., *Contemporary Debates in American Reform Judaism: Conflicting Visions* (New York: Routledge, 2001), 135.
32. Beth M. Gilbert, "Judaism Found", *Reform Judaism*, Spring 1999, 52, 53.
33. Ibid., 51, 52.
34. Ibid., 52, 54. For more information on the Commission on Synagogue Affiliation, see website *http://uhac.org/synaff.*
35. Debra Nussbaum Cohen, "Forty Seven Percent of Rabbis in Two Movements Conducting Intermarriages," *Jewish Bulletin of Northern California*, March 22, 1996, *http://jewishsf.com/bk960322/usrabbis.html.*
36. Jacques Cukierkorn, correspondence with the author, May 2, 2002.
37. Cohen, "Forty Seven Percent of Rabbis."
38. Barry A. Kosmin, Sidney Goldstein, Joseph Waksberg, Nava Lerer, Ariella Keysar, and Jeffrey Scheckner, *Highlights of the CJF 1990 National Jewish Population Survey* (New York: Council of Jewish Federations, 1991), 4,13–16.
39. Cohen, "Forty Seven Percent of Rabbis."
40. Michael Goldberg, *Why Should Jews Survive? Looking Past the Holocausts Toward a Jewish Future* (New York: Oxford University Press, 1995), 136–37.
41. Dana Evan Kaplan, "Reform Jewish Theology and the Sociology of Liberal Religion in America: The Platforms as Response to the Perception of Socioreligious Crisis," *Modern Judaism*, February 2000, 60–77.
42. See Rodney Stark, "The Economics of Piety: Religion and Social Class," in Gerald W. Thielbar and Saul D. Feldman, eds., *Issues in Social Inequality* (Boston: Little, Brown, 1972); "Church and Sect," in Phillip E. Hammond, ed., *The Sacred in a Secular Age* (Berkeley: University of California Press, 1985); "Do Catholic Societies Exist?" paper presented at the annual meeting of the Society for the Scientific Study of Religion, Virginia Beach, Va., 1990; "Antioch as the Social Situation for Matthew's Gospel," in David L. Balch, ed., *Social History of the Matthean Community: Cross-Disciplinary Approaches to an Open Question* (Minneapolis: Fortress Press, 1991); and "The Reliability of Historical U.S. Census Data on Religion," *Sociological Analysis* 53, 1 (1992): 91–95.

    Also see Dean Kelley, *Why Conservative Churches Are Growing: A Study in the Sociology of Religion* (Macon, Ga.: Mercer University Press, 1986), and Laurence R. Iannaccone, "Sacrifice and Stigma: Reducing Free-Riding in Cults, Communes, and Other Collectives," *Journal of Political Economy* 100, 2 (1992): 271–292; "Religious Practice: A Human Capital Approach," *Journal for the Scientific Study of Religion* 29, 3 (1990): 297–314; "Why Strict Churches Are Strong," *American Journal of Sociology* 99, 5 (1994): 1180–1211; and "Risk, Rationality, and Religious Portfolios," *Economic Inquiry* 33, 2 (1995): 285–295.

43. See Roger Finke, "Demographics of Religious Participation: An Ecological Approach, 1850–1980," *Journal for the Scientific Study of Religion* 28, 1 (1989): 45–58; also,Finke and Rodney Stark, "Turning Pews into People: Estimating Nineteenth-Century Church Membership," *Journal for the Scientific Study of Religion* 25, 2 (1986): 180–192 and "Religious Economies and Sacred Canopies: Religious Mobilization in American Cities, 1906," *American Sociological Review* 53, 1 (1988): 41–49.

   Also see Charles Y. Glock, "The Religious Revival in America?" in Jane Zahn, ed., *Religion and the Face of America* (Berkeley: University of California Press, 1959), 25–42, and "The Role of Deprivation in the Origin and Evolution of Religious Groups," in Robert Lee and Martin E. Marty, eds., *Religion and Social Conflict* (New York: Oxford University Press, 1964), 24–36; and Charles Y. Glock and Rodney Stark, *"Religion and Society in Tension* (Chicago: Rand McNally, 1965) and *Christian Beliefs and Anti-Semitism* (New York: Harper and Row, 1966).

   See also William Sims Bainbridge, "Collective Behavior and Social Movements," in Rodney Stark, ed., *Sociology* (Belmont, Calif.: Wadsworth, 1985); and Rodney Stark and William Sims Bainbridge, "Networks of Faith: Interpersonal Bonds and Recruitment to Cults and Sects," *American Journal of Sociology* 85, 6 (1980): 1376–1395; *The Future of Religion: Secularization, Revival, and Cult Formation* (Berkeley: University of California Press, 1985); and *A Theory of Religion* (New York: Lang, 1987).

44. Roger Finke and Rodney Stark, *The Churching of America, 1776 to 1990 Winners and Losers in Our Religious Economy* (New Brunswick, N.J.: Rutgers University Press, 1992), 5. On Stark as a sociologist of American religious history, see David G. Hackett, "Rodney Stark and the Sociology of American Religious History," *Journal for the Scientific Study of Religion* 29, 3 (1990): 372–376. For a more critical view, see Philip K. Goff, "Spiritual Enrichment and the Bull Market: Balancing the Books of American Religious History," *Religious Studies Review* 22, 2 (1996): 106–112. Goff writes that despite the fact that Finke and Stark write well, their book *The Churching of America* "is so wrought with problems that readers will invariably distrust the occasions when Finke and Stark are on the mark" (107).

45. Debra Renee Kaufman, "Better the Devil You Know . . . and Other Contemporary Identity Narratives: Comparing Orthodox to Reform Judaism," in Dana Evan Kaplan, ed., *Platforms and Prayerbooks: Liturgical and Theological Perspectives on Reform Judaism* (Lanham, Md.: Rowman and Littlefield, 2002), 223.

46. Rodney Stark, *The Rise of Christianity* (San Francisco: HarperSanFrancisco, 1997), 175. See the recent set of essays on this book by reviewers Willi Braun, Burton Mack, and Randall Collins, with an introduction by Russell T. McCutcheon, "A Symposium on Rodney Stark's *The Rise of Christianity,*" *Religious Studies Review* 25, 2 (1999): 127–139.

47. Benton Johnson, Dean R. Hoge, and Donald A. Luidens, "Mainline Churches: The Real Reason for Decline," *First Things* 31 (1993): 18.

48. Jack Wertheimer, *A People Divided: Judaism in Contemporary America* (Hanover, N.H.: Brandeis University Press, 1997), 96.

49. Jacob Neusner, "When Reform Judaism Was Judaism," in Kaplan, *Contemporary Debates*, 69–89.
50. Wertheimer, *A People Divided*, 96.
51. The only restriction would be that it may not cross over certain "red lines," such as introducing overtly Christian elements, which would be objectionable primarily for crossing the boundary out of Jewish identity. It would also be theologically inconsistent, but that would be far less likely to bother the congregational leadership.
52. Walter Jacob, "Standards Now," *Reform Judaism*, fall 1992, 64. Jacob has continued the work of his predecessor, Solomon Freehof, at Congregation Rodef Shalom, who published a number of collections of Reform Responsa literature. See Walter Jacob, ed., *American Reform Responsa* (New York: CCAR Press, 1983), *Contemporary American Reform Responsa* (New York: CCAR Press, 1987), and others.
53. Wade Clark Roof, *A Generation of Seekers: The Spiritual Journeys of the Baby Boom Generation* (San Francisco: HarperSanFrancisco, 1993), 30.
54. Eric H. Yoffie, correspondence with the author, April 27, 2000.
55. "The Orlando Biennial Album," *Reform Judaism*, spring 2000, 37.
56. Eric H. Yoffie, "The Importance of Outreach in Maintaining Reform's Autonomy, Diversity, and Pluralism," in Kaplan, *Contemporary Debates*, 150.
57. Ibid., 151.

Chapter 9 *The Struggle for Women's Equality*

1. For an overview of this subject, see James Davison Hunter, *Culture Wars: The Struggle to Define America* (New York: Basic Books, 1991). For another view, see Todd Gitlin, *The Twilight of Common Dreams: Why America Is Wracked by Culture Wars* (New York: Holt, 1995).
2. For a history of Jewish women in twentieth-century America, see Joyce Antler, *The Journey Home: Jewish Women and the American Century* (New York: Free Press, 1997). For a slightly dated but still useful description of American Jewish feminism, see Sylvia Barack Fishman, *A Breath of Life: Feminism in the American Jewish Community* (New York: Free Press, 1993).
3. Judith Hauptman, "Conservative Judaism: The Ethical Challenge of Feminist Change," in Robert M. Seltzer and Norman J. Cohen, eds., *The Americanization of the Jews* (New York: New York University Press, 1995), 296.
4. Simeon J. Maslin, "Yes, There Is a Reform Divorce Document," *Reform Judaism*, spring 2000, 47.
5. On this conference, see *The German Rabbinical Conferences, 1844–1846*, with an introduction by M. Meyer, trans. Z. Jacobson (Jerusalem: Dinur Center, Hebrew University, 1986), 47–65.
6. Isaac Mayer Wise, *Minhag Amerika: Tefillot Beney Yeshurun/Daily Prayers* (Cincinnati: Bloch, 1857). A revised edition was issued as *Minhag Amerika/The Daily Prayers for American Israelites* (Cincinnati: Bloch, 1872).
7. Kaufmann Kohler, "Conference Paper," in Walter Jacob, ed., *The Changing World of Reform Judaism: The Pittsburgh Platform in Retrospect* (Pittsburgh: Rodef Shalom Congregation, 1985), 96.
8. Rachel Adler, paper delivered at Brandeis-Bardin Institute, June 1983.
9. I use the term "myth" as religious studies does to refer to a commonly held understanding of the origins and history of a particular faith. The use of the term does not imply that such a religious story is fictitious.

10. On the history of women in the rabbinate, see Pamela Nadell, *Women Who Would Be Rabbis* (Boston: Beacon Press, 1998). Also see Ellen M. Umansky, "Women's Journey Toward Rabbinic Ordination," 27–41, and Jonathan D. Sarna, "From Antoinette Brown Blackwell to Sally Priesand: An Historical Perspective on the Emergence of Women in the American Rabbinate," 43–53, both in Gary P. Zola, ed., *Women Rabbis: Exploration and Celebration* (Cincinnati: HUC–JIR Rabbinic Alumni Association Press, 1996).

11. Frank's papers can be found under her married name, Ray Frank Litman, at the American Jewish Historical Society in New York.

12. "Majority Report of the Committee on the Question of Graduating Women as Rabbis," HUC Correspondence, Miscellaneous File, Jacob R. Marcus Center of the American Jewish Archives, HUC-JIR, Cincinnati, Ohio.

13. *CCAR Yearbook* 22 (1922): 51.

14. Chaim Stern, ed., *The Gates of Prayer for Shabbat and Weekdays: A Gender-Sensitive Prayer Book* (New York: CCAR Press, 1994).

15. "The Inaugural Rabbi Sally J. Priesand Visiting Professor of Jewish Studies: Dr. Tikva Frymer-Kensky," *Chronicle*, no. 58 (1995): 7.

16. Author interview with Jean Rosensaft, Senior National Director for Public Affairs and Institution Planning, HUC-JIR, New York, February 20, 2002.

17. The issue of the feminization of the American Christian clergy has been discussed for a number of years. See, for example Paula D. Nesbitt, *Feminization of the Clergy in America: Occupational and Organizational Perspectives* (New York: Oxford University Press, 1997).

18. Fishman, *A Breath of Life*, 201.

19. Vicki Cabot, "On Shabbos the Rabbis Wear Skirts," *Greater Phoenix Jewish News*, September 11, 1992, 10–11.

20. Author interview with Michael and Linda Lieberman, April 5, 2002.

21. Melanie Aron, correspondence with the author, July 8, 2002.

22. Emily Feigenson, "A Message from the Rabbi," *Leo Baeck Temple Bulletin* (Los Angeles), May 2000, 2.

23. Ibid.

24. Janet Marder, "How Women Are Changing the Rabbinate," *Reform Judaism*, summer 1991, 5.

25. Lisa Keys, "Feting a Feminist Rabbi Who Broke 'Stained–Glass Ceiling,'" *Forward*, May 18, 2001, *www.forward.com/issue/2001/01.05.18/news5.html*.

26. An early and still influential attempt is Judith Plaskow, *Standing Again at Sinai: Judaism from a Feminist Perspective* (San Francisco: Harper and Row, 1990). See also Lynn Davidman and Shelly Tenenbaum, eds., *Feminist Perspective on Jewish Studies* (New Haven: Yale University Press, 1994). One of the most influential feminist scholars is Daniel Boyarin; see his *Carnal Israel: Reading Sex in Talmudic Culture* (Berkeley: University of California, 1993).

27. Miriam Peskowitz and Laura Levitt, eds., *Judaism Since Gender* (New York: Routledge, 1997).

28. Ellen M. Umansky, "Piety, Persuasion, and Friendship: A History of Jewish Women's Spirituality" in Ellen M. Umansky and Dianne Ashton, eds., *Four Centuries of Jewish Women's Spirituality* (Boston: Beacon Press, 1992), 23.

29. Rachel Adler, *Engendering Judaism: An Inclusive Theology and Ethics* (Boston: Beacon Press, 1999).

30. See Sylvia Boorstein, *That's Funny, You Don't Look Buddhist: On Being A Faith-*

ful Jew and a Passionate Buddhist (San Francisco: HarperSanFrancisco, 1997); Melinda Ribner, *New Age Judaism: Ancient Wisdom for the Modern World* (Deerfield Beach, Fla.: Simcha Press, 1999).

31. Marcia Falk, *The Book of Blessings: New Jewish Prayers for Daily Life, the Sabbath, and the Moon Festival* (Boston: Beacon Press, 1996)

32. Lynn Gottlieb, *She Who Dwells Within: A Feminist Vision of a Renewed Judaism* (San Francisco: HarperSanFrancisco, 1995).

33. Rachel Adler, "In Your Blood, Live: Re-visions of a Theology of Purity," *Tikkun*, January–February 1993, 38–41.

34. Susannah Heschel, review of *Engendering Judaism* by Rachel Adler, *Journal of the American Academy of Religion* 67, 2 (June 1999): 473–476.

35. Adler, *Engendering Judaism*, xiv.

36. Rachel Adler, "*The Jew Who Wasn't There*: Halakhah and the Jewish Woman," in *The Jewish Woman: An Anthology. Response* (1973), 77–82; reprinted in Jacob Neusner, ed., *Signposts on the Way of Torah* (Belmont, Calif.: Wadsworth, 1998), 82–87.

37. On Nevison, see "Cantor Ordered to Stand Trial," *Newsday*, April 17, 2002, *http://newsday.com/news/local/newyork/ny-cantor0418.story*; on Jacobs, see Debra Nussbaum Cohen, "Last in a Series: 'Conspiracy of Silence' Fuels Rabbis' Sexual Misdeeds," *Jewish Bulletin of Northern California*, 1996, *http://www.jewishsf.com/bk961101/1blast.html*; on Neulander, see Richard Jerome, "Judgment Day," *People*, November 12, 2001, 69–70; Suzanne Pollak, "Rabbi's Murder Trial Shines Spotlight on Jewish Mourning, Intermarriage," *JTA–Global Jewish News*, *http://www.jta.org/story.asp?story=8813*.

38. Andy Altman-Ohr, "Kirschner Assesses Scandal and His Life," *Jewish Bulletin News of Northern California*, April 28, 2000, *http://www.jewishsf.com/bk000428/pagenews.shtml*.

39. Debra Nussbaum Cohen and Natalie Weinstein, "Rabbi Robert Kirschner Apologizes," *Jewish Bulletin of Northern California*, October 18, 1996, *http://www.jewishsf.com/bk961018/1brabbi.html*.

40. Fred Rosenbaum, *Visions of Reform: Congregation Emanu-El and the Jews of San Francisco, 1849–1999* (Berkeley: Judah L. Magnes Museum, 2000).

41. Altman-Ohr, "Kirschner Assesses Scandal."

42. Cohen, "Last in a Series."

43. For a broad view of American political sex scandals from the early Republic until the 1960s, see John H. Summer, "What Happened to Sex Scandals? Politics and Peccadilloes, Jefferson to Kennedy," *Journal of American History*, December 2000, 825–854.

44. Burton Lehman, correspondence with the author, December 4, 2000.

45. Steward Ain, "HUC Head Resigns; Sexual Misconduct Cited," *New York Jewish Week*, December 8, 2000, 1, 32.

46. Ibid.

47. Douglas LeBlanc, "Bishop to Be Punished Nineteen Years After Affair," *Christianity Today*, February 5, 2001, 20.

48. Debra Nussbaum Cohen, "How Serious Is Sexual Misconduct?" *New York Jewish Week*, April 13, 2001, 8.

49. Ami Eden, "Reform Leader's Departure Seen Leaving Huge Gap at Seminary," *Forward*, December 22, 2001, *www.forward.com/issues/2000/00.12.15/news5. html*; Susannah Heschel, "The Glass Ceiling at Hebrew Union College," letter to the editor, *Forward*, January 19, 2001, 8.

50. "From a Minyan of Men to Women's Studies," *HUC–JIR 2000–2001 Annual Report*, 6, author's files.

51. Author interview with Efrat Zohar, Miami, May 2001.

52. "Faculty Spotlight," *Chronicle*, no. 59 (2001): 10–11.

53. E. J. Kessler, "Women in their Place," *Forward*, April 7, 2000, 9.

54. Ibid.

55. During the 2000 presidential elections many polls found a dramatic difference between men and women, not only over which candidate they supported for president, but also in how they perceived the outcome of political events such as debates. A far higher percentage of women supported Al Gore over George W. Bush because they perceived him as being more "compassionate."

56. Aviva Cantor, *Jewish Women/Jewish Men: The Legacy of Patriarchy in Jewish Life* (San Francisco: HarperSanFrancisco, 1995).

Chapter 10 The Acceptance of Gays and Lesbians

1. Mark Washofsky, *Jewish Living: A Guide to Contemporary Reform Practice* (New York: UAHC Press, 2001), 321.

2. Norman Lamm, "Judaism and the Modern Attitude to Homosexuality," *Encyclopedia Judaica Yearbook 1974* (Jerusalem: Keter, 1974), 203.

3. Denise L. Eger, correspondence with the author, July 2, 2002.

4. David M. Feldman, "Homosexuality and Jewish Law," *Judaism* 32 (fall 1983): 429.

5. Margaret Moers Wenig, "Truly Welcoming Lesbian and Gay Jews," in Aron Hirt-Manheimer, ed., *The Jewish Condition: Essays on Contemporary Judaism Honoring Rabbi Alexander M. Schindler* (New York: UAHC Press, 1995), 327.

6. Denise L. Eger, "Embracing Lesbians and Gay Men: A Reform Jewish Innovation," in Dana Evan Kaplan, ed., *Contemporary Debates on American Reform Judaism: Conflicting Visions* (New York: Routledge, 2001), 180.

7. Melissa Minkin, "Celebration of 'Life': The First Lesbian and Gay Synagogue Marks Its 30th Anniversary, *Jewish Journal of Greater Los Angeles*, June 28, 2002; *www.jewishjournal.com/home/searchview.phd?id=8797*.

8. Ibid.

9. "Judaism and Homosexuality," *CCAR Journal*, summer 1973, 33.

10. Author interview with Rabbi Allen B. Bennett, July 3, 2002. Additional quotes from Bennett, and Bennett's quoting of Alexander Schindler and Joseph Glaser in this section, are taken from this interview.

11. Interview with Camille Angel, San Francisco, September 23, 2002.

12. The four articles were: Robert Kirschner, "Halakhah and Homosexuality: A Reappraisal"; Eugene B. Borowitz, "On Homosexuality and the Rabbinate, a Covenantal Response"; Yoel H. Kahn, "Judaism and Homosexuality"; and Peter S. Knobel, "Homosexuality: A Liberal Jewish Theological and Ethical Reflection."

13. *Report of the CCAR Ad Hoc Committee on Homosexuality in the Rabbinate*, 1990, CCAR Archives, New York.

14. Janet Marder, "Our Invisible Rabbis," *Reform Judaism*, winter 1990, 5–12.

15. Ibid.

16. *Report , , , on Homosexuality in the Rabbinate.*

17. T. J. Michels, "Tarzana Rabbi to Give First Public Talk Here on Coming Out," *Jewish Bulletin*, October 26, 2001, 32A and 33A.

18. Berger and Kravitz are quoted in Marder, "Our Invisible Rabbis," 9.
19. Jack Wertheimer, *A People Divided: Judaism in Contemporary America* (Hanover, N.H.: Brandeis University Press, 1997).
20. Marder, "Our Invisible Rabbis," 12. Also see Marc Angel, Hillel Goldberg, and Pinchas Stolper, "Homosexuality and the Orthodox Jewish Community," *Jewish Action* 53, 2 (1992): 54.
21. Moshe David Tendler, "Extravagant Forbearance," *Jerusalem Report* 49, October 8, 1992.
22. Eger correspondence.
23. "On Gay and Lesbian Marriage," resolution adopted at the 107th CCAR Convention, March 1996, CCAR Archives, New York.
24. "Civil Marriage for Gay and Lesbian Jewish Couples," resolution adopted by the General Assembly, Union of American Hebrew Congregations, Dallas, Texas, October 29–November 2, 1997, UAHC Archives, New York.
25. CCAR, *Ad Hoc Committee on Human Sexuality Report to the CCAR Convention,* June 1998, CCAR Archives, New York.
26. Stewart Ain, "Reform Divided over Gay Unions" *New York Jewish Week* April 24, 1998, 1, 16.
27. Author interview with Dow Marmur, CCAR Conference, Anaheim, Calif., June 1998.
28. "Same Gender Officiation," resolution adopted at the 111th CCAR Convention, March 2000, CCAR Archives, New York.
29. Lisa Edwards, "From the Rabbi's Study," *G'vanim,* May 2000, 1; Valerie Lieber, "Perspectives," *Newsweek,* April 10, 2000.
30. "Same Gender Officiation."
31. Julie Wiener, "Critical Response: Reform Vote on Gay Ceremonies 'Not a Jewish Move,' Orthodox Say," *Jewish Journal of Greater Los Angeles,* April 28, 2000, 22–23.
32. Ibid., 22, 23.
33. "Same Gender Officiation."
34. Julie Wiener, "Reform Rabbis Back Gay Unions," *Jewish Bulletin of Northern California,* March 31, 2000, 1, 49.
35. Howard Voss-Altman, "A Revolutionary Moment," *North Shore Congregation Israel Bulletin (Chicago),* May 5, 2000, 1, 3.
36. Stewart Ain, "Shifting Stance on Intermarriage," *New York Jewish Week,* October 24, 1997, 12.
37. Voss–Altman, "A Revolutionary Moment," 1, 3.
38. Daniel L. Rabishaw, "How Do Reform Jews Make Jewish Decisions?" *Congregation Beth Israel Bulletin* (Houston), May 1, 2000, 1.
39. Ibid.
40. Paul Menitoff, "Boycott the Boy Scouts", *Reform Judaism,* Winter 2000, 104.
41. Jade Chang, "Between Heaven and Earth: A New Home for L.A. Congregation," *Forward,* February 15, 2002, 17.
42. Ibid.

Chapter 11   The Battle over the Future of Reform Judaism

1. Daniel Freelander, correspondence with the author, October 23, 2000.
2. Simeon J. Maslin, ed., *Gates of Mitzvah: A Guide to the Jewish Life Cycle* (New York: CCAR, 1979).
3. Shimeon J. Maslin, correspondence with the author, January 15, 2001. The

four essays were: Herman E. Schaalman, "The Divine Authority of the Mitzvah"; David Polish, "History as the Source of the Mitzvah"; Roland B. Gittelsohn, "Mitzvah Without Miracles"; and Arthur J. Lelyveld, "Mitzvah: The Larger Context."

4. Richard N. Levy, "The Reform Synagogue: Plight and Possibility." Jacob Neusner (ed.), *Understanding American Judaism: Toward a Description of a Modern Religion, Vol. 2, Sectors of American Judaism: Reform, Orthodoxy, Conservatism, and Reconstructionism.* (New York: Ktav, 1975), 64. The entire article appears on pages 63–83. Originally published in *Judaism*, Vol. 18, No. 2 (1969): 159–176.

5. Beth Sampson Bauer, Paul Uhlmann Jr., and Henry A. Fribourg, Letters to the Editor, *Reform Judaism*, spring 1999, 6, 7, 8.

6. David Davidson, "The UAHC Board Comments," in *Reform Judaism*, spring 1999, 17.

7. E. J. Kessler, "Reform Gets Set to Turn Toward Jewish Tradition, Draft Principles Suggest," in *Forward*, September 18, 1998, 1.

8. Ibid.

9. *New York Times*, May 27, 1999; D. Van Biema, "Back to the Yarmulke . . . ," *Time*, June 7, 1999, 65; S. J. Willis, "Reformed Reform? Jewish Leaders Say Platform Misunderstood," *Las Vegas Sun*, June 14, 1999.

10. *New York Jewish Week*, May 28, 1999; Lance Sussman, correspondence with the author, August 6, 1999.

11. Willis, "Reformed Reform?"

12. Author interview with Rabbi Paul Menitoff, April 2001.

13. J. B. Stiffman, "The Vitality of Reform Judaism," *Shaare Emeth Temple Bulletin* (St. Louis), June 11, 1999, 2.

14. Willis, "Reformed Reform?"

15. Aaron Mark Petuchowski, "The Value of a Snapshot," *Temple Sholom Bulletin (Chicago)*, July 1999, 1–10.

16. Steven Fuchs, "A Reaction to a Statement of Principles for Reform Judaism Adopted at the 1999 Pittsburgh Convention of the Central Conference of American Rabbis," *Connecticut Jewish Ledger*, June 4, 1999; reprinted in the *Congregation Beth Israel Newsletter* (Houston), August 1999, 1.

17. G. Bullard, "Reform Judaism Adopts New Platform," *Detroit News*, May 26, 1999.

18. Harry K. Danziger, "Between You and Me," *Temple Israel of Memphis Voice*, midsummer 1999, 1.

19. Eric H. Yoffie, teleconference speech, August 17, 1999.

20. M. L. Shook, "With Heart and Mind," *Temple Israel Dateline* (Creve Coeur, Mo.), July–August 1999, 4.

21. Ibid.

22. Leon Morris, "Not Your Grandfather's Reform Judaism," typescript, author's files.

Chapter 12   **Where Do We Go from Here?**

1. Charles S. Liebman and Steven M. Cohen, *Two Worlds of Judaism: The Israeli and American Experiences* (New Haven: Yale University Press, 1990), 128.

2. Alexander Schindler, State of the Union Message, UAHC Biennial Conference, Houston, November 1983.

3. Ibid.

Index

About the Author

Dana Evan Kaplan is the Oppenstein Brothers Assistant Professor of Judaic and Religious Studies in the Department of History at the University of Missouri-Kansas City and is a Research Fellow at the Miller Center for Contemporary Judaic Studies and the Institute for Cuban and Cuban-American Studies at the University of Miami. He has led Reform congregations in Australia, Israel, and South Africa and is now Rabbi of Congregation B'nai Israel in Albany, Georgia. His books include *Contemporary Debates in American Reform Judaism: Conflicting Visions*, *Platforms and Prayerbooks: Theological and Liturgical Perspectives on Reform Judaism*, and the *Cambridge Companion to American Judaism* (forthcoming). Some of his publications can be found on his website *www.DanaKaplan.com*.